Devised Performance in Irish Theatre:
Histories and Contemporary Practice

Devised Performance in Irish Theatre:
Histories and Contemporary Practice

Edited by

Siobhán O'Gorman and Charlotte McIvor

Carysfort Press

A Carysfort Press Book in association with Peter Lang
Devised Performance in Irish Theatre:
Histories and Contemporary Practice
Edited by Siobhán O'Gorman and Charlotte McIvor

First published in Ireland in 2015 as a paperback original by
Carysfort Press, 58 Woodfield, Scholarstown Road
Dublin 16, Ireland

ISBN 978-1-78874-791-2
©2015 Copyright remains with the authors
Typeset by Carysfort Press
Cover design by eprint limited

This book is published with the financial assistance of
The Arts Council (An Chomhairle Ealaíon) Dublin, Ireland

Caution: All rights reserved. No part of this book may be printed or reproduced or utilized in any form or by any electronic, mechanical, or other means, now known or hereafter invented including photocopying and recording, or in any information storage or retrieval system without permission in writing from the publishers.

Contents

Acknowledgements ix

1 | 'Devising Ireland: Genealogies and Contestations' 1
Charlotte McIvor and Siobhán O'Gorman

Section One: Devising as Collaborative Art

2 | 'Spectres of Connolly: *The Non-Stop Connolly Show* Reconsidered' 33
Michael Jaros

3 | 'A Portrait of the Citizen as Artist: Community Arts, Devising and Contemporary Irish Theatre Practice' 47
Charlotte McIvor

4 | '"Whose art is it anyway?" A Critical and Historical Analysis of Upstate Theatre Project' 67
Irene White

5 | 'Interview with Una McKevitt (Una McKevitt Productions)' 97
Jesse Weaver

6 | 'A Song about Survival: Talking Shop Ensemble Responds to the Irish Debt Crisis' 111
Laura Farrell-Wortman

Section Two: Formal Politics

7 | 'A Theatre of Truth? Negotiating Place, Politics and Policy in the Dublin Fringe Festival' 127
Miriam Haughton

8 | 'Mapping Contemporary European Theatre(s): Reconsidering Notions of Devised and Post-dramatic Theatres' 143
Noelia Ruiz

9 | 'An Interview with Gavin Quinn (Pan Pan Theatre)' 159
Noelia Ruiz

Section Three: Regional Practices

10 | 'Staging Blue Raincoat's production of WB Yeats's *The Cat and the Moon* (2009) and *At the Hawk's Well* (2010)' 173
Rhona Trench

11 | 'Repeating, Revising and Devising: Communities in Contemporary Galway Theatre' 189
Siobhán O'Gorman

12 | 'Interview with Máiréad Ní Chronin (Moonfish Theatre)' 211
Charlotte McIvor

Section Four: Northern Approaches

13 | 'Reawakening Belfast's Streets: Tourism and Memory in Site-Specific Northern Irish Theatre' 229
Eleanor Owicki

14 | 'Politics, Pride, and Performance: TheatreofplucK's Devised Queer Dramaturgies in Northern Ireland' 243
Caitriona Mary Reilly

15 | 'Interview with Will Chamberlain (Belfast Community Circus)' 261
Siobhán O'Gorman

Contributors 279

Index 285

List of Illustrations

Cover: Performers depict Connemara in Moonfish's devised stage adaptation of Joseph O'Connor's novel, *Star of the Sea*, presented in co-production with An Taibhdhearc at An Taibhdhearc, Galway as part of the Galway Arts Festival, 2014. Photo by Marta Barcikowska.

1: Sorcha Kenny in ANU Productions' *Laundry*. Photo: Pat Redmond

2: Lloyd Cooney and Caitriona Ennis in ANU Productions' *Boys of Foley Street*. Photo: Pat Redmond

3: John Finegan as Desmond O'Prey and Ciaran Kenny as Teddy O'Sullivan in Upstate's 2006 revival of *Hades*. Written and Directed by Declan Gorman. Part 1 of Upstate Live's The Border Chronicles Trilogy.

4: A scene from *The Mango Tree* (2011), produced by Upstate, facilitated and directed by Stephen Murray, and devised and performed by Bianca Browne, Sarah Bromley, Michael Duffy, Derek Cummins, Denise Geraghty, Rosemary Traynor, Thomas Segun, Mary Oki, Beauty Ogbewe, Robert Carlos Tunde. Photo by Matt Dillon.

5: Andrew Bennett, Una McKevitt, Gina Moxley, Samantha Pearl, Daniel Reardon and Dick Walsh in Pan Pan's *Americanitis* presents *The Seagull & Other Birds* (Dublin Theatre Festival 2014), Space Upstairs, Project Arts Centre. Directed by Gavin Quinn and designed by Aedín Cosgrove. Photo by Ros Kavanagh.

6: Blue Raincoat's *At the Hawk's Well* (2010) with John Carty, Sandra O'Malley, Fiona McGeown (Chorus), Marketa Formanova (Hawk Woman), Ciaran McCauley and Niall Henry (Old Man and Young Man) at The Factory, Sligo. Image (2010) by kind permission of Joe Hunt and Blue Raincoat.

7: Blue Raincoat's *The Cat and the Moon* (2009), with Ciarán McCauley, Fiona McGeown, Sandra O'Malley as the Chorus. The performance pictured took place in The Factory, Sligo. Image (2010) by kind permission of Joe Hunt and Blue Raincoat.

8: Zita Monahan in of one the many shifting roles of Martin Sharry's *King Alfred: A Mystery Play*, directed by Dick Walsh at the Town Hall Studio, Galway (2012). The play was developed from collaborative workshops exploring the concept of the 'history play' and local stories about MGM's filming of *Alfred the Great* (1969) in Galway throughout the summer of 1968. Photo by Jaesin Yu, JS Photographic.

9: (L to R) Kate Murray, Jarlath Tivnan, Seamus O'Donnell, Teresa Brennan, Oísín Robbins and Maria Tivnan in Fregoli's *Home*, Nun's Island Theatre, Galway, as part of the Galway Theatre Festival (2012). The piece was devised by the performers under the direction of Rob McFeely. Photo by Rob McFeely.

10: New version of Patrick McCabe's *Frank Pig Says Hello*, directed by Andrew Flynn and staring Jarlath Tivnan as Piglet (centre), presented at Nun's Island Theatre, Galway, as part of Galway Arts Festival 2012. Set design by Owen McCarthaigh, with scenic painting by Ger Sweeny. Costume design by Petra Bhreatnach, lighting design by Mike O'Halloran, and soundscape by Matt Guinnane and Peter Rabitte. Photo by Jane Talbot.

11: The Reliables teach Pius Mulvey (Zita Monahan) a lesson in Moonfish's devised stage adaptation of Joseph O'Connor's novel, *Star of the Sea*, presented in co-production with An Taibhdhearc at An Taibhdhearc, Galway as part of the Galway Arts Festival, 2014. Photo by Marta Barcikowska.

12: Grace Kiely as Grantley Dixon, the journalist, in Moonfish's devised stage adaptation of Joseph O'Connor's novel, *Star of the Sea*, presented in co-production with An Taibhdhearc at An Taibhdhearc, Galway as part of the Galway Arts Festival, 2014. Photo by Marta Barcikowska.

13: Actor Fra Gunn as Barney in Kabosh Theatre's *Belfast Bred* (2010), developed in collaboration with the owners of several Belfast restaurants and playwright Seth Linder, under the direction of Paula McFetridge, Kabosh Artistic Director. Image courtesy of the Northern Ireland Tourist Board.

14: Antoinette Morelli and Gerard Jordan in The *West Awakes* (2010). To create *The West Awakes,* Kabosh partnered with Coiste, an organisation of former republican prisoners and a team of writers including Jimmy McAleavey, Laurence McKeown, Kieron Magee and Roseleen Walsh. Photo by Aidan Monaghan.

15: Poster image for TheatreofplucK's first incarnation of *Divided, Radical and Gorgeous (D.R.A.G.),* performed by Belfast drag performance artist Gordon Crawford, otherwise known as Trudy Scrumptious (pictured here). *D.R.A.G.* was first performed as part of the OUTburst Queer Arts Festival in 2011. Paul Boyd took over the role in the second production of *D.R.A.G.* in 2012. Both were directed Niall Rea. Photo by Simon Crawford.

16: Karl Schappell in TheatreofplucK's *Automatic Bastard* (2005), developed and scripted through a series of workshops held at The Lyric Theatre in Belfast using autobiographical material inspired by the lives of Niall Rea and Karl Schappell. The production was designed and directed by Rea. Photo also by Rea.

17: *Urban Circus,* the 2004 Belfast Community Circus Youth Circus show, directed by Australian circus artist Stephen Burton and performed at the Waterfront Hall, Belfast. Photo by Will Chamberlain.

18: Dublin-based performance company, PaperDolls (Elaine McCague, Emily Aoibheann and Karen Anderson), offering street performance at the Festival of Fools, Belfast, in 2012. Photo by kind permission of Belfast Community Circus.

19: Belfast Festival of Fools 2010: image of *Decadence* by St Petersburg group Mr Pejo's Wandering Dolls, taken from the entrance to St Anne's Square, Belfast. Photo by Grant Goldie.

Acknowledgements

Our sincere thanks go to all those who have contributed to this volume – through writing essays, conducting interviews, blind peer-reviewing submissions, or agreeing to or inclusion of published or unpublished interviews. All of these efforts have served to further existing knowledge of devised performance in relation to Irish theatre and performance, as well as these two fields at large. We are grateful to Lionel Pilkington, Nicholas Johnson, Ramin Haghjoo, Aoife McGrath, Cormac O'Brien, Jesse Weaver, Patrick Lonergan and Eamonn Jordan for their help and support in bringing this collection to fruition. We also acknowledge the advice, assistance and encouragement garnered from a range of other colleagues, in addition to friends and family members. Finally, we would like to thank each other, as co-editors, for making the collaborative process of bringing this body of work together such an inspiring, fruitful and rewarding experience.

1 | Devising Ireland: Genealogies and Contestations

Charlotte McIvor and Siobhán O'Gorman

Introduction

This essay collection situates the histories and contemporary practice of devised performance in the Irish theatre by bringing together a range of perspectives from both academics and practitioners. It responds to a decisive shift in the landscape of Irish theatre, following the increasing recognition afforded by several emerging companies including ANU Productions, Brokentalkers, THEATREclub, THISISPOPBABY and The Company. This contemporary surge of work has influenced not only the evolving needs of Irish theatre and performance criticism but the very pedagogy of theatre training in Ireland with institutions including Trinity College, Dublin, National University of Ireland, Galway, the Gaiety School of Acting and others now offering practical courses that incorporate devised performance techniques at BA and MA levels. The current wave of devised performance builds on a physical and dance theatre movement in Irish theatre that began to coalesce in the 1990s through the work of companies like Barabbas, Macnas, Blue Raincoat, Corn Exchange, Pan Pan, and Corcadorca which was influenced by earlier genealogies of Irish, European and international arts practice. That body of practice in turn built on what Sandy Fitzgerald has interpreted as a cross-border Irish community arts movement, emerging throughout the island of Ireland from the 1970s, characterized by broadly leftist politics and often enmeshed with the interrelated community development sector ('Beginnings' 70).

We have told the history of devised performance in Irish theatre backwards in our opening paragraph because this is often how we have encountered it as scholars, critics, audience members, and educators (who are also practitioners) working at the beginning of the twenty-first century. *Devised Performance in Irish Theatre: Histories and Contemporary Practice* aims to challenge this perception that devised performance techniques are primarily contemporary performance practice in the field of Irish theatre by placing these practices in longer historical genealogies. Our working definition of devised performance for the purpose of this task encompasses material that is collectively created by individuals working together in ways that resist (but do not necessarily reject altogether) the hierarchical organizational structures usually associated with institutional theatre. Devising is an umbrella term that describes a range of collaborative methodologies of creation that are characterized by collective dramaturgical input into the generation of a new 'work,' whether original text, work of dance theatre or even adaptation of a known work. Devised performance methodologies can therefore lead to the creation of work in multiple theatrical genres, including but not limited to physical, immersive, site-specific, improvised, collaborative, community, documentary and verbatim theatre as well as adaptations or the premiere of a new 'play' in the case of companies who bring writers into their devising processes. We highlight the fact that Irish (and other) practitioners employing practices of devised performance also regularly draw on diverse artistic disciplines including but not limited to theatre, dance, visual arts, music and multimedia in order to create original material.

We also reject here the notion that devised performance methodologies have an 'implied binary position to text-based theatre' (Radosavljevic 62), arguing instead that devising can be employed to transform an already existing text (such as in the case of adaptation) or aid in the creation of a new play. This 'implied binary' betrays the reality of what Patrick Lonergan discerns in his popular blog as a much more nuanced relationship between playwriting and devising. Lonergan cites such examples from the Irish context as Deirdre Kinahan and Enda Walsh, who 'began their careers by doing work that would now be seen as devising' ('Eight Irish Dramatists'). He also aptly exemplifies Michael West's *Freefall* (2009), which was devised in collaboration with Dublin-based theatre company The Corn Exchange, but is 'also a brilliantly written play' ('New British Drama'). Ultimately, like Lonergan, we see the '"play vs. devised piece" distinction' as both unnecessary and unhelpful (Ibid.), supporting this contention with a range of additional historical evidence outlined in this introduction and elsewhere in the volume.

We focus primarily on the use of devised performance within Irish theatre practice but recognize and situate the use of multiple artistic genres and disciplines within productions that may be billed primarily as 'theatre,' whether through advertising or programming as part of denominated theatre festivals or the choice of venue. We speak about 'devised performance' to acknowledge the interdisciplinary performance techniques (outlined above) which artists often use to create devised material but situate the work that has been created within an Irish *theatre* context. Most of the work examined in this collection has been produced by companies that would self-identify as 'theatre' companies, present in our annual 'theatre' festivals throughout the country and so on. This collection does not for example deal extensively with performance art,[1] the use of devising and collaborative practice in visual art, the relationship between devising and choreography in modern and contemporary dance, or devising by professional community groups for the purpose of large-scale public festivals or parades celebrating national holidays or community events. Our excavation of genealogies of devised performance practices in Irish theatre ultimately makes possible a more inclusive model of Irish theatre *and* performance history that might provide a methodological model for alternative historiographical approaches to familiar figures, aesthetic techniques or movements within this broad field. Historiographical practice within Irish theatre studies has most frequently tended to valorize authors, the authority of the text and the history of culturally-prominent, authorized venues. Yet devised performance in Ireland involves a variety of spaces, contributors and modes of expression – a variety that this volume seeks to recognise and explore.

While this is a book focused primarily on Irish work and companies, we present these case studies in order to test what Irish work contributes to transnational understandings of devised performance as a formal practice. To this end, we map convergent and divergent genealogies of artistic influences and practical techniques in order to not only account for the success of recently acclaimed new Irish theatre work using devised performance techniques within Ireland, but to situate the Irish practice of devised performance within the scope of global trends and influences in this broad area of work. In doing so, we ask not only how international interlocutors might inspire Irish devised

---

[1] For the history of performance art in Ireland, see Áine Phillip's edited collection, *Performance Art in Ireland: A History* (2015).

performance practice, but what specifically Irish practices of devised performance can contribute to an understanding of techniques, practices and reception within this genre globally.

Genealogies of Devising in Ireland and Beyond

Only a handful of works offer detailed discussions of Irish devised performance as a component within wider frames of theatre and artistic practice. Looking at the subgenre of devised performance within a community arts context, a few important works that serve as a model for this collection must be mentioned. Sandy Fitzgerald's edited collection *An Outburst of Frankness: Community Arts in Ireland – A Reader* (2004) includes essays and a series of roundtables with artist/facilitators and administrators documenting a cross-border of community arts practice from the 1970s to the present with devised performance techniques figuring centrally in these narratives. Upon publication of this ground breaking work, Fitzgerald openly anticipated extensive further exploration of this important field offering that the 'very nature of a reader is to create a debate, both within the texts and among the readership' ('Introduction' 2), and by extension, scholarly communities. Yet, in the context of histories of the Republic, these hopes remain largely unfulfilled despite Fitzgerald's challenge, a challenge this collection hopes to circulate further and answer through some of our chapters. Investigation of devised and/or community practices is a slightly better developed area in a Northern Irish context with major contributions including Tom Maguire's thought-provoking analysis of devised site-specific work in his 2006 *Making Theatre in Northern Ireland: Through and Beyond the Troubles* as well as Bill McDonnell's 2008 *Theatres of the Troubles: Theatre, Resistance and Liberation* which details 'the narrative of the community theatres which developed within working-class Republican and Loyalist communities during the war, and in the first decade of the Peace Process, 1997-2009'(4).

For the Republic, Christie Fox's 2008 *Breaking Forms: The Shift to Performance in Late Twentieth-Century Irish Drama* is the sole substantial monograph on contemporary Irish theatre and performance to examine the working process and output of several companies which use devised techniques including Macnas, Barabbas, and Blue Raincoat; but strangely, this work has not enjoyed substantial circulation within the field. Carmen Szabo's *The Story of Barabbas, The Company* (2012) and Rhona Trench's *Blue Raincoat Theatre Company* (2015), both also published by Carysfort Press, provide thorough archives of these two companies, representing a forward momentum that confirms the need to develop a field-wide account of devised performance practice across contemporary Irish theatre history. The ground breaking work done in Irish dance studies over the last decade suggests that Irish dance studies may be ahead of the curve, and should be more centrally integrated into field debates about devised performance within Irish theatre and performance studies. Landmark works include Deirdre Mulrooney's *Irish Moves: An Illustrated History of Dance and Physical Theatre in Ireland* (2006), which explores the collaborative work of dance artists from Ninette de Valois to Jean Butler, and Aoife McGrath's *Dance Theatre in Ireland: Revolutionary Moves* (2012), which examines contemporary dance companies who use devised choreographic methods such as Fabulous Beast Dance Theatre and CoisCéim.

Edited collections on Irish theatre and performance too have only recently turned in the direction of devised performance with two very recent publications meriting particular note. Most recently, and also published by Carysfort Press, Miriam Haughton and Mária Kurdi's edited collection *Radical Contemporary Theatre Practices by Women in Ireland* (2015) examines the diversity of contemporary Irish theatre-making, but – rather than focusing specifically on devising – its key objective is to provide a necessary investigation of the work of Irish women practitioners. Coming at theatre-making in contemporary Ireland from another angle, *'That Was Us': Contemporary Irish Theatre and Performance* (2013), edited by Fintan Walsh, succeeds in documenting and exploring the changing character of Irish theatre since the economic downturn through the lens of the Dublin Theatre Festival's programming from 2007 to 2013. In addition to examining the continuance of more traditional forms, the collection explores the work of companies such as Brokentalkers and ANU, and to a lesser extent Pan Pan, THEATREclub and Fabulous Beast. However, the essays focus mainly on companies that have been fortunate enough to have had some association with the Dublin Theatre Festival – which also commissioned the publication. As such, *'That Was Us'* inevitably overlooks a range of exciting new fringe and regional work.

In contrast, our contention that community arts have played a key role in the history of devised performance opens the field for the examination of companies operating in diverse locales beyond Dublin, many of whom are examined in this collection, and not all of whom would identify as 'community arts' groups. Examples include: Connemara-based group Fíbín, who employ puppetry and seek to emphasize the visual, corporeal and musical aspects of theatre in order to promote the Irish language; Drogheda's Upstate Theatre Project, a 'community-engaged performing arts organization' which adheres to 'collective and collaborative approaches in keeping with principles of cultural democracy' (Upstate Theatre); Kilkenny's Barnstorm Theatre, which incorporates educational, outreach and creative development programmes as well as devising productions; Galway's Moonfish, which produces classics, new writing and devised work, exploring the possibilities of such media as shadow work, live music and dance; Derry-based Big Telly Theatre, which concentrates on the visual potential of performance by fusing art forms such as theatre, dance, music and circus; and Asylum Productions, based in Midleton, Co. Cork, an artist-led company that re-investigates existing scripts as well as developing new work by merging puppetry, physical and object theatre. The practices and productions of these companies have suffered critical neglect. This may be because they emerge from regions that are not as culturally prominent as the capital cities of Dublin and Belfast, or because their key roles within local communities may negate their image as 'professional' or of national importance. *Devised Performance in Irish Theatre* therefore calls for attention to a variety of devised practices taking place in regional areas, as well as Dublin and other cultural hubs such as Galway, Cork and Belfast.

In terms of the documentation of performance texts created through devised techniques, Walsh's *Queer Notions: New Plays and Performances from Ireland* (2010) includes Una McKevitt's *Victor and Gord, Ali and Michael*, created through a collaborative process, while Thomas Conway's *The Oberon Anthology of Contemporary Irish Plays* (2012) prominently features devised or partially devised texts including Grace Dyas's *HEROIN*, Amy Conroy's *I <3 Alice <3 I*, and finally, *The Big Deal*, edited by McKevitt. Most recently, Charlotte McIvor and Matthew Spangler's *Staging Intercultural Ireland: Plays and Practitioner Perspectives* (2014) includes plays such as Paul Meade's *Mushroom* and Bisi Adigun's *Once Upon A Time/Long Ago and Far Away* (which were created using devised techniques), as well as interviews with practitioners including Declan Gorman and Declan Mallon of Upstate Theatre who work primarily through devising. These emergent trends in publication attest to a growing awareness of devised performance, but also signal the need for continuing comprehensive accounts of this historical and emerging body of practice.

Beyond this national milieu, while several important volumes have been published on devised performance internationally since the 1990s, research on the history of devised practice still remains relatively sparse and focused on the UK with some scholars including Duška Radosavljevic arguing that the term has lost its salience in a European context. Theatre-maker Alison Oddey, who has been engaged in devised work in Britain since the late 1970s, was one of the first to attempt 'a general theory of devising theatre'(xi). In *Devising Theatre: A Practical and Theoretical Handbook* (1994), Oddey focuses on a variety of performance groups active in Britain from the late 1980s to the early 1990s in order to explore the interconnections of diverse devising processes, decision-making procedures and the kinds of performances that emerge as a result. While Oddey's book blends practical, analytical and historical perspectives, works that followed, such as Gil Lamden's *Devising: A Handbook for Drama and Theatre Students* (2000) and Sheila Kerrigan's *The Performer's Guide to the Collaborative Process* (2001), function more exclusively as educational guides. 2005 saw the publication of Deirdre Heddon and Jane Milling's *Devising Performance: A Critical History*, which historicizes devising techniques in the UK, the USA and Australia from the late 1950s to the early twenty-first century and a special issue on devised work from the international journal *Theatre Topics* that includes responses from academics and practitioners. Heddon and Milling's study went some way towards excavating the roots of devising by historicizing its processes from the late 1950s to the early twenty-first century. However, their definition of devising limits it to work that takes place without any pre-existing script, play text or performance score (3), a contention rejected by this collection. Casting a wider historical net, Emma Govan, Helen Nicholson, and Katie Normington, in *Making a Performance: Devising Histories and Contemporary Practices* (2007), locate the 'inception' of devising within the European avant-garde of the early twentieth century but see it in a much more permissive light, as 'a process of generating a performative or theatrical event often but not always in collaboration with others' (6, 4).

Kathryn Mederos Syssoyeva and Scott Proudfit have undertaken a series of edited collections since 2013 outlining the history of what they term alternatively as 'collective creation.' Despite this different organizing term, Syssoyeva defines collective creation as 'the practice of collaboratively devising works for performance' (2). The work of Syssoyeva and Proudfit acknowledges the collaboration inherent in (but hidden by some) devised practices, which might usefully extend the arguable blind spots of earlier systems of classification for what counts as 'devised.' Syssoyeva and Proudfit's first essay collection, *A History of*

Collective Creation (2013), collates international histories of collaborative devising, from experiments led by Vsevolod Meyerhold at the beginning of the twentieth century to the work of theatre practitioners in Quebec, the United States and Europe in the early 1980s (4). Following on from this, their *Collective Creation in Contemporary Performance* (2013) offers a range of responses that together consider collectively devised performance (again in an international context) from the 1960s to the present day. They are in the process of releasing a third edited collection in this series, *Women, Collective Creation, and Devised Theatre*.

Collaborative devising often has been associated with a leftist, countercultural fringe of the late 1960s and early 1970s. However, Syssoyeva and Proudfit resist limiting collective creation to one particular ideological frame or rooting it within any specific historical moment, arguing instead that 'in the history of collective creation, it is polyphony, not consensus, that is the norm – and arguably the beauty – of both form and practice' (Syssoyeva 5). This approach promotes fresh examinations of theatre and performance history, in which – for example – 'a collectively devised mise en scène for an existing dramatic work might constitute a form of collective creation' and 'collective creation might accommodate authorial and directorial leadership' (Ibid).

'Devising' is central to Syssoyeva and Proudfit's definition of 'collective creation' in relation to their examinations of historical and current, transnational performance-making practices. Duška Radosavljevic's *Theatre-Making: Interplay Between Text and Performance in the 21st Century* also embraces the term 'collective creation,' but rejects the term 'devising' as an international and transferable paradigm, citing 'its implied binary opposition to text-based theatre' which creates 'confusion among continental Europeans' as well as 'the overuse of the term in a British context' leading to the conflation of the 'terms devising and ensemble, where it is implied that ensembles typically devise and only exceptionally work with playwrights' (62). Rather than seeking a more complex, inclusive conception of 'devising' from practical and historical perspectives (as we do in this introduction), Radosavljevic advocates for a use of alternative terminology, including 'collective creation' and 'theatre-maker' to describe what she perceives to be the more commonly held working practices of contemporary theatre companies which incorporate 'various kinds of multi-skilled practitioners' who hold multiple roles simultaneously in the company such as actor/artistic director, director/lighting designer and so on (23). She also persuasively makes a case for the Anglophone-centred (and particularly UK) prejudice for devising as the field-wide term to encompass collaborative processes of non-hierarchical collective creation, and evidences internal contradictions into its adoption even in an Anglophone or UK context. She cites the use of 'création collective' (Jacques Lecoq, Ariane Mnouchkine), 'collaborative creation' (The Living Theatre, The Open Theatre, and the Performance Group), 'improvisation' (Eugenio Barba and the 'Stanislavskian tradition'), 'authorial work' or '"autoroski rad," "autorosko divadlo"' ('Eastern and Central European contexts') and finally, 'workshopping' (Joan Littlewood) (59). She does however also concede that 'it might be safely stated that one thing we do owe to the Devisers (capital D) of the twentieth century is an increasing democratization of contemporary theatre – both in terms of its evolving production and reception processes' (84).

Finally, at the intersection of devised performance and community-based arts, Jan Cohen-Cruz's seminal *Local Acts: Community-Based Performance in the United States* (2005) focuses primarily on community-based performance, but she defines this practice as 'artists guiding the creation of original work or material adapted to, and with, people with a primary relationship to the content, not necessarily to the craft' (2-3). Cohen-Cruz's definition demonstrates the continuing overlap between community-based arts and performance devising. James Thompson has also written extensively on community-based and participatory performances organized in prisons, detention centres and sites of war and disaster. His book *Performance Affects: Applied Theatre and the End of Effect* (2009), for example, reflects on his experience as a practitioner in Sri Lanka and Rwanda and seeks a re-evaluation of the goals, ethics, politics and aesthetics of applied theatre projects. In more recent years, there has indeed been what McIvor describes as a 'cluster of publications in the field of theatre and performance studies on the politics of community, arts collaboration and the participation of non-professionals in relationship to the expansion of neoliberal economies' ('*Theatre of Good Intentions*' 523). These works include Shannon Jackson's *Social Work: Performing Art, Supporting Publics* (2011), Claire Bishop's *Artificial Hells: Participatory Arts and the Politics of Spectatorship* (2012), Grant Kester's *The One and the Many: Contemporary Collaborative Art in a Global Context* (2011), Jen Harvie's *Fair Play: Art, Performance and Neoliberalism* (2013), Nicholas Ridout's *Passionate Amateurs:*

Theatre, Communism and Love (2013), and Dani Snyder-Young's *Theatre of Good Intentions: Challenges and Hopes for Theatre and Social Change* (2014). These publications take on a wide range of case studies, usually at the intersection of visual art, community arts and theatre, case studies that all investigate the politics of collaborative or devised arts practice in diverse institutional and interdisciplinary contexts. The sheer range of approaches represented by this group of recent publications not only demonstrate the timeliness of our subject but illustrate that theatre (and arts) practice may be named in multiple and overlapping critical genealogies. This is why we have remained focused on 'devised performance' as our primary optic as we feel it both connects us to these wider interdisciplinary debates on collaborative arts practice, but focuses our own path of inquiry within the context of Irish theatre and performance studies as a subfield.

Innovative, contemporary theatre practices, in addition to recent international scholarship on devising, prompt new understandings of what constitutes 'devised performance' and pave the way for fresh approaches to theatre historiography. Although there is much work yet to be done on devising in Irish theatre and performance history, archival evidence and a selection of publications makes it possible to argue that devising is, in fact, a long-established and ongoing feature of theatrical activity in Ireland – evident not only in amateur and community drama but in folk and ritual practices, pageants, revues and variety shows, work produced in little theatres (including the original Abbey theatre, which was destroyed by fire in 1951), political performances, and the work of female theatre practitioners ranging from Lady Gregory to Carolyn Swift. There are complex links between devising and issues of power, politics, community and identity, both in terms of the activities themselves and how they have – or have not – been historicized. Although the essays in this volume focus on devised performance in Irish theatre from the late 1970s to the present day, we offer next in this introduction a historical overview of Irish performance practices that could be considered as devised. These are only fragments of what is surely a much larger history, presented in the hope of encouraging more detailed historical investigations into the practices of devising works for performance in Ireland and elsewhere.

Devised Performance in Irish Theatre History/ies

We present the above critical international genealogy in order to inform detailed considerations of devised performance in Irish theatre history, contextualized in this introduction and elsewhere in the volume – for example, in essays by McIvor, Michael Jaros and Irene White – within longer histories of Irish theatre practice. In doing so, we want to promote broader, but also more complex, understandings of devising.

As explored above, the term 'devising' is currently met with contention by some theatre practitioners – including Gavin Quinn, director of Pan Pan Theatre, who is interviewed by Noelia Ruiz in this volume, and indeed Ruiz examines the term critically in her own essay with recourse to Radosavljevic's *Theatre-Making*. In some contexts, the contemporary backlash against labelling certain highly collaborative and/or interdisciplinary theatre-making practices as devised might stem for example from the assumed association of devising with the political left. It might also express anxiety about the supposedly utopian goals of sharing power and authorship equally in a collaborative process, regardless of whether or not it is named 'devising.' Antagonism towards this terminology might also be explained by the very popularization of the term 'devising' which includes the ways it has been adopted within mainstream and institutional contexts, especially the university and funding bodies. Radosavljevic records anxiety by UK-based theatre-maker Andy Fields that there is 'no longer anything radical about devising' due to its institutionalization and mainstreamed status as a methodology (60).

Yet, while devising may be an imperfect genealogical term to trace, it does usefully organize what is truly a diverse field of methodological practice that nonetheless has some common origins and practices, such as the influence of mid twentieth-century leftist politics, for example. We have stayed with devising as our key term as we *are* writing from an Anglophone context whose theatre practice has been substantially influenced by the UK particularly for reasons of colonialism, geography and language. Like ourselves in an Irish context, Radosavljevic identifies for example the pivotal impact of theatre-in-education (TIE) in evolving British devising practices (65-68). We therefore respond directly to the genealogy that Radosavljevic critiques as implicit (and in being so, implicitly limited) and consider how Irish practice may expand or challenge devising as a UK, European or international grouping of theatre methodologies that emphasize collective input into the creation of a shared original performance event. To think in terms of 'devising' allows us to think with a more focused and historical remit. Our devising-focused remit recognizes that how we characterize the relationship between the collaboration of multiple artistic stakeholders (in delineated, non-delineated or multiple roles) and the creation of a 'performance text' for live performance must continue to evolve in recognition of not only contemporary but previously obscured or under-theorized historical case studies. Crucially, our remit focuses this inquiry for the purposes of coverage in a way that also invites the term (devising) to be debated openly, as many of our contributors indeed do. Through this collection, however, we call for a recuperation of 'devising' as a strategic way of designating a wide range of largely collaborative performance practices, acknowledging vast distinctions in the ideological, aesthetic and practical issues surrounding their aims.

Drawing on expanded understandings of devising, devised performance can indeed be seen to have roots in Irish history deeper than previously recognized. Lionel Pilkington contends that the indigenous Irish theatre canon excludes pre-existing rural theatrical traditions such as mumming and folk drama ('Theatre History' 27-33). Employing flexible performance models, such practices frequently incorporate group improvisation. J.M. Synge draws on such folk traditions in his work produced at the early Abbey theatre. In his preface to *The Playboy of the Western World* (1907), Synge uses the word 'collaboration' to explain his practice as a dramatist, which was informed by his anthropological studies of rural Ireland. In this context, he admits: 'I have used only one or two words that I have not heard among the country people of Ireland [...] and I am glad to acknowledge how much I owe to the folk imagination of these people' (67). Other practices that have incorporated aspects of devising at the early Abbey theatre include the collaborations of Gregory and W.B. Yeats. Although Gregory is remembered as one of the Abbey's founders, her co-authorship (with Yeats) of the famous *Cathleen ni Houlihan* remained unacknowledged until 1988.[2] This showcases the complex power relations (in this case, gendered) that have, at times, obscured histories of devised performance. Collaborative practice has suffered critical neglect in Irish theatre historiography. So too has the specificity of women's contributions to Irish theatre, especially where collaboration is concerned.

In this book, Eleanor Owicki's essay on Kabosh Theatre and Siobhán O'Gorman's interview with Will Chamberlain, director of Belfast Community Circus, both point to the ways in which devised performance has been used to reimagine Belfast as an undivided city of

---

[2] Yeats and Gregory's co-authorship of *Cathleen ní Houlihan* was revealed in 1988 by James Pethica in his essay '"Our Kathleen:" Yeats's Collaboration with Lady Gregory in the Writing of *Cathleen ní Houlihan*.'

leisure. The use of devising on the island as a politicized practice aiming to (re)construct communities can be traced back at least to the early twentieth century. Following the establishment of the Irish Free State in 1922, state-sponsored events employed devised performance to produce pageants of highly selective, romanticized versions of Irish history in the service of postcolonial nation-building – including appropriations of Celtic mythology and commemorations of the 1916 Easter Rising. Joan Fitzpatrick Dean identifies pageantry as a key feature of Irish history, drawing on the work of Erika Fischer-Lichte to locate the practice within a broader, European context. Fischer-Lichte explores a re-appropriation of pageantry in late nineteenth- and early twentieth-century Europe (33). Dean recognizes religious celebrations – including Christmas and Nativity plays, passion plays, and Easter reenactments – as the most prevalent forms of pageantry in Ireland. However, Dean also identifies distinct 'flurries' of collectively-created pageants celebrating Irish history and culture in the decade following the establishment of the Irish Free State, and again during the 1950s following the establishment of the Irish republic in 1949 (20-21).

The first wave of pageantry of this kind was part of the aforementioned postcolonial 'nation-building.' The second can also be linked to *nation-branding*, contextualized following the European Recovery Programme and the Organization for European Economic Co-operation (both 1948), when the Irish state began to consider the nation in terms of international, economic competitiveness (Ferriter 467-8). Dean rightly asserts that no one was more involved in these mythical/historical pageants than Micheál Mac Liammóir who 'wrote, directed, and starred in the century's most successful public spectacles of Irish history,' devising with his partner Hilton Edwards, *The Ford of the Hurdles* (1929), and different versions of *The Pageant of St. Patrick* which were staged in Dublin as part of the national Tóstal festivals of the 1950s (33). An Tóstal was a succession of festivals that took place between 1953 and 1958. Its agenda is comparable to 'The Gathering 2013' – a series of Irish occasions and festivals held throughout that year, aiming to celebrate Irish culture and to attract visitors including tourists and the Irish diaspora. Similarly, An Tóstal sought to promote Ireland as a tourist destination, as well as to entice the return of Irish emigrants. Patriotic spectacles such as *The Pageant of St. Patrick*, while shaped in the main by key cultural figures such as Edwards and Mac Liammóir, were ultimately created collectively through the contributions of a range of artists and civic personnel.[3] Like Kabosh's partnerships with Belfast industries and tourist organizations, the complexities of which are considered in this volume by Owicki, these activities showcase the ways in which devised performance practices can be harnessed in the service of *both* (re)constructing communities and economic expansion.

The decade following the establishment of the Irish republic was one of ideological conflict in Ireland; these tensions also permeated Irish theatre. Ernest Blythe's policies as managing director of the Abbey theatre between 1941 and 1967 can be seen in some ways to epitomize the struggle to maintain an established national identity based on cultural and economic self-sufficiency. Scholars have contended that the period of Blythe's reign, due to his championing of theatre that showcased 'representative nationalism' (Pilkington, 'Theatre, Sexuality and State' 24) and 'the values of a rural, Catholic Ireland, as interpreted by Fianna Fail' (Trotter 119) was a rather stale one for the Abbey. Meanwhile, from the late 1940s on, small theatre clubs emerged including Globe, Studio, 37 Club, Pike, Orion, Gemini, Pocket, Garrick, Lantern, and Focus. Many of these challenged the seemingly tired images of Irishness played out on the Abbey stage. The activities of these clubs often drew on devised performance, blurring the lines between discrete responsibilities, as well as strict identifications of performers as amateur or professional. Nevertheless, key Irish playwrights have historically maintained an elevated position in Irish theatre studies. This might explain why scholarship on Ireland's little theatres of the 1950s remains relatively sparse. As Pilkington points out, these enterprises 'were much more concerned either with staging productions of United States or European dramatists or with devised performances that stressed the improvisatory responsiveness of theatre to a particular political context' ('Little Theatres').

Ireland's little theatres of the 1950s were influenced by modernist, avant-garde ventures in London and Paris. The Irish genealogies of these theatres can be traced back to earlier initiatives that also incorporated collective creation such as 'Austin Clarke's Lyric Theatre

---

[3] The extent of the interdisciplinary collaboration involved in *The Pageant of St. Patrick*, for example, is clear from the 1955 scripts held at the National Library of Ireland, Dublin, containing narratives, dialogue, musical scores and an additional episode written by G.A. Hayes McCoy. See 'Papers of Micheál Mac Liammóir,' (MS 41, 256/1-6).

(1944-1952), the socialist New Theatre Group (1937-1943) and Erin Brady's Dublin Dance Theatre Club (1948-51)' (Pilkington, 'Little Theatres'). According to Pilkington, 'these groups are criss-crossed by a network of complex inter-involvement, with a plethora of overlaps between those who were involved in these earlier ventures and those involved in later groups like the 37 Theatre Club, the Pike Theatre Club and the Lantern Theatre Club' ('Little Theatres'). For example, dancers who emerged from Brady's Irish School of Dance Art (1939) went on to collaborate with Austin Clarke's Lyric Theatre Company on a devised production, first staged in 1944, blending poetry and dance based on Samuel Ferguson's poem, *The Fairy Thorn* (Mulrooney 99). Dublin's little theatres also incorporated both amateur and professional performers, and, as Pilkington also outlines, were likely influenced by contemporaneous, community initiatives such as the Bernadette Players (1951-1961), originally based in a Rathmines parish hall but moving on to tour shows in community centres around Ireland ('Little Theatres'). The group was established by Father Mick Murphy. Although Father Murphy co-wrote all the shows with Pat O'Rourke, '[o]nly O'Rourke's name was ever associated with the theatre group due to the embargo on priests being associated with theatre' (Pilkington, 'Little Theatres'). This points again to the complex web of ideological issues that can not only underpin the drive to devise, but can hide the extent of such practices historically.

Elsewhere, O'Gorman has contextualized Dublin's Pike theatre within a history of devised performance in Ireland, arguing that collective creation was central to this theatre club's working processes ('Hers and His'). However, as O'Gorman points out, interconnected issues of gender, authorship, authority and attribution often served to obscure, or at least to simplify the intricacies of, collaborative theatre-making. From the outset, Swift was at the forefront of devised performance at the Pike. In addition to translating and adapting existing scripts, she also co-wrote plays such as *Stealing the Picture* (with Joy Rudd), produced by the Pike in the late 1950s. Swift also led the productions of the Pike's late-night satirical revues, called *Follies*, which were central to the club's financial stability throughout the 1950s. These shows also contained sketches devised by other company members, some created collectively, as well as musical scores written or adapted by George Desmond Hodnett. These activities built on the work of organizations such as the Bernadette Players (a group that became well-known for their pantomime-like revues) and was later extended by The Lantern theatre, established in 1957, which offered its own late-night revue series called *Lanternscope*. Revues produced by these clubs dealt with topical subjects, and – due to the incorporation of amateur performers with other commitments – there were ongoing changes to casts. The shifting nature of both subject matter and cast meant that shows had to be changed and updated regularly, with new sketches written quickly to suit specific performers and respond to current events. Creating performances within such circumstances, in addition to the nature of the revue as a form, inevitably entailed extensive group collaboration as a practical necessity.

The Lantern outlived many of Dublin's other pocket theatres and, though it was for its lifetime categorized as amateur, it produced work for the Dublin Theatre Festival and was 'a seedbed for many professional actors and directors' (Eileen Sheridan 3). Beyond *Lanternscope*, The Lantern theatre engaged in other forms of devising. Lantern practitioners such as Patrick Funge, Liam Miller, and Kevin Byrne co-created several shows including *The Road Round Ireland* (1964) based on the writings of Padraic Colum, adaptations of David Krause's biography of Sean O'Casey (1965-1972), and *The Spirit of the Nation*, marking the golden jubilee of the Easter Rising in 1966. In 1968, the Lantern also staged *The Royal Pardon or the Soldier Who Became an Actor* by married collaborators Margaretta D'Arcy and John Arden. D'Arcy and Arden would go on to work together frequently on amateur, community, and activist performance initiatives in Ireland, including *The Non-Stop Connolly Show* (1975) – the focus of Jaros' illuminating essay in this collection. *The Non-Stop Connolly Show* was a day-long passion play involving working-class Dubliners in an alternative commemorative event with socialist goals. Unlike the work of D'Arcy and Arden, shows other than revues devised by the Lantern itself were reminiscent of the aforementioned pageants in that they usually mythologized, rather than challenged, specific aspects of Irish culture.

Focus Theatre (in operation professionally from 1967 to 2012) was established by Deirdre O'Connell; it developed out of the Stanislavski Studio O'Connell had set up in 1963 with a view to training Irish actors.[4] O'Connell was director of Focus till her death 2001, soon after

---

[4] Brian McAvera and Stephen Dedalus Burch's edited collection *Stanislavski in Ireland: Focus at Fifty* makes a start in excavating the enormous history of Focus – a small, unsubsidised but very popular and long-living Dublin theatre, which made an important contribution to Irish actor training.

which Joe Devlin was appointed to the role. In 2005, under his direction, Focus set up its 'Creative Partnership Scheme,' through which the company provided free training placements for practitioners seeking to produce experimental and devised performance projects – including Louise Lowe (artistic director of ANU productions), who was at the time working in Ballymun (Devlin 40). Insightful analyses of ANU's work within pertinent historical and contemporary frameworks are offered in this volume by McIvor and Haughton respectively. To return to Focus theatre, its activities under Devlin appear to deviate from historical perceptions of Focus, which predominantly associate this theatre with staging naturalist classics such as the plays of Henrik Ibsen and Anton Chekhov. However, what is less well-known about Focus under O'Connell's direction is that it publically staged improvisational theatre throughout the 1970s (Moynihan 15-17). These shows often employed Stanislavski's techniques to interpret, respond to and/or deconstruct a range of existing play texts. For example, in a Beckett double-bill of *Krapp's Last Tape* and *Play* produced by Focus during the summer of 1973 (directed by Peter O'Shaughnessy), on 'one evening per week, *Krapp* was replaced by improvisation exercises on *Play*, lasting forty minutes as compared with the twenty-five for *Play* itself' (Murray 118).

Mary Elizabeth Burke-Kennedy's staged appropriations of fairy tales with Focus, and her subsequent work with Storytellers (established in 1986 but ceasing production in 2008) blended adaptation, appropriation, and devised performance techniques, sometimes using masks and puppets. Burke-Kennedy's work reveals how the use and staging of Stanislavskian improvisation at the Focus theatre informed future innovations in Irish theatre practice. Actor Tom Hickey also worked with Focus from its inception. He cites his training and experience there as key to later work in which he became involved – including his collaboration with writer Tom Mac Intyre, director Patrick Mason and a range of performers to devise *The Great Hunger* (1983), an adaptation of Patrick Kavanagh's 1942 poem of the same name. The inception of the play began with Mac Intyre's preliminary script – or 'score' as he preferred to call it – which was accepted for production at the Peacock by then artistic director of the Abbey, Joe Dowling, '[bringing] together a collaborative group who would work on a series of productions at the Peacock till 1988' (Sweeney 51). Following its acceptance by Dowling, Mac Intyre's script was reworked and expanded based on performance work led by Hickey and directed by Mason, and influenced by Mac Intyre's exposure to a range of developments in dance theatre while living in New York during the 1970s. According to Hickey, these activities involved improvisations using objects – an approach with which Hickey was adept as a result of his background in Focus. When asked about the play's authorship, Hickey maintains that, despite the collaborative processes involved, it was still Mac Intyre's script, but that Mac Intyre is a writer who works best in the rehearsal room, watching actors in action. Bernadette Sweeney describes the very physical, imagistic and linguistically-sparse production that emerged as a result as 'a landmark in Irish theatre history,' the influence of which 'stemmed from its departure from a literal interpretation of [what was considered in Ireland as] a literary masterpiece' (50, 51).

However, by the time *The Great Hunger* was produced in Ireland, devised projects that were even more interdisciplinary in style had been taking place for some time within the thriving amateur theatre scene, and were ongoing within professional contexts. Since the early 1970s, brothers Peter and Jim Sheridan had collaborated with their amateur group Slot Players to create such new productions as *Karak* (1970), as well as their own versions of classics including *Doctor Faustus* (1971), and *Oedipus Rex* (1972) – a response to Derry's Bloody Sunday in which twenty-six civil rights protesters and bystanders were shot by soldiers of the British Army. The work of contemporary bands such as The Doors and Pink Floyd, and dance sequences inspired by this music, were key both within Slot Players' devising processes and the productions created by these activities (Sheridan, 'Slot Players'). By the late 1970s, the Sheridans were playing an important role in running the Project Arts Centre's theatre programme, which often included experimental and devised performances. By 1982, Operating Theatre – originally a band – had also launched its interest in performances based on cooperation between different artists and artistic forms with *Ignotum Per Ignotius*, a highly visual piece with a musical score, written by James Coleman in collaboration with the group's co-directors, Olwen Fouéré and Roger Doyle. Operating Theatre followed with *The Diamond Body* in 1984, written with the company by Aidan Matthews and seeking to interrogate discrimination and violence directed towards homosexual and transgender people. In 1983, theatre designers Monica Frawley and Gabby Dowling were awarded an Arts Council 'Special Theatre Project' grant, which led in December that year to the production at Temple Bar Studios of *Forbidden Fruits*, an almost wordless, visual performance piece that required spectators to move between seven performance spaces – each depicting one of the seven deadly sins. Initially mapped out by Frawley and Dowling, the performances were developed collaboratively with a range of visual artists and performers (Frawley, Personal interview). The names of several performers were recognizable both from the Focus theatre, and TEAM Educational Theatre – a company that has been engaged in devising work for, and occasionally with, young audiences since the mid-1970s.

Dowling and Frawley brought to *Forbidden Fruit* experience with other Irish theatre groups, some of which also employed devised performance practices. Dowling had also designed and performed in Moving Theatre's devised, participatory production *Legs 11*, a community play scripted by dramatist Bernard Farrell and performed as part of the 1979 Dublin Theatre Festival. When *Forbidden Fruit* was produced, Frawley had begun to design sets and costumes for the Irish Theatre Company, as well as Druid theatre in Galway. Although Druid is now associated with championing the work of important Irish playwrights, the company showed in its early years interests in Brechtian epic theatre and devised performance practices. Its production of *Island Protected by a Bridge of Glass* (1980) offered a Brechtian take on local folklore, charting the life of the notorious Grace O'Malley (known by her nickname Granuaile), who lived a life of piracy along the coasts of Connacht until her death around the turn of the seventeenth century. The play, though scripted in the main by Hynes, was created in collaboration with other company members. *Island Protected by a Bridge of Glass* blended 'song, dialogue and balletic movement' and included a musical score by Irish folk band De Dannan to offer 'a kaleidoscope of a particular period of Irish history' (Finlan 10). Productions such as *The Great Hunger*, *Legs 11* and *Island Protected by a Bridge of Glass* reveal the ways in which devising in Irish theatre has accommodated designated roles – including singular authorship. Sweeney points out that *The Great Hunger* was 'the product of an all-embracing creative process, which accommodated the artistry of playwright, director and actors' (51). The histories outlined in this introduction, and several essays within the collection, show how this statement might be applicable to a range of devised projects in Irish theatre.

Yet presenting a collaboratively-made play as the work of one particular dramatist can also have serious ramifications when it comes to sharing credit and royalties. The Project Arts Centre's production of *The Liberty Suit*, first performed at Dublin's Olympia in 1977, is a prime example. The play was originally billed as authored by Peter Sheridan, who went on to play an important role in using devised performance to promote community engagement during the 1980s, as discussed in McIvor's essay in this collection. *The Liberty Suit* is a fictionalized biography of Gerard Mannix Flynn who also starred in the first production. Three years later, Flynn famously took Sheridan to the high court for failing to acknowledge his co-authorship of the play. The case was eventually settled out of court with Sheridan agreeing to give Flynn 33.3 per cent of all royalties, and to present the authorship as Peter Sheridan 'in collaboration with' Gerard Mannix Flynn on all promotional materials (Sheridan, *Break a Leg* 231). Despite the case's settlement out of court, these events soured what had been a fruitful artistic partnership. Moreover, as we have discussed earlier in this section, and as O'Gorman points out elsewhere ('Hers and His'), other productions that have employed devising, but were subsequently billed as written or directed by prominent male artists, have at times served to obscure the extent and specificities of women's contributions to Irish theatre histories.

On the other hand, devised performance has also been harnessed to further women's roles in Irish theatre. Feminist theatre groups historically have used devising, both within Ireland and internationally, to offer more democratic alternatives to the hierarchical organizational structures of institutional theatres, which historically have been mostly dominated by male authors and directors. In 1983, Belfast theatre company Charabanc was established in response to five of its female members' frustration with the absence of dynamic roles for women. The company went on to pioneer independent theatre-making in Northern Ireland, often producing collectively devised work. Later, in the Republic of Ireland, Glasshouse Productions (founded in 1990 in Dublin by four women also seeking to expand women's roles in the theatre) opted for a leaderless, democratic organizational structure, workshopping such plays as Trudy Hayes' *Out of My Head* (1991). In the late 1980s and early 1990s, around the time in which Gregory's co-authorship of *Cathleen ni Houlihan* was revealed, the apparent absence of women playwrights in Ireland was becoming a topic for critique. This was also the period in which the now celebrated dramatist Marina Carr emerged. Carr's early plays *Low in the Dark* (1989) and *This Love Thing* (1991) were written based on group improvisations that focused on gender and representation, utilizing items of clothing and other gendered props. As O'Gorman has discussed elsewhere in 'Writing from the Margins: Marina Carr's Early Theatre,' even though Carr was not part of a feminist theatre group, the mode in which she worked with independent companies during the late 1980s and early 1990s – and the gender-conscious material that emerged from such collaborations – allows us to locate her early plays within national and international feminist theatre histories.

Although critics and academics have responded in vigorous and rigorous ways to the contemporary work of companies such as ANU and Brokentalkers, few have traced the genealogies of such practice within Irish theatre and performance. McIvor, in her essay in this volume and elsewhere, locates current trends in devising within a longer history of Irish community arts, emerging from the 1970s through to the 1980s with the work of such groups as Waterford Arts for All, Belfast's Neighbourhood Open Workshop (NOW), as well as City Workshop, Grapevine, and Moving Theatre in Dublin ('Witnessing the (Broken) Nation' 39). Like ANU and Brokentalkers, practitioners involved in this earlier movement incorporated community contributions (biographical accounts, local histories, and/or community performers), employing devising to address deep-seated issues including poverty, disadvantage, sectarian conflict, and institutional abuse. Many of the companies discussed in this volume use devising to produce theatre that contests hegemonic, stratified constructions of community that are grounded in such interconnected identity categorizations as gender, sexuality, social class, ethnicity, and religion. Others, such as Pan Pan Theatre, and Blue Raincoat (whose working processes are outlined by Trench in this volume), foreground the aesthetic and philosophical potentialities of productions underpinned by highly collaborative working processes.

Outline of Sections and Chapters

Our first section, 'Devising as Collaborative Art,' considers the relationship between political activism, collaborative aesthetic practices in devising, and local community engagement. Jaros' 'Spectres of Connolly: *The Non-Stop Connolly Show* Reconsidered' reconstructs British playwright Arden and Irish political activist and artist D'Arcy's 1975 twenty-six hour performance event *The Non-Stop Connolly Show*. In doing so, Jaros argues that 'the theatrical event that D'Arcy and Arden facilitated (which remains largely absent from most theatre histories of the period) represented a significant step towards later community-based theatre and devised performance.' Continuing on with this genealogical approach, McIvor's 'A Portrait of the Citizen as Artist' locates the work of acclaimed contemporary companies including ANU, Brokentalkers and THEATREclub within histories of 'the formation of the community arts sector in Ireland in the mid-late 1970s and early 1980s.' McIvor particularly emphasizes the relationship between community arts and community development during this period, as aesthetic programmes for local community engagement such as Peter Sheridan and Mick Egan's 1980 City Workshop in north inner city Dublin were frequently run in partnership with temporary or Community Employment Schemes run by FÁS, the Irish National Training and Employment Authority, among other partners. Irene White's 'Whose Art is it Anyway?' offers a case study of Upstate Theatre Project, focusing on the development and influence of this Drogheda-based company, which has operated in the border region since 1993. Similarly to Jaros and McIvor's claims for the foundational influence of community arts, White makes a case for Upstate's formative influence on the field of contemporary devised performance in Ireland and details the dramaturgy of its work at the intersection of community and professional theatre practice. This section concludes with Jesse Weaver's interview with McKevitt, a ground breaking contemporary theatre practitioner whose writing collaborations with non-performers stretch the boundaries of both documentary theatre and devised performance practice in Ireland and beyond.

Section Two, 'Formal Politics,' explores the ways in which the politics of theatrical form – and the relationship of form to contemporary politics – are negotiated in work produced by Dublin-based festivals and companies. Laura Farrell-Wortman's '"A Song about Survival": Talking Shop Ensemble Responds to the Irish Debt Crisis,' as its title suggests, explores how Talking Shop Ensemble's *I am a Homebird (It's Very Hard)* (2011) and *Death of the Tradesmen* (2012) have engaged with and challenged contemporary political and economic circumstances. Farrell-Wortman positions the company's specific demographic (comprising Irish artists in their early twenties) as central to how its work responds to issues including unemployment and mass emigration. She argues that Talking Shop Ensemble advocates for the representation of the unique experience of young Irish adults, 'and for the utility of theatre to create community and, perhaps, a light at the end of the tunnel.' In Chapter Seven, 'A Theatre of Truth?' Haughton coins the phrase 'milieu of truth' to describe 'the general climate of exposure dominating contemporary Irish public and political life,' following revelations of child abuse committed by representatives of the Roman Catholic Church, the economic downturn, and the publication of the Ryan and Cloyne reports in 2009 and 2011 respectively. She argues that the Dublin Fringe Festival offers a key forum for producing challenging creative responses to this 'climate of exposure,' especially by promoting multidisciplinary performances that explore 'critically and creatively notions of truth and fact, and how these notions operate in public and private experience.' Honing in on the work of ANU, a now prominent company that was nurtured by the Dublin Fringe Festival, Haughton offers a perceptive case study, illuminating the ways in which these issues are negotiated in contemporary theatre practice. Chapter Eight is Ruiz's insightful essay, 'Mapping Contemporary European Theatre(s),' which explores the international landscape of experimental, collaboratively-made theatre, focusing on genealogies, different political ideologies and debates in terminology, and using Pan Pan Theatre as a case study. This is aptly followed by an interview with Gavin Quinn, also conducted by Ruiz. Quinn is a founding co-director of Pan Pan, a company that has provided innovation in the development of Irish theatre since the early 1990s.

The third section is entitled 'Regional Practices,' and offers case studies of work produced at a significant geographical distance from the capital cities of Dublin and Belfast. In Chapter Ten, 'Staging Blue Raincoat's productions of W.B. Yeats's *The Cat and the Moon* (2009) and *At the Hawk's Well* (2010),' Trench examines the ways in which collaborative processes combined with techniques in corporeal mime can be used to devise new mise-en-scènes for existing play scripts. Blue Raincoat has been drawing on its company members' training in physical theatre to produce innovative work in Sligo since the early 1990s. Contextualized within Pierre Bourdieu's concept of *habitus* as defined in *The Logic of Practice* (1980), Trench argues for the generative nature of Blue Raincoat's specific *habitus*, which blends the particularities of the company's base in Sligo with its members' long-term collaborations using techniques acquired in Europe. Following this, O'Gorman's 'Repeating, Revising and Devising' examines three devised productions that took place in Galway in 2012: Fregoli's *Home*, Side-Show's *King Alfred: A Mystery Play* and a reimagining of Pat McCabe's *Frank Pig Says Hello* by Galway Youth Theatre and Galway Arts Centre Community Drama. Like Trench, O'Gorman seeks to extend our understanding of devising to a practice that can be used in response to existing scripts, and that can accommodate designated roles such as author, director and/or designer. And, like Trench, O'Gorman examines how local, national and international influences shape a company's theatre-making processes and resulting productions. She concludes that, although 'devised performance within regional urban centres such as Galway is characterized by negotiating marketability, practicality and conceptions of artistic integrity,' it has the potential 'through its processes and outcomes, to challenge broader cultural stratifications and promote a revisionist questioning of deep-seated national values.' This section concludes with McIvor's interview with Máiréad Ní Chronin, co-director of Galway-based Moonfish Theatre, which has since its inception in 2006 produced theatre in Irish and English (sometimes blending both) that often seeks through its scenography to immerse its audience within sensuous experiences. Like the other responses in this section, this interview foregrounds the interconnections of theatre-making processes, performance practices, production contexts and aesthetics in contemporary devised theatre.

In the final section, we travel across the border to examine the ways in which contemporary devised performance practices have been used to negotiate the complexities of Northern Irish identity in the wake of the 'Troubles' – the ethno-nationalist conflict that affected Northern Ireland (sometimes spilling over into the Republic) from the late 1960s to the late 1990s, with sporadic outbursts of violence occurring before and after this time period. Owicki's 'Reawakening Belfast's Streets: Tourism and Education in Site-Specific Northern Irish Theatre' examines two plays staged on the streets of Belfast in 2010: *Belfast Bred* and *The West Awakes*, produced by Kabosh Theatre in association with the owners of select Belfast restaurants and Coiste (which offers tours organized by former republican prisoners) respectively. Owicki argues that, although these works sometimes evade 'the more divisive or controversial events that affected the areas depicted,' perhaps 'an attempt to find other narratives can be beneficial and healing.' In Chapter Fourteen, Caitriona Mary Reilly also focuses on alternative narratives of Northern Irish identity. Her essay, 'Politics, Pride and Performance' examines two works by Northern Ireland's first publicly-funded gay theatre company, TheatreofplucK: *Automatic Bastard* (2006) and *Divided, Radical and Gorgeous* (2011). Reilly makes the important argument that the company's production of theatre with a queer slant has offered a different kind of 'trouble' by disrupting hegemonic Northern Irish identities. The section is rounded off with O'Gorman's interview with Chamberlain, who discusses his role as the current director of Belfast Community Circus, which was established in 1985 with a view to providing positive shared experiences for young people from different communities. The organization launched its street theatre festival, the Festival of Fools, in 2004. Chamberlain reflects on the transformative potential of circus and street theatre in relation to divided and disadvantaged communities.

Conclusion

Studying devised performance entails a rethinking of authorship, calling attention to Irish theatre's long histories of collaboration. Obsessions in Ireland with 'ownership' and 'property' historically 'have been inextricably tied in to questions of Irish independence and national self-determination' (O'Connell xv). These preoccupations, which arguably have contributed to the current fragility of Ireland's economy, have also infected dominant Irish theatre histories. The need to demarcate intellectual property by ascribing works to individual authors has led to a theatrical canon that, at times, forgets its own history. This anxiety to credit creative offerings to specific individuals within a hierarchical framework of author, director, and various members of a production team (tiered on the basis of the perceived 'value' of their inputs) is on-going. It can be detected in the emphasis on playwrights and directors in Irish theatre criticism. O'Gorman has been reviewing Irish theatre for various journalistic public forums since 2008. In her experience of writing reviews, she has frequently had to contact companies when their programme has not provided adequate information about the individual assignment of standard production roles, and has often had companies respond by arbitrarily assigning roles such as costume designer to core members of the group for the sole purpose of answering to the theatre review format. While theatre criticism provides a significant archival function, unfortunately its prevailing structures of emphasis may also contribute to public amnesia by continuing to require the situation of individuals within roles that may not always function so discretely from one another. By focusing on devised performance, we embrace the flexibility and fluidity of roles, the collectivity of creative processes, to recognize forgotten historical contributions and celebrate the work of diverse participants as theatre-makers past and present.

Perhaps the lack of a sustained theorizing of Irish devised theatre's goals, aesthetics and impacts up until now stems from the ways in which some of this work resists containment within linguistic parameters and, hence, is even more 'ephemeral' than the traditional 'play.' In Conway's introduction to *The Oberon Anthology of Contemporary Irish Plays*, he offers, somewhat paradoxically, that the volume entails a published record of recent productions that 'ride in no slipstream of the identifiably Irish play' and offer 'a commitment to become in the theatre' (7). Our own volume seeks to explore rigorously the slipstream that Conway identifies that indeed has changed the face and working processes of Irish theatre in 2015, as well as broadening who can be credited as the 'authors' of contemporary Ireland as lived on the stage. This slipstream can only be navigated through a thorough historical approach to devised performance cognisant of national and international trends in theatre practice that influenced its development, and its implications for the future of Irish theatre as a genre in its own right. In navigating this history, *Devised Performance in Irish Theatre*'s coverage can only be partial, and it is hoped that this collection is the springboard for diverse future inquiries.

Bibliography

Cohen-Cruz, Jan. *Local Acts Community-based Performance in the United States*. New Brunswick, NJ: Rutgers UP, 2005. Print.

Conway, Thomas, ed. *The Oberon Anthology of Contemporary Irish Plays*. London: Oberon, 2012. Print.

Dean, Joan Fitzpatrick. 'Rewriting the Past: Historical Pageantry in the Dublin Civic Weeks of 1927 and 1929.' *New Hibernia Review* 13.1 (2009): 20-41. Print.

Devlin, Joe. 'The Journey to Stanislavski and Beyond.' *Stanislavski in Ireland: Focus at Fifty*. Ed. Brian McAvera and Steven Dedalus Burch. Dublin: Carysfort, 2013. 27-58. Print.

Edwards, Hilton, Micheál Mac Liammóir and G.A. Hayes-McCoy, *Pageant of St.Patrick* (1955). Held in 'Papers of Micheál Mac Liammóir' at the National Library of Ireland, Dublin. MS 41, 256/1-6.

Ferriter, Diarmaid. *The Transformation of Ireland, 1900-2000*. London: Profile, 2004.Print.

Finlan, Michael. 'New Play at Druid Theatre.' *The Irish Times* 14 May 1980: 10. ProQuest Historical Newspapers. Web. 10 Nov. 2014.

Fischer-Lichte, Erika. *Theatre, Sacrifice, Ritual: Exploring Forms of Political Theatre*. London: Routledge, 2005. Print.

Fitzgerald, Sandy, ed. 'The Beginnings of Community Arts and the Irish Republic.' *An Outburst of Frankness: Community Arts in Ireland: A Reader*. Dublin: Tasc at New Island, 2004. 64-79. Print.

---. 'Introduction.' *An Outburst of Frankness: Community Arts in Ireland: A Reader*. Ed. Sandy Fitzgerald. Dublin: Tasc at New Island, 2004. 1-3. Print.

---. *An Outburst of Frankness: Community Arts in Ireland: A Reader*. Dublin: Tasc at New Island, 2004. Print.

Fox, Christie. *Breaking Forms: The Shift to Performance in Late Twentieth-Century Irish Drama*. Newcastle upon Tyne: Cambridge Scholars Pub., 2008. Print.

Frawley, Monica. Personal interview with Siobhán O'Gorman. 25 Sept. 2014.

Govan, Emma, Katie Normington, and Helen Nicholson. *Making a Performance: Devising Histories and Contemporary Practices.* London: Routledge, 2007. Print.

Haughton, Miriam and Mária Kurdi. *Radical Contemporary Theatre Practices by Women in Ireland.* Dublin: Carysfort, 2015. Print.

Heddon, Deirdre, and Jane Milling. *Devising Performance: A Critical History.* Basingstoke: Palgrave Macmillan, 2006. Print.

Hickey, Tom. Personal interview with Siobhán O'Gorman. 19 March 2014.

Kerrigan, Sheila. *The Performer's Guide to the Collaborative Process.* Portsmouth, NH: Heinemann, 2001. Print.

Lamden, Gill. *Devising: A Handbook for Drama and Theatre Students.* London: Hodder & Stoughton, 2000. Print.

Lonergan, Patrick. 'Eight Irish Dramatists Discuss Irish Playwriting Today.' *Scenes from the Bigger Picture.* Wordpress, 1 July 2013. Web. 17 Dec.2014.

Lonergan, Patrick. 'New British Drama and Playwriting in Ireland.' Web log post. *Scenesfrom the Bigger Picture.* Wordpress, 24 June 2013. Web. 17 Dec. 2014.

Maguire, Tom. *Making Theatre in Northern Ireland: Through and beyond the Troubles.* Exeter: U of Exeter, 2006. Print.

McAvera Brian and Steven Dedalus Burch, eds. *Stanislavski in Ireland: Focus at Fifty.* Dublin, Carysfort, 2013. Print.

McDonnell, Bill. *Theatres of the Troubles: Theatre, Resistance and Liberation in Ireland.* Exeter: U of Exeter, 2008. Print.

McIvor, Charlotte and Matthew Spangler. *Staging Intercultural Ireland: Plays and Practitioner Perspectives.* Cork: Cork UP, 2014. Print.

McIvor, Charlotte. '*Theatre of Good Intentions: Challenges and Hopes for Theatre and Social Change by Dani Snyder-Young.*' Rev. *Contemporary Theatre Review* 24.4 (2014): 523-25. Print.

---. 'Witnessing the (Broken) Nation: Theatre of the Real and Social Fragmentation in Brokentalkers' *Silver Stars, The Blue Boy* and *Have I No Mouth.*' *'That Was Us': Contemporary Irish Theatre and Performance.* Ed. Fintan Walsh. London: Oberon, 2013. 37-56. Print.

McGrath, Aoife. *Dance Theatre in Ireland: Revolutionary Moves.* Basingstoke: Palgrave Macmillan, 2012. Print.

Moynihan, Mary. 'Loving the Art in Yourself: A Short History of Focus Theatre.' *Stanislavski in Ireland: Focus at Fifty.* Ed. Brian McAvera and Steven Dedalus Burch. Dublin: Carysfort, 2013. 5-25. Print.

Mulrooney, Deirdre. *Irish Moves: An Illustrated History of Dance and Physical Theatre in Ireland.* Dublin: Liffey, 2006. Print.

Murray, Christopher. 'Beckett Productions in Ireland: A Survey.' *Irish University Review* 14.1 (1984): 103-25. Print.

O'Connell, Cathal. *The State and Housing in Ireland: Ideology, Policy and Practice*. New York: Nova Science, 2007. Print.

Oddey, Alison. *Devising Theatre: A Practical and Theoretical Handbook*. London: Routledge, 1994. Print.

O'Gorman, Siobhán. '"Hers and His:" Carolyn Swift, Alan Simpson and Collective Creation at Dublin's Pike Theatre.' *Women, Collective Creation, and Devised Theatre*. Ed. Kathryn Syssoyeva and Scott Proudfit. New York: Palgrave Macmillan, Forthcoming.

---. 'Writing from the Margins: Marina Carr's Early Theatre.' *Irish Studies Review* 22.4 (2014): 487-511. Print.

Pethica, James. '"Our Kathleen": Yeats's Collaboration with Lady Gregory in the Writing of *Cathleen ni Houlihan*.' *Yeats Annual* 6. Ed. Warwick Gould. London: Macmillan, 1988. 3-31. Print.

Phillips, Áine, ed. *Performance Art in Ireland: A History*. Bristol: Intellect, 2015. Print.

Pilkington, Lionel. 'The Little Theatres of the 1950s.' *The Oxford Handbook of Modern Irish Theatre*. Oxford: Oxford UP, Forthcoming.

---. 'Theatre, Sexuality and State: Tennessee Williams's *The Rose Tattoo* at the Dublin Theatre Festival, 1957.' *Interactions: Dublin Theatre Festival 1957-2007*. Ed. Nicholas Green and Patrick Lonergan. Dublin: Carysfort, 2008. 21-33. Print.

---. 'Theatre History and the Beginnings of the Irish National Theatre Project.' *Theatre Stuff: Critical Essays on Contemporary Irish Theatre*. Ed. Eamonn Jordan. Dublin: Carysfort, 2000. 27-33. Print.

Radosavljevic, Duška. *Theatre-making: Interplay between Text and Performance in the 21st Century*. Houndmills, Basingstoke, Hampshire and New York: Palgrave Macmillan, 2013. Print.

Sheridan, Eileen. 'The Lantern Theatre 1957-1975.' Unpublished dissertation, held in 'Records of the Lantern Theatre' at the National Library of Ireland, Dublin. MS 40,215/7.

Sheridan, Peter. *Break a Leg: A Memoir*. Dublin: New Island, 2012. Print.

Sheridan, Peter. 'Slot Players.' Telephone interview with Siobhán O'Gorman. 10 Nov. 2014.

Sweeney, Bernadette. *Performing the Body in Irish Theatre*. Houndmills, Basingstoke and Hamshire: Palgrave Macmillan, 2008. Print.

Synge, J. M. *The Complete Works of J. M. Synge*. Ed. Aidan Arrowsmith. Ware, Hertfordshire: Wordsworth, 2008. Print.

Syssoyeva, Kathryn Mederos, and Scott Proudfit, eds. *A History of Collective Creation*. New York: Palgrave Macmillan, 2013. Print.

---, eds. *Collective Creation in Contemporary Performance*. New York: Palgrave Macmillan, 2013. Print.

Syssoyeva, Kathryn Mederos. 'Toward a New History of Collective Creation.' *Collective Creation in Contemporary Performance*. Ed. Kathryn Mederos Syssoyeva and Scott Proudfit. New York: Palgrave Macmillan, 2013. 1-11. Print.

Szabo Carmen. *The Story of Barabbas The Company*. Dublin: Carysfort, 2012. Print.

Thompson, James. *Performance Affects: Applied Theatre and the End of Effect*. Houndmills, Basingstoke and Hamshire: Palgrave Macmillan, 2009. Print.

Trench, Rhona. *Blue Raincoat Theatre Company*. Dublin: Carysfort, 2015. Print.

Trotter, Mary. *Modern Irish Theatre*. Cambridge: Polity, 2008. Print.

Upstate Theatre Project. 'About Us.' Upstate Theatre Project. Web. 17 November 2014.

Walsh, Fintan, ed. *'That Was Us': Contemporary Irish Theatre and Performance*. Oberon: London, 2013. Print.

---, ed. *Queer Notions: New Plays and Performances from Ireland*. Cork: Cork UP, 2010. Print.

Section One: Devising as Collaborative Art

2 | Spectres of Connolly: *The Non-Stop Connolly Show* Reconsidered

Michael Jaros

Introduction

In a 2008 edition of the journal *Interventions,* dedicated to James Connolly's lasting influences in the 21st century, David Lloyd opines in the afterword, 'why still read Connolly?' The 'question remains,' he maintains, 'is [Connolly's] work too specific, too particular [...] to have any capacity to transfer to the present moment?' (117). Addressing those who remain skeptical of Connolly's lasting influence, he answers with a resounding no: Connolly's life and work in fact 'reopen a sense of possibility in Irish history' (118). Writing at the beginning of the slide into the present financial crisis, Lloyd notes that Connolly provided a way of:

> thinking beyond the economic and political paradigms of the neo-colonial, global capitalism that has renovated the forms of domination in our time, forms in which the Irish elites have been too keen to participate. Part of rethinking Connolly historically will prove inseparable from imagining, as he did, futures that run against the grain of the present (118).

Lloyd speaks here about Connolly's *texts*, but how might one imagine embodying Connolly's legacies in theatrical *performance,* especially within the historically loaded cityscape of Dublin itself? What might a successful act of recovering Connolly look like? Given Connolly's own historical involvement in the street theatre of social protest, the traditional theatre – which fellow socialist Bertolt Brecht so memorably dubbed the 'sausage machine' of material culture ('Emphasis' 8) – might not be the most fertile place to search.

In Easter Week of 1975, British playwright John Arden and his partner, Irish political activist Margretta D'Arcy, staged their twenty-six-hour long political passion play, 'a drama of continuous struggle in six acts,' aptly titled *The Non-Stop Connolly Show*. The work was an outright rejection of the material conditions of theatrical production, which they equated with the 'meaningless foam rubber of the jumbo jet culture' (*Awkward* 4). The daylong performance sought actively to involve the working-class Dublin community in an alternative commemorative event, a 'giant pop festival of the left' ('Socialist' 118) that would bring Connolly's neglected socialism to the forefront of Irish cultural discourse. It is my contention that the theatrical event that D'Arcy and Arden facilitated (which remains largely absent from most theatre histories of the period) represented a significant step towards later community-based theatre and devised performance. Despite their somewhat fraught attempts to remain in authorial control of the production, the work shared with earlier devised work an ideological opposition 'to the economic imperatives of the commercial theatrical marketplace' (Heddon and Milling 19), and also sought actively to involve the community in the collective creation of the overall festival. D'Arcy and Arden's work, then, is an important benchmark in the transition from authorial to collective forms of creation in political theatre in Ireland, one that in fact sought to embody a genealogy of performance begun by Connolly himself in his own street theatre protests at the beginning of the twentieth century.

Spectres of Connolly

There have certainly been other, more recent attempts to memorialize Connolly in performance that were politically and socially engaging. 2013 was itself the centenary of one of the most famous labour protests in Irish history, the Dublin Lockout, the largest labour strike in Irish history, in which Connolly was integrally involved. Consequently, the Abbey staged its new version of James Plunkett's work about Dublin's urban poor during the Lockout, *The Risen People* (originally produced by the Abbey at the Queen's Theatre in 1958) to an underwhelming reception. During the Dublin Fringe Festival that year, ANU productions' *Thirteen* (discussed below) more successfully revived the spirit of the Lockout by converting Dublin's city centre into a series of performance zones that attempted to return the space and stakes of the Lockout to the post-Celtic tiger present. However, several productions of the preceding decade call for a more sustained discussion, if only to contrast their overall scopes and methodologies with the type of performances Arden and D'Arcy advocated. In 2009, Frank Allen's play *12 Days in May* was staged at Liberty Hall in Dublin, the present headquarters of the Services, Industrial, Professional and Technical Union (SIPTU). The staging location was quite strategic, as this Liberty Hall was built over the original structure which had been the home of the Irish Transport and General Workers' Union, from which Connolly had himself marched forth at the head of the Irish Citizen Army (ICA) to participate in the 1916 Rising. Decimated by British shelling, the building had been faithfully restored after the Rising, and was in use until being condemned in the 1950s, leading to the present, modernist structure on the Liffey. Allen's *12 days* depicted the last twelve of Connolly's life, following his arrest during the Easter Rising. The play, which was in general reviewed unfavourably, featured a prone Connolly in bed, already a monument devoid of any sense of dynamism. Connolly's life and actions, which covered two continents and many decades, were reduced to the recognizable frame of a family drama. Nevertheless, the specter of Connolly seemed to hover over the performance; one blogger noted that she herself attended the play 'on a day when public sector strikes were happening all over the country' (Sharon). Allen's play, put on within Connolly's own union hall, seemed disengaged from its immediate cultural context: the real theatre was transpiring in the streets outside.

Three years earlier, in 2006, Connolly's corporeal absence dominated Ken Loach and Paul Laverty's widely-distributed film *The Wind that Shakes the Barley*, the story of which unfolds in the aftermath of the Easter Rising in County Cork, where the character Dan, an erstwhile member of Connolly's Citizen Army, speaks for the slain Connolly's betrayed legacy in the subsequent birth of the Irish Free State. At one point, Dan, and the protagonist of the film, Damien, both chant a passage from Connolly's political writings as if it was a communal litany.[1] Both die in the subsequent birthing of the state, which is rendered cinematographically as the first fated step on the path to Celtic Tiger consumerism: without a Socialist Republic, Dan

---

[1] 'If you remove the English army tomorrow and hoist the green flag over Dublin Castle, unless you set about the organization of the Socialist Republic your efforts would be in vain. England would still rule you. She would rule you through her capitalists, through her landlords, through her financiers, through the whole array of commercial and individualist institutions she has planted in this country and watered with the tears of our mothers and the blood of our martyrs' (Connolly 124).

maintains, in a forceful paraphrasing of Connolly's writing, all that a revolution will have changed are the 'accents of the powerful and the colour of the flag.' Connolly's words here become a forsaken gospel that Loach and Laverty suggest was all too prescient.

Walter Benjamin's well-known work, 'Theses on the Philosophy of History,' informs Lloyd's opening quote about *reading* Connolly, and any attempt at *performing* Connolly must also approach Connolly's legacy radically, must render it 'charged with the time of the now and blasted from the continuum of history' (Benjamin 261). Achieving such contemporaneity means eschewing monumentality in favor of active, collective engagement, while at the same time avoiding predictable dramatic narratives that seem ill-fitted to the purposes at hand. *12 Days in May,* itself developed from an abandoned film script, and *The Wind that Shakes the Barley,* although helmed by a critically acclaimed director (Loach) with established Labour ties, both envelop their stories of the betrayal of Connolly's Socialist Republic in the readily digestible melodrama of familial relations. In both the above works, Connolly is not an active participant in the dramatic action, but is dying or already dead, a fossilized monument with some testament to give to the present.

Connolly and Political Performance

Connolly was himself no admirer of monumentality. He preferred a less prescriptive dialogue with public space and memory: Catherine Morris recently highlighted how Connolly employed theatrical tactics throughout his career as a socialist agitator, from helping Maud Gonne organize the 'funeral for the British Empire' in 1897 as a counter-performance to Queen Victoria's Jubilee, to his use of a coffin parade during the 1911 Belfast lock-out, demonstrating in these and other cases his 'commitment to exploring how the emergent nationalist culture in Ireland could depict itself in public space' (104). Connolly's first editorial in *The Workers Republic* (1889) argues against the statue-raising madness of the 1798 centenary, especially the failed efforts to raise money for a statue to Wolfe Tone for St. Stephen's Green. Connolly protests that such monuments to 'dead heroes represented empty gestures and the worst forms of intellectual bankruptcy' (qtd. in Morris 107). Theatrical gestures directly attached to collective action seemed much more his forte: a decade and a half later, as if to demonstrate this point, he staged his own play, *Under Which Flag,* at Liberty Hall a month before the Easter Rising. Although melodramatic in its composition, and with a theme of nationalist sacrifice very similar to Lady Gregory and W.B. Yeats' famous 1902 play *Cathleen ni Houlihan*, its engagement with the present historical moment was radical: the author and several of the chief actors in the play would be dead in several weeks. After the conclusion of the play's premiere performance, lead actor Seán Connolly (no relation to James), carried the flag used in the production to the roof of Liberty Hall. It was this same flag that the actor would carry in his assault on Dublin's city hall weeks later during the actual Rising, where he was shot dead by British sniper fire while attempting to raise it on the roof of that second building (Ritschel 67). The union headquarters at Liberty Hall became not only a munitions dump for the ensuing rebellion, but a complex site of historical reckoning, where the theatre of the Rising itself was literally rehearsed.

In staging a play about the 1867 Fenian Rebellion a few weeks before an actual rebellion would occur within the same space, Connolly seemed to understand the importance of establishing his own place of memory; he created it not by building monuments, but instead through an embodied engagement with urban space. Pierre Nora notes that such places of memory are complex sites of historical engagement: these places exist because of 'their capacity for metamorphosis, an endless recycling of their meaning and an unpredictable proliferation of their ramifications' (Nora 19). Importantly, they are not *only* stone and mortar, or marble, or bronze, but are also comprised of the plurality of human interactions that occur within those spaces, interactions either directly or indirectly associated with remembrance. If, then, as David Lloyd says, the figure of Connolly himself is 'a sign of the unclosed field of possibilities for the imagination of what the unfinished project of decolonization might continue to mean in Ireland' (118), then it follows that a place of memory associated with him would be complex. What might such a space, which Nora notes is 'forever open to the full range of its possible significations, yet still concentrated in its own name' (24), in this case 'Connolly,' look like?

The Non-Stop Connolly Show

The Non-Stop Connolly Show sought to open up such a space of possibility at a critical moment in Irish history. In 1975, the Irish economy was a shambles, unemployment was rampant, and violence in Northern Ireland seemed certain to continue for decades. Cultural critic Conor Cruise O'Brien was to issue his famous warning about the 'unhealthy intersection' between art and politics that August,[2] and the seasons at the Gate and Abbey theatres were fairly traditional and tame, composed primarily of works by Henrik Ibsen, Somerville and Ross, with the notable exception being Brian Friel's *Volunteers* at the Abbey (Johnston 410-11). This was the cultural moment within which Margaretta D'Arcy and John Arden staged their work, which started Easter Sunday, 1975, and ran into the next Monday.

The critical reviews that emerged in the wake of the play were mixed at best, but focused almost exclusively on the text versus the twenty-six-hour long performance. Writing in *Theatre Quarterly,* Paddy Marsh sought to evaluate the play from a standpoint of its literary merit, as if a play of such length, featuring both professional and semi-trained actors, performed in the streets and in a flexible stage-space in a union hall – and for an audience more akin to one at a rock concert – could be reviewed as if it were a two and a half hour domestic drama at the Gate Theatre. *The Guardian* theatre critic was less merciful, calling it 'unbelievably inept' pedantry; she focused specifically on the script's length and the performance's lack of organization that, in her opinion, 'managed to make deeply moving events into stultifying boredom' (Cooke).

A few years after the premiere, critic Henry Schvey did attempt a broader critical assessment of the play as a collaborative, performance-based enterprise, but still asserted that D'Arcy and Arden's purported trajectory toward radicalism produced not vital, popular spectacle, but 'a pedant's idea of popular theatre' (68). Arden had been collaborating with D'Arcy for some years before the composition of *The Non-Stop Connolly Show.* Together, they had moved away from traditionally organized and funded theatrical productions in both Ireland and the UK towards more community-based performance work. Evaluating their collaborative work together, in opposition to Arden's earlier work as an established British playwright working in more conventional forms, Schvey remarks that they had merely created 'agitprop theatre, having exchanged the Brechtian tradition of intellectual paradox for the Brechtian tradition of the *Lehrstück,* which [...] was intended to teach the tactics of class war' (63). For Schvey, Arden devolved from an

---

[2] O'Brien argued for a severance of literature from politics, calling the meeting of the two an 'unhealthy intersection,' He suggested that the 1916 Rising was largely unnecessary, and would perhaps not have occurred if literature and nationalist politics had not been so entwined. O'Brien specifically related these concerns to the ongoing crisis in Northern Ireland at the time (O'Brien).

intellectually complex playwright into a collaborator working on community-based propaganda, whereas Bertolt Brecht's career evolved away from the agit-prop, educational work of his youth towards his later 'mature' works. Despite his attempts to evaluate D'Arcy and Arden's work in some other way but aesthetically, he ultimately fails to do so, reconfirming earlier criticisms of the work's (read: script's) aesthetic limitations, and essentially upholding the cult of the playwright.

D'Arcy and Arden were in fact very much aligned with Brecht's attempts to bring new, working-class audiences into the theatre with the goal of inciting social change. They had little to no interest in rendering Connolly for traditional, upper-middle class audiences. Brecht's collaborative *Lehrstücke* had likewise been aligned against conventional notions of the material theatre in his own time; they assaulted the theatre as both an institution and a business model, one that was uncannily successful at defanging radical forms of performance within its apparatus (Brecht, 'Modern' 34-35). From the outset, D'Arcy and Arden's production plan was similarly directed against the bourgeois theatre culture of the capital. 'It was not credible,' they maintained, 'that plays on this subject, and on so large a scale could be produced in the ordinary context of Irish middle class theatre practice' (D'Arcy and Arden, 'Socialist' 118). They advertised in trade union papers and in the 'industrial' section of the *The Irish Times,* and secured funding from the ITWGU and Sinn Fein. They invited no major critics to the production, nor did they seem to care if they came. The audience they wished to attract was working class, people who were 'primarily socialists and republicans' ('Socialist' 135). After the initial production, they also hoped to tour parts of the production in the theatrically disenfranchised housing estates of north Dublin.

The festival itself was conceived as primarily a participatory, collaborative event. Interspersed with smaller plays from the British company Red Ladder and the Puny Little Theater from Dublin, screenings of films by Sergei Eisenstein, and even meals catered by the union, the entire theatrical event was conceived, as D'Arcy notes, as more of a pop festival than a sit-down theatrical experience (118). People arrived with sleeping bags, and came and went throughout the long evening as they pleased, with audience attendance reaching over 400 people at its height. The actors themselves were taken from a small smattering of Dublin's professional cadre, including those in the fringe theatre scene of the time and members of the workers' cultural group, who had little to no experience in theatre (and who sang songs in the interim); the children required by the script were provided by members of the Fianna youth group. As directors, Arden and D'Arcy brought in Robert Walker from Britain, along with future film director Jim Sheridan, who was, along with his brother Peter, to become quite involved in the Dublin fringe theatre scene at the Project Arts Centre a year later (Morash 248). This large-scale, improvisational collaboration, did not seem a far cry from what Arden himself had written earlier about Brecht's learning plays, describing them as 'workshop[s] where every worker was independently and communally dedicated to the construction of an image of society that should express both the fallibility of humanity and also its potential majesty' (Arden, 'Brecht' 40). For D'Arcy and Arden, this meant building up an interactive theatre of the working class in Dublin. Fred Johnston, who acted in the production, remembers *The Non-Stop Connolly Show* as a 'whole-hearted public involvement,' the 'play as argument, as public and accessible discussion forum' in opposition to the critical sphere of the 'play as art.' Actor-audience interaction remained flexible, and one would sit through 'all or part of it, one would partake as one wished' (412).

Liberty Hall did not offer the cast a traditional theatrical space, but instead a giant room in which roughly-assembled platforms shared space with banners, projection screens, and giant puppets (strongly influenced by D'Arcy and Arden's experiences with Vermont's Bread and Puppet Theatre). Performers playing Tory aristocrats donned grotesque masks to resemble birds of prey, and the demon-king 'Grabitall' wore the same mask throughout. Such carnivalesque tactics very much echoed the performance conventions of the protest marches Connolly had himself helped to orchestrate at the beginning of the century. This six-part series of plays, however, had the sweeping scope of a religious passion play, with an ongoing allegorical battle between Socialism and Capitalism, of which the Easter Rising was only one event among many. The actor playing Connolly linked the events together, as he moved between Scotland, Europe, America and Ireland.

The Non-Stop Connolly Show was conceived, then, as a communal workshop, an extension of Brecht's ideas into D'Arcy and Arden's own time. Specifically, this meant creating a cultural intervention in the urban space of downtown Dublin, a memorial counter-performance to the official celebrations of the 1916 Easter Rising underway at the same time. It sought to open the space to a larger range of meanings than those provided by these official celebrations. This meant involving the actors and audience in a radical counter-performance to the traditional commemorations of Easter Week at work outside the union hall. The day-long event itself commenced with a parade: before the production began, the cast, as D'Arcy and Arden recall, 'marched in costume to the beat of a drum up O'Connell Street to the post office and round the side streets, carrying banners and some of the large puppets which were to be used in the plays' (D'Arcy and Arden, 'Socialist' 125-6).

The parade route moved in the same direction up O'Connell Street to the General Post Office that the official processions of Easter Week also took. By the 1970s, these celebrations had become rather stale affairs, especially toned down during the Troubles. 'Conservative nationalist parties,' Declan Kiberd remarks, 'encouraged the people to become drunk on remembrance' (4). These official parades, for Kiberd, covered over the Republic's failure to implement so many of the social promises of the foundational revolution. In this context, Kiberd goes on to say, 'it might have seemed reasonable to some that the fittest way to honour a man like James Connolly was a strategic forgetfulness of his life and sacrifice' (5). D'Arcy and Arden's work certainly sought to highlight the disparity between the goals of the rebellion and the modern realities of the postcolonial state, specifically the separation of Republicanism and Socialism, by gathering a 'congregation of protest against the current Fine Gael/Labour "revision of history" attitudes, which deprecate the 1916 Rising on specious grounds' (D'Arcy and Arden, 'Socialist' 135). Remembering 1916 had first been made 'safe,' in their view, and was now in danger of becoming superfluous; the two authors wanted to address the radical nature of Connolly's involvement in the Rising.

The performance of *The Non-Stop Connolly Show* was certainly aligned against such forgetting of Connolly's various sacrifices, but it also sought to make him more than a monument or disembodied words, as Allen and Loach's versions would subsequently do. Instead, D'Arcy and Arden wished to bring Connolly and his radicalism back to the place he had first made important historically. 'Not only the Rising,' D'Arcy and Arden note, 'but also the demonstrations and riots of the 1913 Lockout took place in these very streets just around the post office.' Within this space, they remarked, they were 'deliberately setting out to re-create a national – and local – folk hero, who has long been enshrined in an iconic portrait, but whose detailed life is not well-known, still less his particular political activities and controversies' (D'Arcy and Arden, 'Socialist' 126). It is clear from such statements that the creators' investment in staging a series of plays about Connolly was directly tied to the space within which the production transpired.

O'Connell Street had itself already been prone to more radical forms of performance than mere commemorative parades, most famously with the IRA's detonation of the Nelson Column in 1966, itself a counter-performance to the official celebrations of the 50-year anniversary of 1916. Two years before D'Arcy and Arden staged their play at Liberty Hall, the Ulster Volunteer Force had detonated a bomb that had shattered almost all the windows in the thirteen-story structure.

Conceived and staged within such a contested space, Connolly became both a local and a global figure, moving through a forest of the giant puppets of the Capitalist establishment, both in Ireland and abroad. But consistently, the various lives of Connolly were all linked to the present moment of Easter week in 1970s' Ireland. In such a vein, the twenty-six-hour performance ended with Connolly directly addressing the audience:

> We were the first to roll away the stone
> From the leprous wall of the whitened tomb
> We were the first to show the dark deep hole within
> Could be thrown open to the living sun
> We were the first to feel their loaded gun
> That would prevent us doing it anymore –
> Or so they hoped. We were the first. We shall not be the last.
> This was not history. It has not passed. (448)

Connolly's final, messianic words from the stage blasted forth, calling for an engagement with modern history in the very space within which an earlier, radical history had transpired. The passion play of the 'continuous struggle' of socialism moved beyond the six-act work and into the present. Even in the face of the work's harsh critical reception, D'Arcy and Arden look back on *The Non-Stop Connolly Show* as their greatest achievement with regard to what they in later years came to term 'The Matter of Ireland' ('Introduction' 4) The existing government of Ireland did not fall, and a Socialist Republic was not born from the event, but D'Arcy and Arden did successfully stage a performance absolutely outside the material theatrical conditions of the day, and helped to provide a pathway towards collectively engaging with urban space through performance. Although the funds did not materialize after the initial performance's expenditure for the production to be toured to various working class neighbourhoods both within and outside Dublin, the production had in effect shown that creating large-scale, site-specific, and socially conscious theatre was possible, and that there was a demand for it.

Conclusion

Many of the people who were directly involved in *The Non-Stop Connolly Show*, from playwright Tom Kilroy, to Jim and Peter Sheridan, were among those who would continue to populate the avant-garde theatre in Ireland in the later 1970s and early 1980s, and were no doubt influenced by their participation in the event. The production, D'Arcy and Arden remark later, 'certainly gave people a feeling that the presentation of plays with some solidity of content was possible without having to accept the normal apparatus of "production technique" and that fairly spontaneous street or yard performances could be a regular feature of Irish urban life' ('Socialist' 133). The daylong performance about Connolly's unfinished revolution sought to enter into a complex dialogue about history and meaning in the Dublin capital at a critical moment in its history. *The Non-Stop Connolly Show's* lasting importance, then, is located not in the aesthetic merits of the performances and certainly not in the script itself, but in how those twenty-six hours during Easter-week provided a benchmark for a potentially viable theatrical event that was both participatory and specific to the sites that it occupied. As Johnston recalls more than thirty years later, it created 'a discussion on whether or not the ordinary people mattered; whether they had a participating role in a politics and a history which was slowly being removed from their reach' (418). In October 2013, to mark the 100th anniversary of the 1913 Dublin Lockout, ANU Productions made the urban spaces of downtown Dublin resonate again through their site-specific work about the 1913 Dublin Lockout, *Thirteen*. Performed as part of the Dublin Fringe Festival, the work took place in locations around the city (including within the 'bowels of Liberty Hall'), for thirteen days of the fringe festival. Conceived, as the creators note, to allow 'audiences to immerse themselves in the tumultuous events of 1913 as they unfold in present day Dublin' ('ANU'), the company sought to again make history contemporaneous, linking the fraught stories of 1913 to the modern inequalities of post-Celtic tiger Dublin. In such a production, one hears a ghostly echo of Connolly's last words from D'Arcy and Arden's script – 'this is not history. It has not passed.' As an important stepping-stone to such later work, *The Non-Stop Connolly Show* clearly deserves a more pronounced space in Irish performance history.

Works Cited

'ANU, Thirteen.' *fringefest.com/strands/thirteen*. 9 Jan 2014. Web.

Arden, John. 'Brecht and the British.' *To Present the Pretence: Essays on the Theatre and Its Public*. London: Methuen, 1977. 37-41. Print.

Benjamin, Walter. 'Theses on the Philosophy of History.' *Illuminations*. Trans. Harry Zohn. New York: Schocken Books, 1968. 253-64. Print.

Brecht, Bertolt. 'Emphasis on Sport.' *Brecht on Theatre: The Development of an Aesthetic*. Trans. John Willett. New York: Hill and Wang, 1964. 6-9. Print.

---. 'The Modern Theatre is the Epic Theatre.' *Brecht on Theatre*. 33-42. Print.

Brecht, Bertolt and Hanns Eisler. 'Open Letter to the Artistic Board of the "Neue Musik", Berlin, 1930.' *Brecht: Collected Plays Vol. 3*. Ed, Trans John Willett. London: Methuen, 1997. 343-44. Print.

Connolly, James. *Selected Writings*. Ed. P Beresford Ellis. London: Pluto Press, 1997. Print.

Cooke, Harriet, '*The Nonstop Connolly Show,* Reviewed by Harriet Cooke.' *The Guardian*. Reprinted in Paddy Marsh. 'Easter at Liberty Hall: The Arden's Non-Stop Connolly Show.' *Theatre Quarterly*: 5:20 (1975): 141. Print.

D'Arcy, Margaretta and Arden, John. 'Introduction: by J.A.' *Awkward Corners*. London: Methuen,1988. 4-8. Print.

---. *The Non-Stop Connolly Show*. London: Methuen, 1977. Print.

---. 'A Socialist Hero Onstage.' *To Present the Pretence: Essays on the Theatre and Its Public*. London: Methuen, 1977. 92-138. Print.

Johnston, Fred. 'The non-stop Connolly Show: A Political Passion Play.' *Studies*: 96:384 (2007) 407-19. Print.

Heddon, Deirdre and Milling, Jane. *Devising Performance: A Critical History*. London: Palgrave, 2005. Print.

Lloyd, David. 'Why Read Connolly?' *Interventions:* 10:1 (2008): 116-123. Print.

Marsh, Paddy. 'Easter at Liberty Hall: the Ardens' Non-Stop Connolly Show.' *Theatre Quarterly*: 5:20 (1975) 133-41. Print.

Morash, Christopher. *A History of Irish Theatre, 1601-2000*. Cambridge: Cambridge UP, 2002. Print.

Morris, Catherine. 'A Contested Life: James Connolly in the 21st Century.' *Interventions:* 10:1 (2008): 102-15. Print.

O'Brien, Connor Cruise. 'An Unhealthy Intersection.' *The Irish Times* 21 August 1975. Print.

Nora, Pierre. 'Between Memory and History: *Les Lieux de Memoire.*' *Representations*: 26 (1989): 7-24. Print.

'Review: 12 Days in May.' Soundtracksforthem.com. 8 June 2013. Web.

Ritschel, Nelson Ó Ceallaigh. 'James Connolly's *Under Which Flag*, 1916.' *New Hibernia Review:* 2:4 (1998): 54-68. Web.

Sharon, '*Twelve Days in May.*' *Culch.ie.* 10 May 2012. Web.

The Wind that Shakes the Barley. Screenplay by Paul Laverty. Dir. Ken Loach. Pathé International, 2006. Film.

3 | A Portrait of the Citizen as Artist: Community Arts, Devising and Contemporary Irish Theatre Practice

Charlotte McIvor

Introduction

In 2011, The Dublin Theatre Festival featured the work of three key emerging companies who engage with devising at the centre of their working practice: ANU Productions (*Laundry* and *World's End Lane*), Brokentalkers (*The Blue Boy*) and THEATREclub (*Heroin*). These productions explored the histories of Dublin's Monto red light district and inner city prostitution, Magdalene Laundries, abuse in state-run industrial and reformatory schools, and the heroin epidemic. Working through devised techniques, these companies mixed multiple genres in their work including documentary theatre, immersive theatre, dance, physical theatre and installation but were most crucially connected by their use of community cast members in performance or as collaborative partners through research, interviews or work with community groups as part of their devising practice. I use 'community' here to imply non-professional participants unified in these cases as communities of place and interest. This chapter explores the relationship between community engagement and devising in Irish theatre history through connecting the formation of the community arts movement in late-1970s Ireland to contemporary devising practice focused on engagement with community as a core working practice.

For ANU, Brokentalkers and THEATREclub, the inclusion of community cast members in performance or as collaborative partners through research, interviews or work with community groups as part of their devising practice have become hallmarks of their work, as was evident at the 2011 Dublin Theatre Festival and in all their output since. ANU Production's *World's End Lane* and *Laundry* were dependent on a relationship with the community as 'vital to how these pieces are developed and staged' ('Re: Community Engagement and "Laundry"'). This relationship included the use of physical space in the community, personal interviews and local records for research by the company as part of the devising process through partnership with the North Inner City Folklore Project among other groups. *Laundry* was developed in partnership with fourteen community participants and also featured performances by some community cast members including Laura Murray and Tony Murphy, who owned and managed the Scrub a Dub Launderette used as one of the sites for the performance.

Heroin was conceived while THEATREclub's Grace Dyas was working under the auspices of CREATE's 'Artist in the Community' scheme through the Arts Council in Rialto. She writes: 'I started to devise a piece of work with the Men's Group at Rialto Community Drug Team. They wanted to make a piece about street language [...] If I would help them with their piece, they would help me with mine' (Dyas). Unlike ANU or Brokentalkers, THEATREclub do not feature community cast members in their productions, but rather partner with them exclusively for the creation of the work.

For Brokentalkers, as Chris McCormack observes, their work gives a 'voice to people in society you don't often hear, whether it's the immigrants in *Track*' an audio tour of Dublin narrated by Chinese narrators 'or the kids in Dublin Youth Theatre' in *This is Still Life* 'or the gay men in *Silver Stars*,' played by a group of mostly community performers who performed in Séan Millar's song cycle under co-artistic directors Keegan and Cannon's direction. In each of these examples, non-professional or 'community' participants were collaborators and partners in the creation and/or performance of the work. Keegan elaborates on Brokentalkers' reasons for this approach:

> We always kinda felt, still do, that theatre is quite an elitist closed-off art form that involves a clear separation between the artist and the audience, and we always had a problem with that. We always thought that it is within everybody's capabilities to be creative and to express themselves. (McCormack)

Like THEATREclub's *Heroin*, engagement with interviewees in the creation of the work happened prior to the performance of *Blue Boy*. In performance, Brokentalkers partnered instead with professional dance theatre company junk ensemble in the presentation of the work.

For prominent *Irish Times* columnist Fintan O'Toole, the 2011 Dublin Theatre Festival was highly significant as it made evident a split in contemporary Irish practice – an opposition he termed as 'smooth' vs. 'rough' theatre. Smooth described the Abbey's co-production of Sean O'Casey's *Juno and the Paycock* with the National Theatre of Britain and the Gate's Production of Hugo Hamilton's *The Speckled People* while the rough belongs to theatre that is 'hard, edgy, and highly political and is happening, to a large extent, outside conventional theatre spaces.' (O'Toole). He went on to state, 'What makes this festival so important is the way it has brought together a number of younger artists who are not just dancing on the grave of the well-wrought play but actively inventing new ways in which theatre can function in a public and highly political space.' (Ibid.) The seemingly 'new ways' in which ANU, Brokentalkers and THEATREclub use theatre to function in a 'public and highly political space' depends centrally on their involvement of community members as participants in the co-creation and devising of the work. But rather than signalling new trends in contemporary Irish theatre making, this chapter suggests that the intersection between community participation and devising in their work makes visible a sustained and politically engaged genealogy of devising practice related to community arts active since the late-1970s at least.

This chapter therefore challenges O'Toole's assertion that the 2011 Dublin Theatre Festival marks a move toward the creation of 'new ways' that Irish theatre can function in a public and highly political space by historicizing the formal practices of contemporary companies including ANU, Brokentalkers and THEATREclub in longer Irish genealogies of community arts. I trace the influences of community arts on contemporary (devised) theatre practice in order to propose strategies for how artists, critics and audiences might more thoroughly account for how these emerging companies participate in longer debates about the role of the Irish artist, and the arts in the lives of Irish citizens.

In doing so, this chapter is necessarily limited to considering primarily the use of drama and theatre in the Irish community arts movement. Yet even with this more narrow focus, this chapter will be in no way a comprehensive history of groups who have worked in this way since the 1970s, a history that yet and urgently has to be written. I also distinguish here quite explicitly between 'amateur' and 'community' drama. In Ireland, amateur drama generally implies the mounting of scripted work by non-professional (i.e. non-paid) performers. However, community drama, according to Declan Gorman, 'refers to original work for performance that has been generated from within communities, often in the context of community development or educational objectives' (11). Finally, from its origins, Irish community arts has been characterized by a cross-border history and network of direct influences between artists and organizations, North and South. A full consideration of this dynamic interplay lies outside the scope of this chapter, but will figure occasionally throughout.

Community Arts and Irish Theatre History

Community arts refers to work produced collaboratively by what CREATE, the Irish national agency for collaborative arts in social and community contexts, describes today as 'communities of place' or 'interest' working usually in partnership with a professional artist or group of artists ('About Create'). Speaking from an Irish perspective, Rhona Henderson refers to it more broadly as 'socially engaged arts' (159) while Susan Coughlan characterizes it as 'a political and social movement with a desire for cultural democracy at its heart' (115). Recently, Irish debates over terminology have considered whether 'collaborative' or 'participatory' arts might be more flexible and inclusive categories to describe this field. This chapter primarily mobilizes community arts as the key term to describe this area of practice due to its utility in tracing the genealogy of the field, which has only more recently turned towards 'participatory' and 'collaborative' as synonyms. Sandy Fitzgerald, a leading innovator in the field of Irish community arts, including as founder and former director of the City Arts Centre in Dublin, even argued in 2004 that 'this change' in terminology 'went unnoticed and unchallenged by the community arts sector itself' (79).

The interplay between devising and community engagement in the work of ANU, Brokentalkers and THEATREclub decisively reveal the origins of Irish experimentation with devised performance techniques in the formation of the community arts sector in Ireland in the mid-late 1970s and early 1980s. This genealogy of influence however has been neglected in critical discussions and reviews of these contemporary companies' work.[1]

It has not been observed for example that ANU Productions' Monto Cycle that includes the works *World's End Lane, Laundry, The Boys of Foley Street,* and *Vardo Corner* reprises the structure and themes of Mick Egan and Peter Sheridan's Monto Trilogy devised with Dublin's

---

[1] See Haughton 65-93, Singleton (2013) 21-36 and Weaver.

City Workshop in the north inner city in the early 1980s. The Monto Trilogy includes the works *The Kips, The Digs, The Village, A Hape A Junk* and *Pledges and Promises* and is described as 'created through improvisation and research by members of the City Workshop' and 'scripted by Mick Egan and Peter Sheridan' (Egan, Sheridan et. al 1). Sandy Fitzgerald narrates the aims of this 'groundbreaking drama project' as to 'show that a community arts project could work, not as art for the people, but by the people' (258-259). The participants were 'housewives, unemployed dockers, and kids out of school' brought together by 'the newly established Department of Education Teamwork Scheme' and Peter Sheridan (Fitzgerald 72). ANU's cycle and the City Arts Workshop's trilogy cover almost identical thematic areas: the history of prostitution in the area, the Magdalene Laundry, heroin addiction and issues of labour and the history of the Dublin docks and unions (the subject of ANU's 2013 cycle *Thirteen*).

The critical silence on ANU's Irish influences and predecessors reflects the place of community arts in the study of Irish theatre and performance. Sandy Fitzgerald forcefully claims that 'arts commentators rarely mention community arts, and when they do, damn with faint praise, condescension or outright hostility'(1). Few major works or edited volumes have dealt with this area of practice. Exceptions include David Grant's 1994 *Playing the Wild Card: A Survey of Community Drama and Smaller-scale Theatre from Community Relations Perspective,* Fitzgerald's own 2004 edited volume, *An Outburst of Frankness: Community Arts in Ireland – A Reader* and Bill McDonnell's 2008 *Theatres of the Troubles: Theatre, Resistance and Liberation in Ireland,* a study of the role of Republican and Loyalist popular theatres during the Troubles. In addition, the origins of Northern Ireland's all-female Charabanc Theatre Company as a collaborative and community-based group, has been the subject of sustained scholarly attention (Lojek, 82-102; Dicenzo, 175-184; Martin, 88-99). However, only *An Outburst of Frankness* addresses community arts work in the Republic of Ireland in any detail.

As a further example, the 2012 *Collaborative Arts Performance Pack* by CREATE, the national agency for collaborative arts in social and community contexts, features case studies of four Irish-based artists or companies including Brokentalkers, Louise Lowe (representing ANU), Dylan Tighe (Co-Artistic Director of The Stomach Box) and Helene Hugel (Artistic Director of Helium) and four international groups Young@Heart (United States), Rimini Protokoll (Germany), Clod Ensemble (UK) and the Red Room (UK). It was designed to be used by anyone in order to 'satisfy your curiosity about contemporary performance techniques and to stimulate new approaches toward making work in collaboration with a range of participants and audiences.' (CREATE, 'Script' 7). For CREATE, Irish contemporary performance technique *is* collaborative practice, an assertion that like O'Toole's, associates this practice with the now without citing an established Irish genealogy of this work. In doing so, however, CREATE suppresses the vital history of their own organization.

A need for organization and centralization of resources in the community arts sector led to the 1983 formation of CREATE's first iteration as 'Creative Activity for Everyone' (CAFE). This was an umbrella organization for community arts on the island of Ireland as a whole. CAFE originally described 'its main objective as "community and individual development with creative activity as a means to that end"' and is credited with 'holding the first community arts conference, the setting up of the first community arts database, the publication of a funding handbook and the organizing of the first community arts workers course' (Fitzgerald 259). This organization would be officially rebranded as CREATE in 2003.

Their 2012 interactive guide on collaborative arts *as* contemporary performance technique (written by *The Irish Times* chief theatre critic Peter Crawley) indeed states that it is not an 'exhaustive history of performance' or 'a history of socially engaged practice or of community arts' (CREATE, 'Script' 7). Yet, the complete absence of earlier Irish histories of community arts (and indeed the organization itself) limits the ability of the pack's targeted audience (those interested in working through collaborative performance techniques) or scholars to historicize the practice of these contemporary companies in not only an artistic, but a political and social context, for both practical and academic purposes.

The wider marginalization of community arts practice in a critical context might be explained by reservations about the aesthetic quality of the work or a lack of access to texts, other performance ephemera or recordings of live performances. Indeed, the characteristic hallmark of a community arts project across national contexts is the habitual emphasis of process over product and the involvement of 'non-artists' (i.e. untrained and not professional) in creating and presenting work for public consumption. As Brian Singleton recently argued regarding Irish theatre studies, 'Often the justification for canon formation is determined by the literary quality of the playtext all the while ignoring completely the extent and the significance of the cultural and sometimes political intervention an actual performance might have generated in a particular historical moment' (*Masculinities and the Contemporary Irish Theatre* 13). He too claims that Irish 'popular and community theatres are barely afforded a mention in most histories' (ibid.). Declan Gorman forcefully argues that 'the virtual exclusion of community drama from the theatre publishing industry is overtly or unconsciously a political act by the industry' (22). Baz Kershaw concurs in a British context noting that an 'incomprehension of the cultural significance of the movement' of alternative and community theatre 'is the result of an analytical perspective which insists on treating performance in terms of its *theatrical* significance' (43). I would push on Kershaw's assertion to argue that in an Irish context, community arts as it operated in tandem with the experimental theatre sector in the 1970s-1990s was and continues to be a site where some of the most cutting edge developments in innovative theatrical strategies are tested.

The Irish Community Arts Movement

The founding and growth of Irish community arts in the mid-late 1970s responded directly to sectarian conflict, poverty and drug issues, serving divided communities, encouraging cross-community work and working in at-risk neighbourhoods. Sandy Fitzgerald details:

> Very real community actions, such as the housing movement of the time, gave people some confidence and strength to move forward. Again, as had happened in England, the intersection of small groups of people who had artistic skills with community groups led to the realisation that being creative was also about having a voice and affecting change ... People became politicized and informed but they also became witnesses for themselves and their communities. They wanted to tell their story and they began to feel the power of these stories. (70)

In a 2003 public forum on the history of community arts, Mowbray Brates, co-founder of NOW in Belfast, summarized the aims of community art's emergence in Ireland in this way:

> There seems to be two broad strands [...]. People who would be looking to push the boundaries of art, liberating art from museums and theatre spaces. Then there would be the direction of political activism and community development, the use of art in a creative way to further political campaigns, specific single issues. And I suppose then there would be people who would want to look at democratizing culture. (Fitzgerald 11)

Artists and groups working in the community saw the arts as a way to give a voice to those marginalized within the broader society. The arts could potentially give individuals or groups the opportunity to tell their story in various artistic mediums but could also provide training in practical work skills, or empower the process of community development through linking practical initiatives to community arts.

In 1980s' Dublin in particular, many individuals came to community arts practice through temporary or Community Employment Schemes run by FÁS, the Irish National Training and Employment Authority. These schemes aim to reverse the trend of high unemployment among young adults, as well other long-term unemployed persons. These programmes are 'designed to help people who are long-term unemployed and other disadvantaged people to get back to work by offering part-time and temporary placements in jobs based within local communities' (Citizens Information: Public Service Information). Before working through these schemes, some artists still working today, including Ollie Breslin, current artistic director of Waterford Youth Arts, had never encountered the arts. Breslin observes:

> Unemployment to me [was] the key. At that time unemployment was huge and I think that was really a big part of why a lot of these things happened because there was a radical side to the arts. I suppose people were fed up with the system and wanted to make a statement against the system and manifest it in some way. (Fitzgerald 11)

Fitzgerald notes, 'there was time when the FÁS grants to the arts far outweighed the total Arts Council budget and these grants were almost exclusively for community arts projects because of their intrinsic social and community perspective' (77). He elaborates: 'The leaders in this early movement in community arts were invariably artists who had come from disadvantaged communities, people who had broken through the system despite all obstacles, to emerge as actors, writers, directors, photographers, film-makers and musicians' (Ibid.).

The definition of community development as defined in a 2006 report from Combat Poverty continues to echo the original aims of community arts in Ireland. According to Brian Motherway, community development refers to a 'process whereby those who are marginalized and excluded are enabled to gain in self confidence, to join with others and to participate in actions to change their situation and to tackle the problems that face their community' and prioritizes 'collective action for social change, with an emphasis on empowerment and participation, and a focus on process as well as outcomes' (Motherway,

Preface; i). In a 1994 report on a partnership between CAFE (Creating Art for Everyone) and the Combat Poverty Agency which studied the work of five community arts projects, one of the major aims of the project was listed as identifying 'ways in which the community arts could be used to tackle poverty and disadvantage' (CAFE (Creative Activity for Everyone) and Combat Poverty Agency, 1-2). Dublin's Fatima Mansions, for example, has been the site of community-based actions towards regeneration since the 1980s that have consistently drawn on the arts through the support of Fatima Groups United, 'the representative body of residents and community groups through which the grassroots energy, needs and views of the community are represented and supported' ('About Us'). Significant arts actions include the 1997 community wide Halloween Parade, 'Burning the Demons: Embracing the Future' which utilized street theatre and was described by the Rialto Learning Community as marking 'a new departure in community organizing and the beginning of a fifteen-year journey towards social, economic and cultural change' ('The Rialto Youth Project Arts Programme'). From 2004-2009, Fatima Groups United worked with funding from the Irish Youth Foundation to draft a cultural arts strategy aimed at creating 'a new and sustainable arts provision ... to be fully integrated and managed within a community framework' ('Arts and Cultural Strategy').

I will now turn towards the evolution of drama and theatre in the Irish community arts sector, focusing on devising as a core early technique in this area. In doing so, I establish the history of devising as not only a formal, but a politicized practice in Irish theatre. Community arts' politicization of formal theatre practices, such as devising among other interdisciplinary arts techniques, challenged dominant theatre-making trends (i.e. the literary theatre with its comparably or superficially clear hierarchy of production roles) as a reflection of wider social inequalities and uneven hierarchies.

Devising and Community

Group devising through improvisation and/or collective writing (which may later be shaped for performance by a facilitator) figures centrally in terms of drama and theatre produced within the framework of community arts. As Deirdre Heddon and Jane Milling observe in regards to the United States and the UK primarily, 'Devising emerged as a core feature and methodology within the burgeoning field of community arts in the 1960s' (130). Their observation holds true in

Ireland as well, perhaps owing to the direct and indirect influence of the British community arts movement.

The influence of both devising techniques and community arts would begin to make an impact in Ireland in the mid-late 1970s leading to the formation of TEAM Educational Theatre, 'Waterford Arts for All, and Grapevine and Moving Theatre in Dublin, all operating by the end of the 1970s' and beginning of the 1980s (Fitzgerald, 70). The 1978 founding of the Neighbourhood Open Workshop (NOW) in Belfast was another key event of this period. While initially founded by a 'group of people working as volunteers on summer play schemes in Belfast,' the creation of NOW would lead to the development of the Crescent Arts Centre '(at the time Belfast's only "neutral" community arts centre),' the 'Play Resource Warehouse in Belfast' and 'the Belfast Community Circus School' (256). NOW's artistically interdisciplinary and community development engaged evolution demonstrate the central role of the community arts movement in innovating new aesthetic techniques and methods as well as intervening in local politics.

Dublin's TEAM Educational Theatre Company, which grew out of a partnership with the Abbey Theatre, was devising plays with and for young audiences as early as the mid-1970s. They began devising *with* groups before shifting to a practice of commissioning playwrights primarily to produce theatre *for* young audiences. In the mid-1970s, TEAM first worked mainly through devising between facilitators and groups of schoolchildren. Their facilitators included Peter and Jim Sheridan, as well as Annie Kilmartin (founder of Moving Theatre), resulting in the devised works *Wonder Ponder Time, Women at Work, That's Mad* and *Sunflower* (Irish Theatre Playography). As TEAM's work evolved, the company worked less with devising and more often through commissioning playwrights including Frank McGuinness, Mary Elizabeth Burke-Kennedy, Paula Meehan, Jim Nolan and Maeve Ingoldsby. Moving Theatre, like City Workshop, had an aim to 'devise plays about issues that touched the hearts of its audience' (Fitzgerald 259). Unlike City Workshop and more similarly to TEAM, Moving Theatre devised theatre *for* rather than *with* audiences, but they also ran the MADCAP (Moving Arts and Drama Community Action Programme) aimed at community participants, blurring lines between community arts and professional work, as ANU does 30 years later.

The work of City Workshop and Moving Theatre illustrates that many early Irish devising practices responded formally to the political concerns of artists and groups who viewed community arts and development as interlinked movements, while the example of TEAM situates Irish genealogies of devised theatre centrally within the ambit of community and/or educational theatre. Devising as utilized by these three companies (and especially City Workshop and Moving Theatre) plays out the desire for artistic democracy in conjunction with activist practices that sought to intervene in local social and political structures. Other Irish artists at the time such as Tom Mac Intyre, Patrick Mason, and Tom Hickey were experimenting with devising techniques such as in their landmark 1983 collaboration on adapting Patrick Kavanagh's poem *The Great Hunger* at the Abbey, but their work falls outside the scope of this chapter as it is situated more firmly in relationship to the 'impact of movement and European performance techniques on the Irish theatrical style' (Fox 7), an interrelated but distinct genealogy of the evolution of devised theatre practice in Ireland.

A quite partial list of notable theatre groups and centres in the Republic working through a community arts practice from the late 1970s to the present include in Dublin: TEAM Educational Theatre (1975); Dublin Youth Theatre founded by Paddy O'Dwyer (1977); Peter Sheridan's City Workshop (founded with the support of Mick Egan as well) (1980); Annie Kilmartin's Moving Theatre (1982); Wet Paint Arts founded by Niall O'Baoill with significant contributions by Kathy McArdle and David Byrne (1985), and the Balcony Belles, established out of the North Wall Women's Centre in Dublin's Sheriff Street and facilitated by Fiona Nolan. Declan Gorman also names the Rialto Youth Project, the Parents Alone Resource Centre, and KLEAR, 'a woman's adult education project in Kilbarrack' as initiatives that used drama through the work of facilitators Joni Crone, Kathy McArdle and Jo Egan respectively (12-13). Elsewhere, notable groups include, in Galway, Macnas founded by Ollie Jennings, Tom Conroy, Páraic Breathnach, and Pete Sammon (1985); in Waterford, Waterford Arts for All (1979); and in Drogheda, Upstate Theatre Project founded by Declan Gorman and Declan Mallon (1997). This list does not include short-term community arts theatre projects funded through more limited grants or initiatives including the North Clondalkin Arts and Drama Group as only one example.

Formally, as a sampling, Gorman describes the early 1990s work of Balcony Belles as 'topical and folk-historical dramas set in the inner city of Dublin' and the Rialto Youth Project's late 1990s plays produced under the guidance of Kathy McArdle and John Bissett as 'social realist plays [...] that compare with the best international published works in this tradition' (12). Their plays include *Here Today, Where Tomorrow*; *In the System* and *Inside Out*. More recent community drama work from Upstate, which Gorman co-founded, has explored site-specificity in works like *Journey from Babel* and *Ship Street Revisited* and were devised by community participants working with directors Gorman and Declan Mallon (*Journey from Babel*) and director Paul Hayes and playwright Colm Maher (*Ship Street Revisited*).

From its origins, debates about how to make theatre in the field of community arts were intimately related to discussion of who should have access to the arts and what access meant at Irish state policy level beyond this sector on its own. Tellingly, the growth of community arts dovetailed with the expansion of the Arts Council's remit and resources from the 1970s-90s, resulting in an overall expansion of the place and role of the arts in Irish society, in terms of rhetoric and funding resources. For theatre in particular, the growth of the independent theatre sector that climaxed in the 1990s owes its existence to the collision of community arts with debates over the role of the arts and Arts Council funding in serving Irish society at large through the professional arts sector.

Form and Funding

Shifts in Irish arts policy on the themes of access and outreach began in the mid-1970s, emerging alongside and in dialogue with the influence of the burgeoning community arts sector. Sandy Fitzgerald highlights the appointment of the Arts Council's first regional arts officer, Paul Funge, in 1976 as a move that 'represented a formalization of the acceptance of "arts-as-development" rather than "arts-as-separate" within society' (255). Paula Clancy looks even earlier to the 1973 Arts Act which expanded the scope and function of the Arts Council, adding cinema for example to a list of arts forms that previously included only 'painting, sculpture, architecture, music, drama, literature, design in industry and the fine arts and applied arts generally' ('Arts Act 1951'). At the time of its passage, then Taoiseach Liam Cosgrove observed:

> There is a danger that many people may regard the arts as the preserve of a privileged coterie. We must actively promote and encourage a wider approach than this: a philosophy that art in all its forms is a means by which a fuller and more satisfying life may be achieved by the people at large. (qtd. in Clancy 86).

It is not made explicit in Cosgrove's statement whether he is talking about increasing access only or access and participation opportunities in the arts, but the push for increased participation in the arts characterized the community arts movement that emerged in the immediate aftermath of his statement. For activists and artists like

Sandy Fitzgerald, Mowbray Bates, Jim and Peter Sheridan, Annie Kilmartin and Ollie Breslin, access meant 'validation of the idea that ordinary people can take an active role in building culture' through direct participation as arts-makers and the 'encouragement of critical thought and action amongst both the people participating and the observer' (Ibid. 89). By 2003, the most recent Arts Act stipulated for the first time that the Arts Council must not just stimulate 'public interest in the arts' but 'promote knowledge, appreciation or *practice* of the arts' ('Arts Act 2003') [*emphasis mine*].

Baz Kershaw's influential *The Politics of Practice: Radical Theatre as Cultural Intervention* makes a persuasive case for the impact of British radical theatre rooted in a community and alternative ethos on the 'culture of a nation' (Kershaw 50) during the period of the 1970s-80s, a similar period under consideration here. Kershaw documents that during this period the British 'alternative theatre movement had grown from almost nothing to the position of contributing almost a third of the product of subsidized theatre, for just over a tenth of the total subsidy' (Ibid.). Sandy Fitzgerald makes a similar claim for the total proliferation in Irish arts between the late 1970s and the present, claiming:

> [...] the unprecedented growth in creative activity and cultural development within the thirty-two counties of Ireland is heavily indebted to community arts, spanning, as it does, an exhausting array of activity including arts centres, festivals, youth projects, disability projects, community training programmes, artist in residence schemes, prison workshops and school programmes. (Fitzgerald 1)

Fitzgerald highlights here a proliferation in art forms and community spaces as a hallmark of the Irish community arts movement. The Irish community arts coalesced in a moment characterized by unemployment, emigration and the heightening of conflict in the North that eventually gave way in the 1990s to the advent of the Celtic Tiger. Unprecedented increases in arts funding during the 1990s were accompanied by new state-level attention in arts policy to the social as well as aesthetic function of the arts in Irish society. During the Celtic Tiger, as Brian Singleton notes, 'public funding of theatre through the Arts Council rose by 300 per cent' during the 1990s before peaking at €81.62 million in 2008 (*Masculinities and the Contemporary Irish Theatre* 6). It would be inaccurate to say that the community arts movement was entirely responsible for the 1990s and early-mid 2000s growth in independent theatre companies that increased arts funding made possible. However, the broadening of infrastructural support for the arts locally through sustained efforts by the Arts Council, and related state supported agencies like CREATE, is undeniably indebted to the field of community arts and its agitators.

Devising the Contemporary Through Community (Arts): The 1990s to now

The connections between the expansion of the independent theatre sector and the community arts movement provides the most crucial link that brings us from ANU and their contemporaries back to Sheridan and his predecessors and collaborators. However, study of the independent Irish theatre sector at large has been limited and new work in this area by Christie Fox, Bernadette Sweeney, Brian Singleton, and Aoife McGrath, as well as Willie White and Peter Crawley's edited collection *No More Drama*, has focused primarily on physical and dance theatre, often first emphasizing European influences on the evolution of Irish theatrical form since the 1990s. The role of the political has also been discounted during this period with Singleton claiming with regret that in the 1990s, 'political performance, though, was a rare commodity and theatre tended to shy away from national political debates for the most part' (*Masculinities and the Contemporary Irish Theatre* 6). Turning to the popular and community theatres Singleton lamented earlier as excluded, however, might yield a different history of this period when considered in relationship to the evolution of the independent theatre sector. This alternative genealogy suggests that contemporary Irish companies that utilize devised technique alongside community engagement do not represent an entirely new wave of theatre making, but continue and rejuvenate a mode of politicized experimentation with theatre and performance form that has been ongoing since the 1970s.

The range and energy of activity in community arts practice from the 1970s onward was matched by experimentation with performance in the streets and fringe theatre spaces in cities including Dublin, Galway, Cork and Waterford. This work involved many artists also working in community arts or social protest movements such as Peter and Jim Sheridan, Mannix Flynn, Annie Kilmartin, Thom 'The Dice Man' McGinty, Fiona Nolan, and slightly later, Declan Gorman, Raymond Keane, Donal O'Kelly, Charlie O'Neill and their contemporaries. According to Charlie O'Neill, these artists' performance experiments addressed explicitly political subjects such as nuclear proliferation, poverty, unemployment, and women's rights (O'Neill). Of this group,

Gorman and Charlie O'Neill have been the most persistent chroniclers of these events through articles, editorials and reports on the role of the arts such as those O'Neill has produced for Fatima Groups United and the Rialto Youth Project, including his most recent role as the editor of *An Arts Plan for Rialto 2012-2016* and Gorman's various news and website articles, as well as his critical introduction to Upstate's self-published anthology of several community drama works, *Out in the Country*.

In an early 1990s piece of writing produced for Calypso Productions, a theatre for social change company originally co-founded by O'Neill and Donal O'Kelly among others, Gorman traced the trajectory of community arts and political theatre in Ireland straight back to the foundation of the Abbey.

> In Ireland, the National Theatre Society was closely linked to the emergence of a liberation movement in the early years of the century. More recently, in the 1950s, Brendan Behan's *The Quare Fellow* is said to have influenced the decision by the British Government to abolish hanging. In the 1970s Jim and Peter Sheridan pioneered a wave of modern Irish social realism in the Project Arts Centre, cultivating awareness and public outrage at the injustices of urban life with controversial plays on the burning issues of the day. In the '80s it was the turn of Passion Machine and Wet Paint with dramas set amongst the marginalized youth of Dublin. Co-Motion, meanwhile, explored international issues, presenting such work as Peter Weiss' anti-colonial play *The Song of the White Man's Burden*. By 1989 visual artists and theatre workers from all the main Irish companies were collaborating with advocates of social justice to mount the massive Parade of Innocence street theatre campaigns, highlighting miscarriages of justice. (Gorman, 'Theatre for Social Change')

Gorman's positioning of the 1990s as a decade inaugurated through a passion for the intersection between theatre, community arts and political activism is a counter-narrative to more recent accounts of this period in Irish theatre history which have instead focused on the important turn to 'forms that were non-realistic, and often highly physical, and approached texts with a corporeal irreverence,' (Singleton, *Masculinity and the Contemporary Irish Theatre* 6) deemphasizing the importance of political performance during this period.

Indeed, a physical and dance theatre movement in Irish theatre coalesced in the 1990s through the work of companies like Barabbas, Blue Raincoat, Corn Exchange, Fabulous Beast, Macnas, and Pan Pan. Fox names this body of work 'the Irish theater of movement' and she argues this shift 'changed the nature of theater in Ireland, permitting a recognition that actors had bodies and that these bodies might be useful in communicating the effects of ... societal changes' related to the upheaval of the Celtic Tiger in the 1990s (3). She continues:

> [T]he new theater de-privileged text and emphasized physical performance. Much of it was in search of a distinctly Irish type of physicality or gesture [...] created from a synthesis of ancient Irish performance forms such as mumming and European forms such as the commedia dell'arte and French mime. (5)

Fox connects this shift to a break from Irish literary traditions that she maintains have dominated theatre criticism even more so than theatre production. Fox's study connects formal innovation primarily to increasing European influences on Irish artists through exposure to work in the Dublin Theatre Festival and Galway Arts Festival, newly available funding from the Arts Council for artist exchanges and visits in the 1990s and Irish artists training in Europe, particularly in French mime, as with Mikel Murfi, one of Barabbas's founders. Crucially, Fox also traces the turn towards a broader adaptation of a 'collaborative method which, combined with devised theater and a decentring of the text, mirrored the disintegration of Ireland as a shared place or communally recognizable society' (7). It is precisely this collaborative method that I have linked back to the community arts movement, and its early experiments with devised techniques of theatre making. The work of this sector not only mirrored the disintegration of Ireland back to itself, but used the arts to interrogate the sources of this disintegration from the perspective of those experiencing it within marginalized community contexts. Not only this, the frequent alliance between community arts and community development positioned the arts as having an importance to serve not just as a mirror of the nation, but as a set of tools for rebuilding the nation from the bottom up.

Conclusion

A history of the community arts sector ultimately offers an overtly politicized framework through which to understand how the arts have functioned in Ireland since the mid-1970s. The 1990s and 2000s in particular brought massive changes, not only economic expansion and collapse, but unprecedented inward-migration and the revelation of multiple damaging Catholic Church scandals. It is these more recent events that ANU, Brokentalkers and THEATREclub respond most explicitly to, and this is perhaps why their work has not been placed in reference to earlier histories of community arts as they make a mutual turn towards political critique and formal methods that empower both minority histories and members of the community themselves as collaborators and performers. They respond to their own immediate context and diverse (and international) artistic influences but do so by drawing centrally on the minority theatre history of community arts. By locating contemporary theatre practice that uses collaborative and devised techniques in the history of community arts (and development), it is possible to theorize more concretely about not only how the arts might be economically beneficial to the economy as a resource, as a 'welcome mat for the heads of state, investors, stars and tourists' as argued by the National Campaign for the Arts 2013 'Republic of Culture' video. Instead, community arts methodologies provide critical tools through which the arts have been used to consciously call into question the limits of participation and inclusion in Irish society. By drawing on the insight of these tactics, the Irish arts may ultimately move closer to achieving another goal of the 'Republic of Culture' campaign, the creation of a 'truly inclusive and creative state and not just an economy' (Ibid.)

Works Cited

Arts Council. 'Participatory Arts-Summary Policy Paper.' Dublin: Arts Council, 2005. Print.

CAFE and Combat Poverty Agency. Creating A Difference: Report of the Creative Activity for Everyone/Combat Poverty Agency- Community Arts Pilot Programme 1993-1994. Dublin: CAFE/Combat Poverty Agency, 1995. Print.

Clancy, Paula. 'Rhetoric and Reality: A Literature Review of the Position of Community Arts in State Cultural Policy.' *An Outburst of Frankness: Community Arts in Ireland – A Reader*. Ed. Sandy Fitzgerald. Dublin: TASC at New Island, 2004. 83-114. Print.

Coughlan, Susan. 'The Old Triangle: Funding, Policy and Community Arts.' *An Outburst of Frankness: Community Arts in Ireland – A Reader*. Ed. Sandy Fitzgerald. Dublin: TASC at New Island, 2004. 115-133. Print.

Citizens Information. 'Community Employment Scheme.' *Citizens Information – Public Service Information*. 20 September 2012. Web. 10 October 2013.

Create. The Collaborative Arts Performance Pack. Dublin: Create, 2012. Print.

---. 'About Create.' Create – the national development agency for collaborative arts in social and community contexts. Web. 7 October 2013.

DiCenzo, Maria. 'Charabanc Theatre Company: Placing Women Centre Stage in Northern Ireland.' *Theatre Journal* 45.2 (1993): 175-184. Print.

Dyas, Grace. 'This is about everything that ever happened.' *Irish Theatre Magazine.* 7 December 2010. Web. 10 October 2013.

Egan, Mick and Peter Sheridan with members of the City Workshop. *The Kips, The Digs, The Village.* TS. Collection of Peter Sheridan, Dublin. Print.

Fatima Groups United, Ltd. 'About Us.' *Fatima Groups United, Ltd.* Web. 4 October 2013.

Fitzgerald, Sandy, ed. *An Outburst of Frankness: Community Arts in Ireland – A Reader.* Dublin: TASC at New Island, 2004. Print.

Fox, Christie. *Breaking Form: The Shift To Performance in Late Twentieth-Century Irish Drama.* Cambridge: Cambridge Scholars Publishing, 2008. Print.

Grant, David. *Playing the Wild Card: A Survey of Community Drama and Smaller-Scale Theatre from a Community Relations Perspective.* Belfast: Community Relations Council, 1993. Print.

Gorman, Declan. 'Introduction: From Tales of the Tower Blocks to Yarns From the Farm: The Macra Community Plays in Context.' *Way Out in the Country: An Anthology of Community Plays.* Eds. Declan Gorman and Declan Mallon. Drogheda: Upstate Theatre Project, 2001. 11-23. Print.

---. 'Theatre for Social Change.' *Calypso Productions.* Web. 23 June 2012.

Haughton, Miriam. 'From Laundries to Labour Camps: Staging Ireland's "Rule of Silence" in Anu Production's *Laundry.*' *Modern Drama* 57.1 (Spring 2014): 65-93.

Heddon, Deirdre and Milling, Jane. *Devising Performance: A Critical History.* Houndsmill, Basingstoke, Hampshire: Palgrave Macmillan, 2006. Print.

Henderson, Rhona. 'Community Arts as Socially Engaged Arts.' *An Outburst of Frankness: Community Arts in Ireland – A Reader.* Dublin: TASC at New Island, 2004. 159-178. Print.

Irish Theatre Playography. 'TEAM Educational Theatre.' *Irish Theatre Playography.*

Kershaw, Baz. *The Politics of Performance: Radical Theatre as Cultural Intervention.* London and New York: Routledge, 1992. Print.

Lojek, Helen. 'Playing Politics with Belfast's Charabanc Theatre Company.' *Politics and Performance in Contemporary Northern Ireland.* Ed. John P. Harrington and Elizabeth J. Mitchell. Amherst: University of Massachusetts, 1999. 82-102. Print.

Lowe, Louise. 'Re: Community Engagement and "Laundry."' E-mail to Charlotte McIvor. 30 May 2012.

Martin, Carol. 'Charabanc Theatre Company: "Quare" Women "Sleggin" and "Geggin" the Standards of Northern Ireland by "Tappin" the People.' *TDR: The Drama Review* 31.2 (Summer 1987): 88-99. Print.

McCormack, Chris. 'Brokentalkers' Gary Keegan and Feidlim Cannon talk *The Blue Boy.*' *Musings in Intermissions.* 27 September 2011. Web. 24 June 2012.

McDonnell, Bill. *Theatres of the Troubles: Theatre, Resistance and Liberation in Ireland*. Exeter: University of Exeter Press, 2008. Print.

Motherway, Brian. *The Role of Community Development in Tackling Poverty in Ireland: A Literature Review for the Combat Poverty Agency*. Dublin: Combat Poverty Agency, 2006. Web. 5 June 2012.

National Campaign for the Arts. 'Republic of Culture.' Online video clip, *National Campaign for the Arts.* Web. 10 October 2013.

Oddey, Allison. *Devising Theatre: A Practical and Theoretical Handbook*. New York and London: Routledge, 1996. Print.

O'Neill, Charlie. Personal interview. 23 February 2009.

O'Toole, Fintan. 'The New Theatre: Magical, Visible, Hidden.' *The Irish Times.* 15 October 2011. Web. 27 June 2012.

---. 'Course of true theatre never should run smooth.' *The Irish Times.* 28 October 2011. Web. 31 May 2012.

'The Rialto Youth Project Arts Programme.' *Rialto Learning Community.* Web. 20 September 2013.

Sheridan, Peter. *Break A Leg: A Memoir*. Dublin: New Island, 2012. Print.

Singleton, Brian. 'ANU Productions and Site-Specific Performance: The Politics of Space and Place.' *'That Was Us': Contemporary Irish Theatre and Performance* Ed. Fintan Walsh. London: Oberon, 2013. 21-36. Print.

---. *Masculinities and the Contemporary Irish Theatre*. Houndsmill, Basingstoke, Hampshire: Palgrave Macmillan, 2011. Print.

Weaver, Jesse. 'Geography and Community: Louise Lowe's artistic four-part vision.' *Irish Theatre Magazine.* 21 September 2012. Web. 25 August 2014.

4 | 'Whose art is it anyway?': A Critical and Historical Analysis of Upstate Theatre Project

Irene White

Introduction

A survey of contemporary Irish theatre practice indicates that an ever-growing number of theatre companies are using devised performance as they seek to develop new approaches to theatre-making and explore new theatrical forms. Within this mix is the work of Brokentalkers, ANU Productions and Una McKevitt. Not only do these companies and artists place devising at the centre of their performance practice but they share the stage with untrained performers. This chapter begins from the premise that while these approaches are becoming more widespread and visible, they are not new. Their origins, in fact, are deeply rooted in the field of community-engaged theatre. As Charlotte McIvor argues elsewhere in this collection, for example, the concept of devising as a politicized practice merging professional and non-professional artists has been in operation in community arts practice in Ireland since at least the 1970s.

Upstate Theatre Project has been one of the long-standing innovators in the area of community-engaged theatre from the 1990s onwards. This chapter proposes that the new thinking among some professional theatre-makers mirrors the model of collaborative, participatory practice developed by Upstate over seventeen years, and represents a logical progression of that socially-engaged tradition. It also suggests that an appreciation and acknowledgement of the aesthetic value of community art informs the current devising movement within the professional sector. It is notable for example that many recently acclaimed independent devising artists including

Brokentalkers' Gary Keegan and Feidlim Cannon, and ANU Productions' Louise Lowe, have found a natural home in Upstate.

Upstate is an Arts Council-funded 'community-engaged performing arts organization' which has operated in the border region between the Republic of Ireland and Northern Ireland since 1997 (Upstate Theatre Project, 'About'). Specializing in devised performance, Upstate enjoys an international reputation in the fields of professional and community-engaged theatre and has made a significant contribution to both participatory arts and professional theatre practice in Ireland. Founded by Declan Gorman and Declan Mallon, the company has successfully and consistently interwoven participatory engaged practice with professional theatre practice in the creation of local, regional and national theatre productions. Upstate's recent collaborations with some of the newly emerging artists referred to above has raised the company's profile further as those artists have achieved national and international recognition in their own right. It is not surprising that Upstate should gravitate towards these young artists who challenge form and style, and whose shared ethos demonstrates a resolute belief in the aesthetic value of collaborative community art; nor is it surprising that such artists should be drawn to work with the Drogheda-based company. Upstate's unique geographical and cultural position in the Irish theatrical landscape makes the company's model a useful lens through which we can view the place of community-engaged theatre and devised practice in Ireland. The company is uniquely positioned for a number of reasons. It is one of the longest established community-based theatre organizations and the only theatre company to consistently provide community arts in a regional and cross-border context in the Republic of Ireland. Furthemore, while Upstate's practice has always encompassed both professional and community theatre, their funding status has changed from that of a professional touring company to an arts participation organization in 2010. This makes them a compelling case-study of how the funding landscape has changed in Ireland since the 1990s and the place of collaborative, community and/or devised practice relative to these shifts.

This study is informed by my own longstanding association with Upstate. My relationship with the company began as a local citizen and audience member based in Drogheda and developed from there to my current position as a voluntary board member of the company. From my position on the board, I have watched Upstate develop its practice over the past seven years. Prior to joining the board, I was engaged on an occasional basis as assistant director and stage manager with the professional touring wing of the company before going on to work as a facilitator and director on some of the company's cross-border projects. This trajectory has given me insight into the company's work and its role within the local community, along with its position in the wider regional context and its contribution to political and social affairs in the border area in the early years of the Northern Ireland peace process. My involvement with Upstate has raised my own awareness of the possibilities and challenges of theatre making, the frustrations and satisfactions of the devising process, and the scope and constraints within which a theatre company must operate.

The research for this chapter was conducted through a series of interviews with Mallon, Director of Upstate; Gorman, former Artistic Director of Upstate; and members of Upstate's artistic team of recent collaborators, including Lowe and Stephen Murray (ANU Productions), Cannon (Brokentalkers), and Paul Hayes (Catastrophe). A number of the community projects' participants also contributed to the research through a focus group. I offer an analysis of Upstate's work at various stages of the company's history, as well as examining the relevance of its model in relation to the developing collaborative, participatory practices currently in vogue in contemporary Irish theatre. The techniques and practices utilized by Upstate's artists are presented here as a backdrop to the contemporary growth of devised performance in Irish theatre. It is not possible, within the confines of this chapter, to provide an exhaustive account of the considerable body of work produced by Upstate over the past seventeen years. Instead this essay will provide a brief overview of a selection of productions from the company's oeuvre in an effort to give the reader a flavour of the variety and breadth of work Upstate has produced.

The discussion begins with an analysis of *The Border Chronicles* trilogy, a series of original devised plays comprising *Hades* (1998), *Epic* (2001) and *At Peace* (2007), that sought to document life in the region known as the border area of Northern Ireland and the Republic of Ireland during a period of immense political, social, cultural and economic change. This selection is taken from work produced by Upstate Live, the company's professional touring wing. The discussion will also examine four productions produced by Upstate Local, the company's community-engaged wing: *Tunnel of Love* (1999), *Come Forward to Meet You* (2011), *Ship Street Revisited* (2012) and *The Far Side* (2013). These productions have been chosen as their chronological order spans the arc of the company's lifetime and thereby offers a glimpse of how the work has developed over time. *Tunnel of Love*

(1999) was the first devised piece created by the company; the other three plays form a trilogy that emerged from Upstate's Shared Heritage Programme which commenced in 2011. This programme, inspired by the archive collected by Drogheda Local Voices, (a project documenting recordings of the town's social history) set out to explore Drogheda's oral histories through contemporary storytelling. The trilogy is also of interest because it provides a snapshot of the work created when Upstate teamed up with some of the newly emerging artists referred to above. This new phase of work developed after the company's restructuring in 2011. The seven plays discussed here therefore illustrate the diverse array of styles and approaches adopted by the company; they highlight the principles and ethos that inform Upstate's work and they offer the reader a broad spectrum of the methodologies and techniques associated with devised practice.

The Early Years of Upstate Theatre Project

Established as an independent regional theatre company in Drogheda, Co. Louth, Upstate's aim was to bridge the gap between what founders Gorman and Mallon saw as a false divide between professional theatre and community-engaged theatre. From its inception, the company sought to reflect a broad understanding of the place of 'theatre' and 'drama methodologies' in a wider social context. In Gorman's words, 'Upstate Theatre Project was founded initially to explore the interface between art and progressive social values' ('Aesthetics'). The organization's vision reflected a culturally democratic viewpoint that 'conceives of the arts as a form of political as well as of aesthetic power' (Benson, 1992, 31). A distinguishing feature of Upstate's practice is its emphasis on art for all – its determination to create art and arts practices inclusive of all citizens. The philosophy of cultural democracy is summarized by Ciarán Benson as follows: '[...T]he case for cultural democracy is moral and political, and grounded in the dominant ideas of modernity. It resists the conception of art and of artists as detached from ordinary life, and argues instead for transcending the divide which has grown up between art and society' (32).

In keeping with the principles of cultural democracy, the company's policy articulates Upstate's aim to improve arts access and provision for all members of the community and, specifically, to expand its audience base to non-theatre goers and to encourage local citizens to participate in the creation of communal art. Upstate's four-strand policy declared the company's socially engaged agenda under the four distinct headings of Local, Learning, Lab, and Live. The company's first publication, *Up and Running: A Review of the First Two Years* (1999) defined each of these areas as follows: Upstate Local, encapsulated 'the company's community drama animation programmes, whereby Upstate works in partnership with local groups to develop drama activity and to devise original dramas of interest to them' (3); Upstate Learning was the branch that would provide 'a range of training and education programmes' (3); Upstate Lab aimed to offer an 'innovative workshop programme, dedicated to researching new approaches to staging and playwriting. Regular action research work is carried out in collaboration with professional actors, designers, choreographers etc., and with local groups and trainees' (3); and finally, Upstate Live, was the term used to refer to the professional touring wing of the company.

The four-strand policy reveals an aspiration to merge community-engaged theatre with professional practice through collaborative, participatory processes. The provision of experimental workshops and related training and educational supports is an indication of the company's vision and recognition of the strategies required to realize its mission. While the company initially pursued all four areas, Lab and Learning appeared to become less prominent, and Local and Live became the principle strands of the company's practice. This division of practice was most unusual; it distinguished Upstate from other theatre companies operating at the time. It was also a somewhat odd decision given that, on the one hand, the company sought to 'bridge the gap' between professional theatre and community-engaged theatre, and on the other, it drew a distinction between 'pure' professional practice (Live) and collaborative community/professional practice (Local). Both wings were dedicated to working with the community in the creation of original devised theatre. Gorman explains that the Live/Local divide was a first step towards integration against the backdrop of 'widespread indifference that abounded in arts funding, media and industry circles generally to community-engaged practice in the 90s. It was driven by an ethos of affording equal esteem to diverse ways of making art' (Personal interview). The division of practice, therefore, seems to have been largely a political decision.

While Gorman and Mallon make a clear distinction between the devising processes adopted by Upstate Live and those adopted by Upstate Local, they refuse to distinguish the work in any way that would elevate one over the other. Gorman avows: 'I reject any hierarchical placing of value on work by differing population groups where the work is genuinely creative and motivated by the desire to make change through art – whatever that might mean' (Personal interview). He emphasizes that there are many models of devising and Mallon concurs stating, 'there's no one model that we would champion; the method and technical approach will continuously shift in order to suit participants and the aesthetic ambitions of the project' (Personal interview). In the case of Upstate Local, the plays were devised, written and performed by participating members of the local community who were provided with professional facilitation and essential training, whereas the plays produced by Upstate Live, while inspired and informed by the community, were written or adapted from classic texts, directed by Gorman and performed by professional casts, with the occasional inclusion of non-professional or training actors, who then toured the shows locally, nationally and internationally.

The plays of Upstate Live were devised through a process of inquiry and engagement with the community that Gorman describes as akin to action research (Personal interview). Through a range of methods including workshops, focus groups and interviews, members of the community shared their views and ideas which were then explored in dramatic form through drama workshops and public readings before being scripted by Gorman who is explicitly identified as the author. The devising methods used were similar in many respects, but differed in terms of the role of the writer and the associated issues of how ownership of work was designated. According to Gorman, this distinction is important and needs to be made clear at the outset of a project. An analysis of a selection of devised work produced by Upstate Live and Upstate Local now follows.

Upstate Live 1997 - 2010

Although Upstate specialize in devised performance, the organization also has produced and performed a variety of other work including adaptations of well-known works and plays by local and national playwrights. The first Upstate Live production was Gorman's adaptation of Gerhart Hauptmann's *The Weavers* (1997), a 19th-century epic of a local craftsmen's revolution in 1844 Silesia. Gorman's adaptation drew parallels between the traditions of the North East of Ireland and the remote Polish-German region in which the original play was set. Other plays adapted and produced by Upstate Live include Shakespeare's *Macbeth* (1999), Elizabeth Kuti's adaptation of Paul Smith's *The Countrywoman* (2000), and Patrick Kavanagh's memoir, *The Green Fool* (2004). In addition to these adaptations, Gorman directed John McArdle's *Two Houses* (2005), a play for children. In a later phase Upstate Live produced Colm Maher's *The Enemy Within*

(2008), Aidan Harney's *Submarine Man* (2009), and Conall Quinn's *The Ones Who Kill Shooting Stars* (2010) developed under Upstate's Writers' Commissioning Scheme which was established and managed by Hayes during his tenure as creative producer with the company.

In terms of work that derived from a devising methodology, Upstate Live produced a series of plays that would eventually become known as *The Border Chronicles*. Written by Gorman, the plays were based on information gathered through interviews, focus groups and public meetings with local communities across the border region over a ten-year period. Emerging themes were explored in workshops with professional and community actors who probed and experimented with ideas through improvisation and physical movement exercises. This methodology was adopted with a view to creating original artistic work that reflected the specific cultural context of the geographical and political milieu of the border region. As a socially engaged arts organization, Upstate sought to capture and express, in aesthetic form, the community's response to the social and political happenings that prevailed in the area during that period. In this regard, the plays are an example of how action research can potentially translate into devised theatre.

Spanning the period 1997 to 2007, the plays offer an account of life in the border region during a time of major political upheaval that covers the signing of the Belfast Agreement, the uneasy peace that followed this, the beginnings of the 'Celtic Tiger' economic boom and the new phenomenon of significant inward migration. The events that unfolded during that decade are depicted against a backdrop of myths and legends from the ancient civilizations of Greece, Ireland, West Africa and the Baltic region. As the narratives weave back and forth from the surreal world of ancient folklore to the present-day Irish political landscape the parallels between these worlds become apparent.

Taking as its starting point the ancient Greek myths of the underworld, *Hades* (1998), the first play of the trilogy, is set in the fictitious border town of Ballinascaul (Town of Shadows) in the months following the Good Friday Agreement, the treaty which enabled the peace process in Northern Ireland. Inspired by the ancient Greek myths of the underworld, the play is a collection of stories of individuals seeking to overcome the obstacles life has thrown in their path. The characters include a taxi driver and his fifteen-year-old daughter who sneaks out of their home at night; an ex-champion boxer desperately trying to escape the grip of moneylenders; a boy whose true identity were it to become known would cause great scandal in local political circles; and an assortment of local public figures struggling to retain their identity in the midst of the shifting sands of an unfolding peace process. A weave of storytelling, myth, dream and dance, *Hades* won a BBC/Stewart Parker Award in 1999 and drew comment on Upstate's collaborative community approach: '[I]f, as Thomas Kilroy recently stated, a lively, collaborative community theatre is emerging to challenge the traditional pre-eminence of the literary in Irish drama, Upstate Live may well lead the charge' (Byrne 54).

Epic (2001), the second instalment of the trilogy, is set primarily on the Cooley Peninsula in County Louth in the wake of the foot and mouth disease that beset the area in 2001, at a time when border paramiltarism and the threat of a breakdown in the peace process remained prevalent. The play merges the ancient Celtic myth of the Táin Bó Cuailgne with modern reality to portray life in this small farming community following the outbreak of the virus. The four-person ensemble, doubling up in twenty-seven roles, presented a weave of interconnected stories that trace the devastation and disquiet sweeping through rural Ireland as a result of this agricultural crisis. The play begins with two boys witnessing an act of criminality in a remote, sacred mountain setting. A modern curse is unleashed and a virus affecting livestock spreads through the land. A cull of farm animals disturbs the ancient ghosts on the plains of Meath and a mysterious virus begins to spread into the homes and hearts of people causing computer crashes, factory closures and a trail of deceit and destruction across the country. The play, a combination of storytelling, surreal myth and dream captures the social and economic disaster that faced inhabitants of this area of the border, while paramiltaries continue to try to hold their grip on the community.

Echoing the themes of *Hades* and *Epic,* the final part of the trilogy, *At Peace* (2007), adopts a physical performance style that mixes myth and modernity to explore life in a peacetime border community. A multi-ethnic cast of Irish, African, and Eastern European actors and an onstage use of their respective native languages highlighted the increased cultural diversity experienced by the border area as a result of the rapid population shift occurring in Ireland during the early years of the twenty-first century. The play begins with the fictional discovery of human remains found during the building of a cross-border motorway. Work on the by-pass is held up when a Nigerian ground worker discovers the ancient remains in the path of the bulldozers. The disturbing of the bones appears to trigger a series of strange events in the area and ancient myths of Eastern Europe, West Africa and Celtic

Ireland surface as the interconnected stories of a group of Nigerian, Latvian and Irish road workers present on the day of the find unfold.

Together the three plays of *The Border Chronicles* offer a panoramic snapshot of a community in a state of flux, in which issues of identity, values and traditions are thrown into disarray during an era of unprecedented political, social, cultural and economic change. Time and place combine to communicate a distinctive cultural context that not only infuses the work but isolates Upstate's geographical and cultural position in Irish theatre-making.

During this period, Upstate was funded in equal measure by the Arts Council, the statutory body charged with funding the arts in Ireland, and the Programme for Peace and Reconciliation, a European Union programme aimed at stabilizing society in the post-conflict era in Northern Ireland and in the counties that form the Border Region of the Republic of Ireland. Arts Council funding was allocated towards core company costs and the Upstate Live programme, while EU funding supported the development of projects under Upstate Local.

In 2010, the company underwent radical structural changes occasioned by funding cuts and a negotiated arrangement with the Arts Council to cease professional production and regional touring and pursue a purely participatory agenda. Upstate Live ceased to operate and Gorman departed the company to pursue other solo, teaching and public art interests. The company, now under Mallon's direction, continued to be funded by the Arts Council of Ireland but solely under the auspices of the Arts Participation Department. The Arts Council had declined explicitly to support Upstate Local activities previous to this. The upheaval coincided with the arrival of a number of emerging theatre-makers on the Dublin scene who proclaimed their collaborative credentials from an early stage. Some of these practitioners, namely, Cannon and Gary Keegan of Brokentalkers, as well as Lowe, were to become essential in the continuing development of practice and form in Upstate as the company changed from an Artistic Director-led to a curatorial model. Interestingly, Upstate's shift from theatre to participatory arts funding occurred at the same time as these artists, whose practice hinged similarly on collaboratively devised theatre with community actors, were funded under the Arts Council's theatre budget. The reason for this anomaly is unclear but it illustrates how the funding landscape has changed in Ireland in recent years, impacting on the structure of arts organizations and – by extension – the form of works they produce. Upstate's recent phase of work, the company's development under participatory arts funding and its relationship with this new wave of artists forms part of the discussion that follows below. The discussion begins by examining the history of Upstate Local.

Upstate Local 1998 - 2010

In Upstate's formative years, Gorman and Mallon worked together as co-facilitators. Their first large-scale undertaking was a creative partnership with a local branch of the national organization Macra na Feirme (meaning Stalwarts of the Land in Gaelic). This organization provides opportunities for seventeen to thirty-five year olds in rural communities to interact through participation in a range of social and cultural activities including performing arts. Upstate's partnership with the local Termonfeckin branch culminated in the productions *Tunnel of Love* (1999) and *Zoo Station* (2001). These plays, along with an earlier work devised by Gorman and the Monaghan Macra Arts Club, are documented in the company's publication *Way out in the Country: An Anthology of Community Plays* (2001). In this collection, Mallon recounts how Upstate Local sought partnerships with groups interested in devising and scripting original material. He writes,

> [u]ltimately we wanted the challenge of writing about a contemporary community, delving into its psyche, challenging its imagination and hearing its stories by having people from the community write the play themselves ('Way Out in the Country' 203).

A discussion of Gorman and Mallon's artistic partnership and the process of working with the local community in their first devised production, *Tunnel of Love* illustrates how the company's origins in devising began.

Tunnel of Love - Gorman and Mallon

Set in a fictitious rural village, *Tunnel of Love* (1999) depicts life in a small, rural Irish community at the turn of the twenty-first century. The play traces the lives of two fictional families over a two-year period, leading up to and including the day of a troublesome wedding. It is a character-driven, episodic drama that follows a narrative through-line concerning families divided by social and economic difference, punctuated by such features as flashback, direct address and stylized movement tableaux. Part of the story involves a local man who emigrates from Ireland to London to avoid the gossip that will inevitably follow the break-up of his seven-year engagement. In London he falls for a woman a few years his junior who also hails from his home village. They return to marry at home but on their wedding day it is revealed that he has had a dalliance in the meantime with his ex. This familiar plot of deceit and betrayal allowed not only for comic episodes, but a serious investigation of emigration, the male psyche, addiction (in a sub-plot concerning an alcoholic family member) and class division in a small community. Some of the later more physical and ritualistic work of Upstate is prefigured in the visual tableaux in *Tunnel of Love*, in particular a highly stylized beginning and ending in which the traditional wedding game where the couple runs through a 'tunnel' of outstretched guests' arms becomes a portal into dream, memory and altered realities.

Tunnel of Love saw Gorman and Mallon combining their methods, Gorman drawing on a model that he had begun to develop in his earlier work in Monaghan and Mallon bringing his knowledge of youth drama (already a hotbed for devising in Ireland at the time) to the project. They acknowledge that borrowing techniques and methods from other practitioners and theorists helped shape their practice and cite Augusto Boal, Chrissie Poulter and Clive Barker as particular favourites. In line with the principles of cultural democracy underpinning the company's ethos, the duo was acutely aware of the need to develop an inclusive approach that would accommodate the varied needs of diverse communities. Fostering positive relationships and creating an environment of mutual respect that encouraged an exchange of ideas and allowed for meaningful dialogue and critical reflection was a priority. As Gorman and Mallon progressed onto the more complex *Zoo Station*, they saw drama games and exercises as key to achieving such an atmosphere. Consequently, every workshop began with physical and verbal drama exercises – warm-ups, trust and spatial exercises – before moving to more intricate work such as tableaux and improvisations. The company's incorporation of physical theatre promoted an emphasis on physicality and movement, and so workshops and resultant productions typically contained a strong element of choreographed movement. Tableaux depicting abstract physical situations were frequently used as a stimulus for brainstorming ideas which were then developed further into scenarios for improvisations.

Gorman and Mallon describe their work in this phase as character-driven narratives. They cite character as the most important element of the process, deeming it much more important than story. Gorman explains how participants would form a series of tableaux and characters and 'before they knew it, they had created a story and then they had created five stories and then we would say, right, let's take those five stories and see can we find a frame to marry them' (Personal interview). They quickly discovered that a narrative drama form was the key to finding a frame and best suited their purpose and methods. It was an effective vehicle for harnessing the unconnected stories that frequently emerge from collaborative writing processes. Mallon maintains that because the work was character driven there was no difficulty in developing a script; characters would bring stories with them: 'with clearly defined characterization and scene objectives, collective writing was not a problem' ('Way Out in the Country' 204). Nevertheless, the collaborative methods used generally led to a hotchpotch of storylines and characters. So, a form consisting of multiple narratives intertwining and unfolding simultaneously was needed.

Gorman observes that dramas with several narratives benefit from the use of devices such as 'unifiers' and 'clustering' (Personal interview). He explains, 'it is helpful to have at least one unifying device – something that all the characters experience even if independently from other characters. And clustering (the gathering together of characters into logical clusters) is a critical step in developing cohesive narratives' (Personal interview). He also recommends that when it comes to penning a story collectively, it is wise to agree a location and a timeline. Gorman and Mallon used these techniques to guide the writing process. In addition to physical drama exercises, their workshops included a succession of creative writing exercises all of which were inspired by what had transpired on the workshop floor and many of which were in the realm of dream or involved memory exercises or working with objects. Participants, having agreed a location and timeline, frequently sat and wrote in seven-minute bursts. This balance of freedom and structure – a coherent framework that allows multiple narratives to develop – gave participants opportunities for individual and shared creative expression. The method of interweaving improvisation with writing is an effective means of stimulating ideas and eliciting material from the participants. It also ensures that the stories are expressed in the participants' own voices, which has the added advantage of capturing the cadence of the local dialect.

Gorman and Mallon recognized that the techniques they had developed were highly adaptable and they set about honing these methods further to work with intercultural and intergenerational groups. Following their fruitful partnership with Macra, Gorman and Mallon expanded Upstate Local across the region to include the wider border area and parts of Northern Ireland. During the period between 2002 and 2007, Upstate Local developed its community-engaged programmes through the auspices of The Crossover Project. Funded by Border Action through Peace and Reconciliation II, the programme comprised of four adult groups and one youth group in the border counties of Louth and Monaghan in the Republic and in counties Tyrone and Fermanagh in Northern Ireland. This cross-border and cross-community project sought to devise original material reflecting life in rural communities of the border counties through the voices of members of both sides of the divide. The devising process that the company had by now developed provided an opportunity for Catholics and Protestants north and south of the border to come together in the creation of communal art. Although conflict resolution was an obvious objective, Gorman and Mallon were adamant that setting out to 'tackle' issues head on was a tactic that should be avoided. Instead they opted to concentrate their efforts on the creation of art. Gorman asserts, '[w]e always described our quest first and foremost as an artistic one, immediately affirming that no-one has a monopoly on dreaming, on creativity" ('Aesthetics'). Gorman and Mallon maintained that any issues present would inevitably surface through the process. With artistic pursuit firmly the focus, they began their work in the realm of dream. Gorman explains their rationale as follows:

> In the early years of Upstate we began with dreams ... That became particularly important when we moved to The Crossover Project you know, we felt that there were such sensitivities there around Catholics and Protestants and north and south and all that stuff and there was enormous pressure on us to deal with issues and we said, 'No we won't do that, the issues will come trailing in behind us eventually anyway.' Why start with the labels, why start with the presumptions that we are victims or the presumptions that we are enemies? You know? Let's begin in the kind of shared and wonderful world of dreaming because every human being dreams in some way; they dream actively and they dream passively in their sleep. So we would create these kinds of big mad tableaux and I would also introduce very early in the process a creative writing exercise that was based around writing a dream. (Personal interview)

This strategy was an effective leveller; it invited participants to communicate and interact imaginatively and intuitively, and alleviated tensions and prejudices that may have been present. It provided participants with an escape from reality and a safe distance from the conflicts that troubled their everyday lives. The use of tableaux facilitates an easy transition to the type of abstract movement pieces that characterize Upstate's theatre. In those early years, in which peace-building and – later – interculturalism were part of the context, Upstate deliberately avoided sharing personal histories with audiences, although some carefully managed work along such lines did occasionally proceed in more advanced enclosed workshops. This foregrounding of dream-based fictions over lived experience was based on a belief that reconciliation and empowerment should come initially from the collective act of devising and creative writing. Participants were encouraged to 'leave their baggage at the door,' to park their labels, resist categorization and instead to imagine new worlds and fictional scenarios, often parallel to the real, familiar border counties' milieu but nonetheless newly reimagined in a shared process. After five years, with an average of four local productions per year, The Crossover Project came to an end and Upstate shifted its focus from the rural communities of the border region to the world of interculturalism and urban youth in its next phase of work.

The Louth International Theatre Project was launched in 2007 in response to the rapid demographic change that had occurred in the region as a result of the large influx of immigrants into Ireland during the boom years of the Celtic Tiger economy. This intercultural initiative aimed to provide an artistic forum where the growing international population could voice their experience of life as an immigrant in Irish society. The first production to emerge from the venture was *The Journey from Babel* (2009), an off-site performance on the theme of journeys and migration. The play, directed by Gorman and Mallon, was devised by fifteen local people of eight nationalities. Performed in a disused dockside warehouse, this work is a significant transitional moment in the company's development, signalling the move from largely black box-situated narrative dramas to Upstate's current preference for interactive, site-responsive and site-specific work. The transition was influenced partly by Hayes' interest in site-specific work and his appointment as creative producer of the company and partly by the growing trend in site-responsive performances happening elsewhere. *The Journey from Babel* utilized techniques common in contemporary site-specific performance including physical engagement with the audience, separating the spectators into separate groups and promenading from room to room. Other companies specializing in site-specific performance at the time were Northern Irish company, Kabosh, as well as Dublin-based company, Semper Fi, whose production *Ladies and Gents* (2002), first performed in the public toilets on Dublin's St. Stephen's Green as part of the Dublin Fringe Festival, won a Fringe First Award in Edinburgh 2004. *The Journey from Babel* combined documentary historical testimony, video, audio, ritual gestural work and song with narrative fiction and comic relief. While the production did not engage entirely with the specificity of the site where it was performed, its narratives foregrounded the immense import of 'place' by highlighting similarities between the lives of immigrants living in present-day Ireland and historical accounts of migrants globally through the ages – from the biblical Babel myth of the performance's title to the Triangle Shirtwaist Factory fire of 1911 in New York in which 146 migrant workers perished.

The Mango Tree (2011), the second production to emerge from the Louth International Theatre project, combined traditional storytelling with visual artistry to reveal the hidden voices of a diverse community. The stories, told through a series of monologues, explore the isolation and disconnection felt by the inhabitants of an Irish town. In the Director's Note on the show's programme, Stephen Murray writes: 'It seemed important that what we were doing was also a social activity and the process of meeting up, devising and working on the play was resolving the very issues that we were working on.'

During the same period as the Louth International Theatre Project, Upstate was also concentrating its efforts on creating a number of community-engaged theatre projects with the young people of the area. For example, *No Change Given* (2009), directed by Murray and Mallon, was devised over a four-month period by a group of twenty-five teenagers from various parts of Drogheda. The project began with the idea of producing a show on a bus. This starting point prompted consideration of situations that might arise on a bus, and characters emerged through plotting the route the bus would take. The characters were developed and a storyline was established through a series of improvisations examining what might happen both on and off the bus as certain characters entered and exited the action. Scripted by playwright Colm Maher, the play was described in its programme as 'a story of life, love and youth in a walled town. Post boom drama through the eyes of the generation who will have to foot the bill. Not so much life in the fast lane as life in the bus lane.' Significantly, this project was informed by an earlier urban work, *The Bus Project* (2007), undertaken in Ballymun, by Lowe collaborating with Murray as part of the Dublin Fringe Festival.

Kinda Random (2011), directed by long-time Upstate collaborator Tara Jenkins, is a further example of the company's work with the youth of the area. Adopting a documentary-style narrative, the play offers an account of life in a present day Irish town from the perspective of its adolescent community. During workshops the thirteen participants aged between thirteen and seventeen explored and experimented with voice, improvisation, choreography and physical theatre techniques and recorded their responses to questions concerning the lives of young people. Jenkins collaborated with Fintan Brady, a writer and political activist in Belfast, who edited the recordings to create a script based on the participants' responses.

Much of Upstate's intercultural and youth work was experimental. Mallon explains that this is because this type of performance needs 'continually to shift and change to ensure a cultural connection with those participants who may have no interest in dramatic presentation as it is conventionally perceived' (Personal interview). These three projects belong to a middle and transitional phase of the Upstate story and coincide with an internal restructuring that took place when Hayes joined the company in a creative producer role in 2006. From his earlier work with Catastrophe Theatre, Hayes brought with him an enthusiasm for site-specific work; his own first directing project for Upstate was the historical drama *The Enemy Within* (2008) performed across two heritage sites in the town of Drogheda – Laurence's Gate and Millmount's Martello Tower – both significant sites in historical sieges of the town. Across the company's Live and Local strands, the move towards the later site-specific and documentary work was beginning to take hold.

Upstate Under Participatory Arts Funding

As outlined earlier, Upstate underwent structural changes in 2010 following the Arts Council's decision to change the company's funding status from a professional producing touring company to a participatory arts organization. This period in the company's development is marked by the company's recent affiliation with newly emerging artists such as Lowe, Cannon and Hayes. An analysis of three of the works produced by Upstate in conjunction with these artists now follows.

***Come Forward to Meet You* – Artist Louise Lowe (ANU Productions)**

In September 2011 Upstate, as part of the Shared Heritage Programme, invited Lowe to work with a group of local adults to devise a piece of theatre based on the oral history archive collected by Drogheda Local Voices. The culmination of that venture was *Come Forward to Meet You* (2011), a site-specific production performed in Oldbridge House, an eighteenth-century manor located on the site of the 1690 Battle of the Boyne – a battle of considerable political and historical significance nationally and internationally. The British throne, French dominance in Europe and Religious power in Ireland were at stake in this decisive battle between the Catholic King James and the Protestant King William of Orange whose landmark victory shaped the course of Irish, British and European history in the centuries that followed. The annual twelfth of July commemoration of the infamous battle remains a contentious issue in Irish North-South relations. The eighteenth-century manor and estate, now publicly owned and managed by the Office of Public Works (OPW), houses the Battle of the Boyne Visitor's Centre. Large installations detailing European politics at the time of the battle and exhibitions illustrating events from the King's perspective are on display in the Visitor's Centre on the ground floor of the house. The setting of *Come Forward to Meet You* in this important heritage site heightened the theatricality of the production. The play reveals a world normally hidden from view. Confined to the basement, the action invites the public to enter the private sphere of the house.

Billed in the programme as 'a unique collision of oral history and highly physical performance,' the play is based on the oral memoir of local woman Angela Mitchell, who lived and worked on the Oldbridge estate as a servant in the 1920s. As is often the case in devised theatre, the site inspired the story and informed the performance. Lowe remarks that, in her practice, devising begins with 'a space, a place or a theme;' she is confident that in this case the architecture of the space fuelled the making of the piece. Lowe recalls how the group were drawn to Angela Mitchell's story. The reason for this was not clear but she speculated that the predominance of women in the group may have steered an overall affinity with Angela's story.

The action took place in five rooms in the original kitchen area located in the basement of the big house. Audience members, having been assigned a number, were greeted by a butler who escorted them through the courtyard into the house. The performance began in the corridor with a movement piece involving the full cast after which the actors dispersed to various rooms followed by audience members marshalled according to the number they were allocated. In each room, the actors awaited the audience who moved from room to room to watch fragments of Angela Mitchell's life unfold. The action in each room was repeated every time a new audience group entered the space. The memories portrayed included the death and burial of a new-born twin, a seductive dance between a young couple entangled in a forbidden courtship, and the highly-physical and disturbed antics of the butler scaling the walls in the kitchen before he eats the supper prepared by a kitchen maid. The wake of the lady of Oldbridge House was depicted in a darkened room where a servant fervently prayed as she repeatedly circled the coffin of her mistress. Across the hall, a servant in the laundry room was washing sheets and asking audience members, 'Do you believe in ghosts?' as she handed them bars of carbolic soap and buckets of water so that they can help her complete the task. In another room an archived recording of Angela Mitchell's voice was heard describing the events illustrated by the various scenes.

The division of the audience into appointed rooms created an intimate atmosphere and intensified the experience for both the actors and the audience. The use of highly physical movement pieces in confined spaces created a palpable sense of entrapment. Dance regularly infiltrates Lowe's work. In her view, actors discover a character's inner thoughts and emotions through movement. The choreography of this production was testament to this belief as the narrative emerged through the movement and rhythm of the performance and infused the characters' lives with symbolic rituals. Lowe emphasizes the importance of giving each actor a 'task' to complete. For example, one actor might be given sheets to wash, while another actor might have to eat a meal or scrub a table. Lowe focuses the actors' attention on physical tasks as a means of creating the action; she maintains that this tactic is also an effective strategy for reducing performance anxiety amongst both trained and untrained performers. Lowe refers to director Anne Bogart's view that the right people should be in the room at the right time. Lowe explains 'I think I take that notion on strongest no matter where I am, that this is the right place, this is the right time, these are the right people and so we make the right piece for these people in this place at the right time.'

In *Come Forward to Meet You*, there was a pleasing symmetry between the characters being portrayed and the actors portraying them. In this subversive account of life in the big house, the servants, the butler, the kitchen maid, and the laundry worker were centre stage. Such characters represent the traditionally invisible citizens in society. The non-professional community cast played a central role in bringing the stories of otherwise forgotten characters to life. Voices that otherwise would not be heard, both in terms of content and performance, were given a platform.

***Ship Street Revisited* - Artist Paul Hayes (Catastrophe)**

Ship Street Revisited (2012), the second instalment of the Shared Heritage Programme, also focuses on the lives and memories of ordinary people. The former residents and workers of the, now largely derelict, street of the play's title are the subjects of this play. Set in 1940s' Drogheda, the plot weaves around the lives of the tightknit, working class community who resided in Ship Street, an industrial area surrounding the town's port. A cast of fifty community actors brought to life the abandoned street, as well as the forgotten stories of the men and women who worked in the boot and shoe factories, the breweries and the mills. A combination of street performance, traditional drama and storytelling, the performance took audience members on a journey through the street and into the derelict homes of its residents. As with *Come Forward to Meet You*, audiences were divided into small groups and guided to each location by a 'local resident' who chatted with audience members about the trials and tribulations of life on the street. Inside the various houses, audiences were met with a conventional fourth wall performance depicting the lives of those who lived there. Familiar themes of young love, family, emigration, poverty and unemployment emerged from the stories that unfolded inside the walls of each dwelling.

Ship Street Revisited was written by Aidan Harney and directed by Hayes. Harney, a local playwright, had been researching the local oral history archive made available to Upstate as part of the Shared Heritage Programme, and he and Hayes had worked together previously on *Submarine Man* (2009). A number of factors distinguish *Ship Street Revisited* from the other two projects that form the trilogy. The fact that it was written by a playwright, for instance, immediately sets it apart. Harney's script, however, emerged from a devising process and the participants, like those of the other two projects, contributed to the development of the characters and storyline. The main reason for adopting this approach was down to Hayes' methods of devising which differ significantly from those of Lowe and Brokentalkers. ANU and Brokentalkers usually begin devising from scratch and continue in this mode right up until the final rehearsal, whereas Hayes, most likely because of his dramaturgical background, opts to work with a writer and likes to have an early draft of a script beforehand.

This preference for dramaturgy, in fact, represents a continuation of the literary strengths traditionally associated with Upstate, exemplified in earlier works such as *Tunnel of Love* (1999), *Zoo Station* (2001), *Time's Hands* (2007) and *Midland* (2008). This shows how Mallon's curatorial policy embraces new methodologies while maintaining space for the artistic strengths upon which the company was built. Hayes felt it was important to explain this style of practice to the participants of the project. He admits, 'I never said to the cast of *Ship Street* that they were writing their own play, I said they were informing the writing of the play, it's different.' Hayes' and Harney's work is a reminder that devised and more 'literary' theatrical forms are not necessarily diametrically opposed. Gorman makes the point that, although devising for the stage is very seldom about creating a literary piece of theatre, one of Upstate's achievements is marrying devising with literary traditions. He states: 'Some of the work that has been created through processes that could appropriately be described as devising actually have quite a strong literary element in them because we always brought creative writing into the room' (Personal interview).

Although this was Hayes' first time to devise and direct a show with community actors, he had devised a number of shows with his own professional theatre company Catastrophe. Those shows were usually inspired by a site-specific location and written by a writer who created a script based on the characters and themes that emerged during the devising process. Hayes followed the same model for *Ship Street Revisited*, and immediately set about securing a site that would provide him and the writer with a framework. Once the venue had been agreed, participants drawing on local history archives were asked to find a person who grew up in Drogheda in the 1940s, on which each would base her/his character. Following this, the performers began writing scenes involving these characters.

With a total of eighty-five participants, *Ship Street Revisited* was Upstate's most ambitious project to date. Aside from the large number of participants, the show was received well locally. It sold out for twenty nights, drawing predominantly non-traditional audiences (anecdotal accounts from the show's participants suggest that upwards of eighty per cent of the audience were non-theatregoers) and attracting an unprecedented number of social networking comments. Much of the reason for this response from the community was due to local interest in the site-specific location and in the oral history archive on which the play was based. Ship Street is strongly associated with the town's industrial past and holds a special place in the town's history. Many locals have fond memories of the street and the residents who inhabited it.

Ship Street Revisited and *Come Forward to Meet You* reflect a significant shift to site-specific work by the company and a decision to search for locations that both reflect and affect the narrative. The settings of Oldbridge House and Ship Street were instrumental in developing plot and characters during the collaborative process between artists and participants. Moreover, both venues resonated enormously with the told stories and the local community audiences.

The Far Side – Artist Feidlim Cannon (Brokentalkers)

The Far Side (2013), the third project in the Shared Heritage Programme, reflects the other recent shift in Upstate's direction from a dramatic narrative form towards a documentary style of presentation. This production mixed traditional live performance with multimedia to document the lives of seven locals living in present-day Drogheda. Once again, the ordinary events of everyday life were placed centre stage; as part of the process of creating this work, performers shared their memories and dreams of growing up and growing old in their local town. Unlike the first two parts of the trilogy, *The Far Side* does not draw on the local oral archives for its inspiration. Rather it relies on the personal lives and experiences of the performers to create a contemporary, living history. The events and experiences that helped shape their identity, from mealtimes around the family table to dancing in a bingo hall, are remembered and celebrated through a blend of humorous and poignant moments of personal recollections and reflection. The participants' stories were presented through a combination of recorded performance, visuals and music in a celebration of the history of their own lives. The action weaved between past and present as the performers' reminiscences came to life on a big screen providing a documentary account of the social history of Drogheda and, on a wider scale, a contemporary perspective of life in a large Irish town in twenty-first century Ireland.

The Far Side came to fruition under the guidance of artist Cannon who conducted a series of writing workshops with participants over a two-year period. For Cannon, much of the nuts and bolts of devising revolve around keeping a record of what happens throughout the process. Flipcharts and markers are always to hand; images, photos, drawings, snippets of text and spider diagrams indicating kernels of ideas are charted and revisited as the work unfolds. Once again, these approaches mirror and reinvent methods used for over two decades by Upstate artists. In his afterword to *Way out in the Country* (2001), Mallon describes how 'the mapping of characters and clusters of characters, told orally, is charted on a grid' ('The Making of Two Community Plays' 205). In 2007, Upstate commissioned artist Vivienne

Byrne to create a visual installation using hundreds of hoarded pages of literary scribbles, drawings, notes and similar grids and charts collected over ten years of Upstate's community devising processes all across the border region.

Cannon, a self-confessed advocate of the collaborative process, sees devising as a way of challenging the traditional ideologies of text-based theatre. Like Lowe, he is concerned with exploring the ideas that emerge from the people in the room. He cautions that clear communication between the artist and the group is crucial, 'even if you don't know what your show is going to be, tell them that.' Whether this degree of honesty inspires confidence or alarm may well depend on the personalities that make up the group; nevertheless, it is a significant endorsement of the artist's belief and confidence in the process and it serves to highlight the importance of participant voices in shaping the outcome of projects. Such a stance promotes openness to diverse ideas during the theatre-making process and increases a sense of group ownership of the final production.

During the course of *The Far Side* project, Cannon encouraged participants to speak openly and candidly about their experiences and memories of growing up in the town. He asked participants to bring him to places of personal significance in their local area. He and the group travelled around the town on a bus and explored places nominated by participants. Cannon recalls, 'all of a sudden then the workshop became about them and I was the one that was actually participating in it.' This reversal of roles shifts the hierarchy, empowering participants to take the lead. It places the artist in the role of observer and gives the group control over content, freedom to create, and opportunity to reflect.

Published literature on devised and community-engaged theatre practices by such writers as Augusto Boal and Chris Johnston suggests that it is an infinitely more powerful experience for participants if the content comes from them, rather than from an outside source. Boal insists:

> The themes to be treated were always suggested by the group or by the spec-actors; I myself never imposed, or even proposed, anything by way of subject matter – if the intention is to create a theatre which liberates, then it is vital to let those concerned put forward their own themes. (19)

Similarly, Johnston argues that community drama workshops 'are more effective by criteria of self-empowerment if they place the participating group in the role of content-makers' (17). In the case of

The Far Side, Cannon's site-specific exercise appears to have provided participants with rich stimuli for writing. Participants commented that visiting the locations brought forgotten memories to the surface, and listening to other people's memories stirred further memories: 'things will come back to you [...] they're talking about stuff you had forgotten about and then that will bring up another story' (Upstate Theatre Project Participants). Cannon cites this as an important workshop tool as it not only generated material at the time but, like Lowe's 'complete the task' strategy, it is also a useful rehearsal device, helping to alleviate participants' performance anxiety. Cannon's bus exercise also made clear that the stories, memories and reminiscences that the group shared with each other during the devising process should be the focus of the show. Cannon remarks that, in his experience of devising, what happens through preliminary exercises and in the rehearsal room often becomes central to the final production.

Murray notes that a similar process took place amongst the group who devised Upstate's production of *Mango Tree* (2011). He recalls how this intercultural group found it difficult to link the separate stories that members of the group had written, and how that struggle ultimately became the theme of the show. He explains: 'It was about all these different people in a city wanting to connect with each other, but not knowing how to. That became the theme because that's what the workshop felt like sometimes.' Community-engaged performance opens the possibility for everyone involved in creating a performance to have her/his voice heard by the wider community. The challenge of bringing together the disparate voices of a diverse community in many ways seems to inform the work. Sharing personal stories, exchanging ideas, and connecting with others in an act of communal art-making to be shared with the wider community reflects Grayling's idea of the arts as that 'typically brilliant part [...] of the conversation a community has with itself' (38).

The Wider Local and Global Political Significance of Upstate's work

The plays *Come Forward to Meet You*, *Ship Street Revisited* and *The Far Side* offer vibrant and thought-provoking portrayals of contemporary Irish society. In this way, they follow the precedent set by *The Border Chronicles* and much of the early work of Upstate Local. Created and inspired by the community, all these productions were grassroots celebrations of the lives of 'ordinary' people, a commemorating of the stories and memories of people whose lives largely go unnoticed. Although firmly rooted in the local, the plays have a wider social and cultural relevance. By highlighting the collective concerns of individuals and communities, the plays reflect the diverse political and cultural beliefs and values that shape a community; they speak beyond the local to matters of national and global relevance. In doing so, they epitomize Michel de Montaigne's philosophy that 'the most deeply individualized is at the same time the most universal' (de Montaigne, qtd. in Cohen-Cruz 129). The plays reveal the social and cultural attitudes and the political and economic circumstances of frequently marginalized social groups. The plays represent the lives and stories of working class and unemployed people, emigrants and immigrants, lone parents, adolescents, older people and other vulnerable or marginalized groups. These often disenfranchised voices and overlooked narratives of a community have characterized much of Upstate's work. Hayes remarks: 'Every town in Ireland has forgotten streets and forgotten stories [...] one of the things that we managed to do was tell people's stories that would have been forgotten otherwise [...] you can do that in this environment.' Murray agrees, affirming that it is the presentation of lesser-heard voices that distinguishes Upstate's work. He observes that the voices portrayed in an Upstate show usually are not heard in more dominant, literary and commercial theatre forms:

> They [the participant-performers] are giving a voice to something that you're not necessarily going to hear elsewhere. You're certainly not going to hear it in any of the big mainstream theatres and that's a shame ... There's things [sic] that they're saying that should be heard.

Upstate's pluralistic attitude and inclusive practice has resulted in an open-door policy that offers all citizens equal access and equal opportunity to engage with art as a participant in the theatre-making process. Participants are recruited using multiple methods, from ads in local papers to social media callouts to direct referrals from official agencies that work with minority groups and vulnerable people in the community. This policy has a direct knock-on effect on Upstate's audience profile as invariably a diverse range of participants attracts a variety of audience members, many of whom are non-theatregoers, who turn out to support family, friends, neighbours and colleagues. In all of Upstate's work, the company has maintained an inclusive, pluralist policy, and has demonstrated a consistent record of persuading people from all backgrounds and ages to come together to create art. By embedding its practice within local communities, Upstate is positioned to respond to the specific needs and agendas of specific communities, and to provide opportunities to widen participation and include culturally marginalized audiences. As a result, the company frequently works with people who have no experience of theatre or the arts. This adds significant depth to the work according to Murray, who asserts that working with community actors brings a fresh perspective that can revitalize the art form. He observes that experienced actors tend to have a heightened awareness of form and structure that can occasionally inhibit ideas whereas, he explains, participants with no experience of performance 'won't have thought about stuff as much so they'll do something completely different ... completely new. When you are working with groups that don't necessarily have as much of a voice, you don't know what they are going to say.' This raises an interesting dichotomy for artists working in the shared environment of community and professional theatre. Indeed, the raw energy of an unschooled performer speaking or physically acting out something deeply truthful can be immensely powerful; it is one of the strengths of community casting, but the unique craft of the trained actors – and especially actors trained in improvisation – can yield equally evocative material. Murray's observation also highlights a need for responsible direction, a leadership and vision that is sensitive to the needs and abilities of participants, in particular, where vulnerable people such as those with intellectual disabilities or traumatic histories may be concerned.

In Upstate's most recent collection of work, the organization has continued to position social engagement at the centre of its practice. Despite some divergence in terms of the methodologies and approaches adopted by its recently expanded team of artistic collaborators, the company's socio-political ethos remains steadfast. Whatever the tools and methodologies used in the creation of the work, the artists share a common aesthetic outlook; they collaborate with a community whose experiences and knowledge inform the subject, and together, they work to create a collective vision that reflects the world from the community's perspective. Each of the projects demonstrates a consistent attentiveness to process. While the pursuit of a quality aesthetic performance is the impetus behind each project, the end production is, nevertheless, of secondary importance to the process. David Grant alludes to this characteristic of community-engaged theatre in *Playing the Wild Card*:

> In community drama, the process is at least as, if not more important than the end product. This is because the involvement of the participants is the end being served by the project. The

resulting production is a shared celebration of the work done together. (8)

Upstate artists' and participants' comments as shared in the Focus group conducted by this author echo Grant's view. Lowe states that

> the productions by Upstate are a celebration of all the work that everyone's done, they're not what we are working towards ... the end result is a celebration of the process.

Murray remarks:

> It's important that they [the participant-performers] have a show at the end of it but more important is the process and I think if you want to talk about Upstate then that's what counts. With Upstate everything comes from the group.

In the programme note for *Kinda Random*, Jenkins notes that

> the performance of *Kinda Random* is the tip of the iceberg. What has happened between us, in our workshop programme, is the other eighty per cent of the iceberg.

Finally, from the participants' perspective, 'the performance is just the icing on the cake but all those workshops ... all those meetings ... the laughter and the fun ... that journey is very special.'

Although the above quotes reveal consensus on the importance of process, there is also a strong emphasis on pursuing the creation of high-quality art. This intersection between high-quality practice and community-based ethos is crucial to Upstate's work. As Gorman asserts:

> We have worked with communities time and again for whom the adventure of entering a theatre workshop, of dreaming up an image or narrative from nowhere, of progressing this to a stage performance, is a novelty. There has usually been no tradition of this. We are there because through whatever brokerage process these people have asserted their right to make art and to make sense of the world around them through art and we have been invited in to be part of that journey. Once in, we have never shied from insisting on our shared responsibility – we as trained artists, them as participant artists – to make art of the highest possible standards, whatever that might mean in these given circumstances. ('Aesthetics')

The pluralist, collaborative and participatory approach adopted by Upstate and its artists is underpinned by a resolute belief in the aesthetic value of community art. It is this fundamental principle that positions Upstate at the forefront of community-engaged theatre practice in Ireland, and it is this footing that has attracted likeminded artists such as Murray, Lowe, Cannon, Keegan and Hayes to the company. As Cannon observes: 'There's a real quality to the [Upstate's] work, it's not patronizing; it's a piece of art that can be held up against any other piece of art. They're making high quality art that's steeped in their community.' Murray and Hayes agree. Hayes remarks that the work can take any artistic form 'but at the core of it, it should be about communities coming together [...] that would be part of the remit because that goes back to the process.' Murray goes on to point out that community-engaged theatre is needed now more than ever: 'The current climate is probably good for theatre; good for the arts, in that people need to express themselves. People are annoyed, people want a voice, people want to have their say; they want to hear things, to see things.'

The plays discussed here engage with pressing issues in modern and contemporary Ireland concerning such intersecting identity categorizations as race, religion, class, social status and citizenship. The displacement, isolation and alienation experienced by certain communities, and individuals within those communities, suggest a need for greater cohesion and solidarity among citizens in society. Collaboratively made, community-engaged theatre creates opportunities for participants to engage in artistic expression and develop social networks within their local communities. It encourages artists and citizens to take action, to make theatre that inspires social change and to create art that engages and awakens the aesthetic imagination of the community. In so doing, it offers opportunities to awaken a critical consciousness in wider society. Perhaps we can account for the current popularity of devised practice in contemporary theatre, both in Ireland and internationally, on the basis of wider desires to promote an ethos of sharing and communicating across perceived cultural, social and political boundaries in response to increased awareness of poverty, disadvantage, inequality and the socially-divisive impacts of neoliberal capitalism following the most recent global recession.

Conclusion

The current surge in experimentation within contemporary Irish theatre practice suggests a desire for alternative forms that are poised to communicate alternative messages. This development has perhaps been prompted by recognition of the need to develop styles of theatre that serve to better authenticate the live experience for both performers and audience. Why has contemporary Irish theatre practice moved progressively more towards embracing the ethos of community arts orientated practice? Why are prominent artists now more than ever seeking out more inclusive, communal ways of making theatre? The answers to these questions may well lie in the fundamental changes that have swept Irish society from approximately the middle of the twentieth century to the present day. The demise of the power of the Catholic Church, the tired politics of a state beleaguered with a legacy of corruption and greed, the so-called 'Celtic Tiger,' mass immigration, the economic downturn, and the continuing cycles of mass emigration have all contributed to increased disenfranchisement and disillusionment within Irish society. Where is the place of art in such a society? And how can art address such seismic failures? Perhaps placing the creation of art in the hands of citizens, artistically embracing the tenets of cultural democracy and narrowing the gap between art and society might offer ways to ensure that art is given meaningful space to illuminate and interrogate pressing contemporary issues. Devising, by its very nature, is collaborative; it enables artists to be inclusive and it encourages citizens to voice their views. These are important steps towards the creation of a truly participative society.

The growth of devised performance and community collaboration is shaping a new relationship between the artist-citizen and the citizen-artist as well as the public's appreciation of a refined art experience. Community-engaged theatre uses the power of performance to build a bridge between art and society, providing possibilities for participants to create meaning in a personal and communal context. It offers a framework for redefining the parameters of art and extending the civic aesthetic space. There are in contemporary theatre practice opportunities to create aesthetic frameworks that encompass and acknowledge the values and aesthetics of community art. This, in turn, calls for a broadening of academic research on Irish theatre to include a critical discourse on this largely ignored sector. Perhaps the recent surge of devising will encourage more theatre-makers to explore new ways of creating art and new ways of broadening and deepening engagement with a wider audience cohort. In terms of future investment and funding for the arts, there is a strong rationale for allocating resources to support the continued development of inclusive collaborative practices that create art that invites equal engagement from all citizens of society. Upstate offers a sustainable model wherein such art has not only been created but documented and refined in long-term practices which acknowledge that, while projects and personalities come and go, the communities that engage with art, benefit from art and provide the wellspring of artistic inspiration remain rooted in place.

Works Cited

Benson, Ciaran. 'Towards a Cultural Democracy.' *An Irish Quarterly Review* 81.321(1992): 23-33. Print.

Boal, Augusto. *Games for Actors and Non-actors*. 2nd ed. Oxon: Routledge, 2002. Print.

Byrne, Ophelia. 'Hades Review.' *Irish Theatre Magazine* 1.3 (1999): 54-6. Print.

Cannon, Feidlim. Personal Interview. 19 June 2013.

Cohen-Cruz, Jan. *Local Acts Community-based Performance in the United States*. New Brunswick, NJ: Rutgers UP, 2005. Print.

Gorman, Declan. Personal Interview. 18 June 2013.

Gorman, Declan. 'Aesthetics in "Applied Theatre."' Citizenship and Applied Theatre Conference. New York University, 2010. Web. 10 October 2013.

Grant, David. *Playing the Wild Card: Community Drama and Smaller-scale Professional Theatre*. Belfast: Community Relations Council Belfast, 1993. Print.

Grayling, Anthony. 'Art and Western Civilization.' *An Outburst of Frankness: Community Arts in Ireland – A Reader*. Ed. Sandy Fitzgerald. Dublin: TASC at New Island, 2004. 33-42. Print.

Hayes, Paul. Personal Interview. 6 June 2013.

Johnston, Chris. *House of Games: Making Theatre from Everyday Life*. 2nd ed. London: Nick Hern Books, 2005. Print.

Lowe, Louise. Personal interview. 3 June 2013.

Mallon, Declan. 'The Making of Two Community Plays.' *Way Out in the Country: An Anthology of Community Plays*. Eds. Declan Gorman and Declan Mallon. Drogheda: Upstate Theatre Project, 2001. 203-7. Print.

Mallon, Declan. Personal interview. 14 June 2013.

Murray, Stephen. Personal interview. 4 June 2013.

Upstate Theatre Project. 'About.' Web. 14 June 2014.

Upstate Theatre Project Participants. Focus group. 11 June 2013. Upstate Theatre Project. *Up and Running: A Review of the First Two Years*. Policy Document. 1999. Print.

Upstate Theatre Project. *No Change Given*. Programme. 2009. Print.

---. *Kinda Random*. Programme. 2011. Print.

---. *Come Forward to Meet You*. Programme. 2011. Print.

5 | An Interview with Una McKevitt

Jesse Weaver

Director and theatre-maker Una McKevitt first came to prominence in 2009 with *Victor and Gord*, a devised piece of autobiographical theatre centred on the relationship between McKevitt's sister Áine and Áine's childhood friend Vickey. The piece received numerous stagings and expanded to include several other figures from McKevitt's own life and experience. At the core of *Victor and Gord* lay themes and motifs that have permeated McKevitt's subsequent work: unadorned staging, a simplicity of language and presentation, explorations of the everyday and the mundane, and an abiding compassion for the subjects of her work that is devoid of easy sentiment. But perhaps the most interesting aspect of McKevitt's dramaturgy so far has been her primary reliance on non-performers, in many cases casting people from her own life whose stories she has found compelling and moving. In keeping with this particular approach, McKevitt followed *Victor and Gord* with *565+*, a one-woman show performed by Marie O'Rourke for the 2010 Dublin Theatre Festival. *565+* explored the therapeutic role that theatre had played in O'Rourke's life. As with *Victor and Gord*, O'Rourke's biography served as the primary source for the show's material, with O'Rourke's lack of experience as a performer serving as a central virtue.

The Big Deal, which premiered at the Kilkenny Arts Festival in 2011, was somewhat of a departure for McKevitt. Utilizing elements of documentary theatre, McKevitt accessed journal entries, poems, email correspondence and interviews provided by two anonymous contributors to chart the experience of two transgender women. Rather than the contributors appearing onstage, two cisgender actresses represented them in the production, disrupting the dramaturgical approach of casting non-performers in McKevitt's earlier work. Still, McKevitt's staging remained intimate and simple, with the presentation of documented material favoured over a sentimentalized dramatization of it.

The relatively light tone of McKevitt's next devised show, *Singlehood*, stands in direct contrast to that of *The Big Deal*. For *Singlehood*, McKevitt worked with a cast of both performers and non-performers who delivered material gleaned from nearly thirty interviews with people examining their experiences of being single. First performed at the Absolut Dublin Fringe Festival in 2012, the show presented itself as an unapologetic comedy exploring the lives of singles in Ireland and was written collaboratively by McKevitt, Dan Coffey and the cast. Since its premiere the show has played larger and larger venues, but McKevitt's focus on forging an intimate connection with the audience, as with her earlier work, remains a core value.

In 2013 McKevitt collaborated with the German theatre company Rimini Protokoll in staging *100% Cork* for the Cork Midsummer Festival. Modelled on Rimini Protokoll's incisive *100% Berlin*, the show attempted to access and quantify on stage the varied demographics that ultimately constituted Cork City's populace. In doing so, McKevitt cast 100 of the city's own inhabitants, many of whom were non-performers and who represented cross sections of Cork's population.

At the time this interview was conducted, McKevitt was developing a possible staging of Eugene O'Neill's *Long Day's Journey into Night*, an idea she explored while taking part in Pan Pan Theatre Company's 2012 International Mentorship Programme. Attracted by the autobiographical origins of the play, McKevitt was toying with the potential idea of melding the structure of a classic play with her own intimate, ensemble-based approaches to staging. Since this interview, McKevitt has also embarked on a more conscious exploration of the social, political and economic factors that shape identity with a new devised piece called MEN. This particular devising process has McKevitt 'finding new ways to author the show without relying on personal testimonies.' According to McKevitt, the piece will take on a 'revue style,' incorporate found text, and will also use original material provided by a writer, a decidedly new element in McKevitt's process.

Jesse Weaver: Your first show when you left college was *Victor and Gord*, a devised piece about your sister and her childhood friend. Could you talk a little bit about how that show developed?

Una McKevitt: When I finished college, everybody was talking about [pursuing] a Master's or how they would follow up, but I had decided that I would just start making theatre, and continue making it until something happened – and continue whether it happened or not. At that stage I needed to do it for myself because it made me happy. So when I put an idea in for Project Brand New to do a show with my sister and my friend in 2008, it was really fortuitous timing. I had tried devising and writing as my major modules when I was in college because I wanted to write, though I wasn't very good at it. Making stuff up wasn't my forte. I never thought about directing at all. But I enjoyed devising. When I saw Manchester-based Quarantine's *Susan and Darren* in the 2008 Fringe, [a devised piece] about a dancer and his mother, it opened a huge window in my head. I found that I could tell the stories that I respond to in my everyday life. It was a way into storytelling and dramatizing stories that I didn't have before. I wanted to be in theatre and I didn't know what I was good at, but that [*Susan and Darren*] kind of put everything together for me.

J: So you saw *Susan and Darren*. Did that immediately spark *Victor and Gord*? Or were you letting this idea about telling stories from everyday life gestate for a little bit, thinking, 'Well, that's the kind of theatre I want to make, but I'm not sure how to?'

U: It was more that I was thinking that that was the kind of theatre I wanted to make once I actually saw it and experienced it with *Susan and Darren*. I hadn't seen anything like it before. My mother was going through cancer treatment [at the time], so I felt that I was opening up emotionally on some level. *Victor and Gord* is connected to where I grew up and it was, without my realizing it at the time, a kind of tribute to a happy childhood – or a safe childhood. So all those things were all happening at the same time. And then I saw a photograph: my sister Áine had these photographs pinned in her room, and one of them was of her and her friend Vickey with their arms around each other in the front garden. I've known Vickey since we were kids, she's a neighbour, and obviously Áine's my sister. I had always found it funny the way they were friends but constantly grumbling about each other – so you'd hear them grumbling about each other and that's where *Victor and Gord* came from.

J: Victor and Gord seemed to bear a lot of the hallmarks of 'devised performance': there was no pre-written script and the ensemble generated the show's material, which was primarily autobiographical. Is that how you would define devised performance? What is devising to you?

U: That's interesting because I never use the word 'devised.' I'm starting to use the word 'written by.' It's problematic because I feel that I don't write anything, but I select and arrange the material. It wouldn't exist in the form that it is in without me overseeing it, prompting it and eliciting it from the people I'm interested in. 'Devising' is, I feel, an old-fashioned word, even though it's not – it is what I do. It's just that I feel that people don't feel they can connect to [the work] when they hear that something's devised. It's a word that's fit for theatre people, but not for everybody else. But 'devising' immediately brings in the group. It immediately signals that there's more than one person involved. Writing is something I think of someone doing on his or her own. Devising is a team sport. Certainly I'm going into a room always looking for ideas, and that's what devising is as far as I can tell. For me, devising is pursuing stories, looking for stories and then working on them till they shine.

J: I like the word 'pursue.' When I first saw *Victor and Gord*, I was thinking, 'How do you put something like that together?' So when I think of the word 'pursue,' I imagine you in the rehearsal room with the performers discovering and pursuing different ideas that pop up in rehearsal. Is that what it's like?

U: Well, it was easy with *Victor and Gord* because Áine and Vickey didn't want to communicate with each other; their desire not to communicate with each other became a handy tool, as in, 'How do I get them to talk at the same time?' I don't have a book of games and I hate warm-ups. So I literally just said, 'Áine, just list all the things you can remember that are in Vickey's house. And Vickey? You do the same.' So everything in the show just came from trying to get these people who were resistant to it to speak. Whereas, if you have people who are really enthusiastic, and are over-thinking it, and are trying to make things up, it just doesn't work. Having people who genuinely are not trying to contrive anything, and aren't really sure where you're going with it, that's actually very helpful.

Then we moved on to a brother and sister, Ali and Michael. Their relationship appeared to be very different, almost opposite to that of Áine's and Vickey's – my impression was that they were very consciously trying not to take anything away from each other, and instead trying to fortify each other. So that became the obstacle: how do I get them to stop only communicating with each other in this way? We were trying to pursue a way of getting an insight into their relationship that maybe annoys them a little bit, because it seemed so perfect. That will read as really real, if the performers do something they're slightly uncomfortable with – which is where I suppose you can use the term 'exploiting,' maybe. I don't think those are necessarily negative things to do. If you have a good relationship with the performers and they have a solid relationship, there's a lot you could do. I'd never work with a husband and wife or people in a romantic relationship. But when you're talking about very old relationships, there is some sort of safety net there always, so you can push it a little bit and it won't break. Áine and Vickey had always said in the beginning that they will always be friends no matter what, just by virtue of knowing each other, so that was safe.

When you're not working with actors, nobody in the room really knows anything about how things 'should be' – and I include myself in that. All I bring to the room is the concept. You're on an even footing, and there's a big risk because no one knows what's going to happen. Whereas, if I'm directing a [written] play (which I will be doing soon) I have to learn how to respond to actors and what they bring out to me. I guess I have more control when it's a devised process, even though I'm saying it's an even playing field; certainly there are fewer expectations of what 'should' happen and that's very liberating. Making *Singlehood*, for instance, with non-professional performers – some were professional, some weren't – I'd hand someone material and the next day give it to someone else. And we never had to have a discussion about why I did that. Most of them don't have the practice of what usually happens in a rehearsal room, and I don't really have the discipline or the experience of knowing what happens in a rehearsal room either. So for me, that's what 'devising' is. It's also making up how you do it and why you do it.

J: Is there a challenge when dealing with things that are so personal to people? Are there times when you see things you might want to pursue, but you have to let go because it might be too emotional?

U: Yes. Anyone I work with has the final say. They are co-editors, really. I'm never going to ask someone to say something that they don't want to. And they know that early on. That's never a huge problem. I don't want to know things that people don't want to tell me. I'm not that curious. I'm not actually working through the person's entire life, or we're not working through their entire life together.

J: I like your description of the performers as 'co-editors,' working with you to decide what the best way to present the material might be.

U: It's important which words are selected and how they're arranged. Especially with *The Big Deal*. If [the contributors] are not in the room, those are the decisions I make with the actors – the selection and arrangement, the editing of material. But in terms of what's actually left in, what's being said, that's something that the contributors will always have control over. As I see it, that's their function as co-editors: what can I or can't I say about you, how can I or can't I represent you from the material you've given me? And it's my role to have already edited and shared the material before it's presented on stage – and also [figured out] how to frame it. As you know, where you put words is as important as what the words are. And that's really the biggest part of my devising process – working that out with performers and contributors. But in giving this answer, I would have to say that I have to have a relationship with the contributors [where they] are happy and that's been my methodology to date. Saying that, it has fallen down at times and work has been abandoned because consensus can't be reached. But that would be it.

J: I was looking at reviews of your work, and the term 'documentary theatre' comes up every now and again to describe what you do. Is that a possible term to describe how you go about editing material and arranging it?

U: Yes, possibly. I don't shy away from it. I don't use it with *Singlehood*, — or I try not to. Again, like 'devising' I think 'documentary theatre' is a term that belongs to theatre-makers and it doesn't have much to say outside of that to an audience that I'm trying to attract. Whereas with *The Big Deal* it's very important that people know that I'm working with actual documents, diaries, and emails. In that context [the term 'documentary theatre'] is very important. With *Singlehood* we've made a comedy show, though the process is [conducted] through interview and everything is true – and that's something that people find out through the performance when the cast actually share their single stories with the audience. It always depends on what words I use and how the audience responds to it. For instance, when I was in the Fringe, I put in a blurb for *Singlehood* that said, 'This is not a play. There is no literary inventiveness.' This is a phrase which one of our critics in Ireland uses in response to documentary theatre: 'Where is the literary inventiveness?' And it's not there because it's not supposed to be. I've never really understood people wanting documentary theatre to be something that it isn't – wanting it to be literature when it's not. Things should be weighed up on what they're actually trying to be.

J: I wonder if the term 'literary inventiveness' is a hangover from the dominance of a literary tradition in Irish theatre, where the writer and his or her text are the central elements in production. Do you think Irish theatre is still a writer's theatre today?

U: I think it's going to become more so, because I think these new ways of making theatre are good challenges to writing. I'd like to come out of this as a writer someday. In a way, everyone's writing because they're selecting and arranging words, so everyone's writing, whether they're devising or not. And all these other ways of finding texts can only really strengthen the practice of writing, and throw down the gauntlet to writers. If you make something up, it has to be really good, because people have found new ways of finding material.

J: With *Victor and Gord* and *565+* it seems like a lot of the material you found was mined right in the rehearsal room. Is that always the case with the work you make?

U: With *Singlehood* I did go outside of the room. Dave Coffey – who I collaborated with and who was an enormous support throughout the whole process – we did interview nearly thirty people about their experience of being single. We did one shout-out on Facebook and met some people we didn't know – so there were maybe thirty per cent of people we didn't know and seventy per cent we did know through one means or the other. That was my leap in *Singlehood*, to mix the performers' material with other sourced material, which I hadn't done before.

One thing I've come to realize with documentary theatre is that, with certain subjects, there comes a point of exhaustion in terms of the material – well, for *Victor and Gord* it was their whole childhood, so you couldn't really exhaust it. But stories about people's love lives can actually be exhausted quite quickly and are often quite similar, so that took a while to work out – how to not tell the same story over and over again. That is what prompted us to look outside of the performers for material. As a result of that, the performers – some of whom had never been on stage – stopped just performing themselves at a certain point, all because of working on material that we had gathered from outside [their experience]. They also started gaining other skills and had to learn lines, which is something I had avoided; in *Victor and Gord* and *565+* there was no script. I only had scripts after the fact when I needed them for applications and things. It's important for me that people aren't memorizing their own lives – whereas in *Singlehood* it had to be scripted because some of the stories they were telling weren't their own. Now two years later, of course, a lot of the performers' lives have altered, so they're turning their own stories into the stories of other people by changing their own names on stage!

J: How did you find the people to perform in your work? Do you audition people?

U: The only show I've auditioned for is *The Big Deal* and a little bit for *Singlehood*. I can't imagine what to look for when people are auditioning. I respond to people that I find interesting.

J: It was interesting that you went with two female performers rather than two transgender performers for *The Big Deal*.

U: 'Cisgender' is the word – that means people who are born into the gender they're happy with, as opposed to 'trans.' That was a decision that was really made by the contributors. My head was going in all sorts of artistic and conceptual directions in terms of casting, but they were very adamant that two cisgender performers be cast. And I think that was the right decision; otherwise it becomes about the body, when really it isn't about the body. It's about personal identity. There's an awful lot of talk about the body, of course, but the identity is internal, in a way. I think that ultimately the women would have liked to have performed it themselves, but for reasons of anonymity and privacy, that's why they chose not to. I could have cast two transgender actors, but then I think the women who contributed would have felt that it was about those two actors and not about them, because then you have four stories there, really: the actors' stories and the contributors' stories. So two actresses playing women, being women was what it was all about. I don't think I'd ever change that. I wouldn't be allowed to anyway. I'm not there to strip people down and say, 'This is who you really are.' It's important that no one is weakened or lessened. You asked about my work earlier, and for me it's really driven by the idea of what keeps us going, why are we still here, what fortifies us and builds us up. So that's a consideration in working with performers as well. I don't want anyone to come away feeling that they lost something from the experience. They don't have to gain anything, but nobody should lose anything. Again, I can't say how successful I've been at that but the intention is very strongly there.

J: Who are the artists you admire or that you feel influence the work you do?

U: For me, in 2008 and 2009, you could say that maybe [my] influences were Dee Roycroft, Louise Lowe, Jody O'Neill and the people that were making Project Brand New – the three women who ran that, because they were specifically looking for work like *Victor and Gord*. Louise had been looking for a long time for a new way of making theatre that wasn't dependent on the structures we had in place, both form-wise and venue-wise. There was definitely a movement or a feeling among certain artists, anyway, of trying to ... and I don't know what kind of influences they were, whether they were sociological or political, but there were all these regularly funded companies and it was tough for new artists to find a foothold. Certainly there were a lot of us wanting to work outside of the 'well-made play' – which unless they're done really well and performed by brilliant actors often feel turgid and lifeless on the Irish stage. But I was very lucky to benefit from that moment, for someone just out of college to have the opportunity to present something in a professional space during Project Brand New. I don't know if those opportunities have been opened before.

J: You worked with Rimini Protocoll on *100% Cork* for the 2013 Cork Midsummer Festival. Would they serve as an influence on the kind of work you aspire to make?

U: No, they have such a different approach. They're looking at how society responds and behaves – society *en masse* – and I'm not. I'm much more about the individual. Saying that though, I think something shifted in me during my time working with them. I have begun to consider much more the [political, social and economic] influences on the individual and the impact of those influences. *MEN* is certainly a step in that direction.

Usually it's film and TV [that influence me] in terms of trying to keep people's attention, moving quickly from one thing to another, and changing direction without alerting anyone to it or signifying that things are going to go down this or that route now.

J: Do you mean the formal structure of TV, the way that it's put together?

U: Yes, I like things that don't just ask for silence and sacredness. Now *The Big Deal* did – I'll be honest. There are points in there where the silence was just incredible; it required the audience to be silent. But at the moment I'm really interested in theatre that doesn't require that from an audience – in the same way cinema and TV don't. That's how I like to watch theatre. So in *Singlehood* – when we did it at Vicar Street – people go to the loo, people go to the bar, and the show is built to withstand interruption and it thrives on it. We're all in the same room and I'm trying to acknowledge that as an important part of my work.

J: Do you think it's possible to train in devising practice?

U: The more I talk to you about it the more I feel like I'm articulating some kind of 'mystical relationship' to it! There's no methodology, there's no planning, there's no structure. It's like voodoo maybe: let's bring the things together, and then make something out of them. Training? I don't know. Why couldn't you train in devising? It's just building up confidence that you don't have to belong in a canon to make something interesting. I personally think that all education or learning is just about being introduced to things. That's all that's required, so it's very liberating to improvise, devise – especially for Irish people, who are not massively confident when it comes down to putting themselves forward. There's kind of an odd modesty culture in this country, which I came across a lot of in Cork, like, 'Don't blow your own trumpet' – that's like the greatest crime imaginable to a Cork person. And in a way, devising is quite bold and audacious, like, 'I'm going to make something up with other people, something that didn't exist before.'

There is a devising course I did – 'Advanced Devising' at Trinity. We had Chrissie Poulter, and we could do anything we wanted; we just had to show it to her, and she really frustrated me because I felt that she wasn't teaching me anything. But in a way, it was the same with the playwriting course I did. They didn't really teach playwriting either in Trinity, they just told you to write a play. That framework of having to do it and present it was enough. So I do this course and I have to think of something to bring to the table and I have to present something and I have to devise it. We weren't instructed in devising, but we still did it and that worked for me ultimately. It's like a leap of faith.

J: Well, it's not like training to be a mechanic or anything. It's not like you're learning how to put together an engine. It's something that is more individual. So how do you train in something that is so individual?

U: I don't know. I think having a mentor would be helpful if you were starting. For me, everything in theatre is about showing, and everyone you show to is an expert. So that's all you really ever need — to have somebody look at it other than yourself. Even if you couldn't see that person, even if you were blindfolded, even if there were a screen between you and them, they're watching what you made, what you've devised. You'd see it so differently because of their presence, even before they've said a word or you've read their body language. That's all you need: someone to go tell you to do it and someone to watch it. That's all the training that's required.

It's really easy to fall in love with what you're doing. The whole thrill is showing it to people. For me, I immediately start criticizing what I've done when someone else is watching it. I will turn around and ask their opinion, but I've already formulated their opinion in my head. I already see what's wrong with it. It's very hard to explain. You're asking if people could train in devising. I don't think it could hurt, but you just have to do it. I certainly think that if somebody was looking for new ways to make work and they weren't familiar with devising, they should go and do a course. But I certainly wouldn't be able to give any courses in devising.

J: Well, maybe you could, with the first and only lesson being, 'Make something and show me.'

U: Yes, that's all I would do. For me, I'm always trying to kind of prove that I'm human by making work, because I don't feel that I can do that in my real life — I'm a bit emotionally constipated let's say! That's my gateway or my motivation, to show people that I understand what it feels like to have feelings, that I am responding emotionally to everything around me. I'm just not great at showing it in my real life. And I suppose that's why it's been hard for me to relate to or have visions for other plays, because they're not me proving that I'm human; it's someone else's voice. So maybe I'd say that: 'Show me your humanity!'

J: And that's a great place to end, I think. Una McKevitt, thank you very much.

Section Two: Formal Politics

6 | 'A Song about Survival': Talking Shop Ensemble Responds to the Irish Debt Crisis

Laura Farrell-Wortman

In his landmark 2004 book *Reading the Material Theatre*, Ric Knowles argues for a view of theatrical events as 'cultural productions which serve specific cultural and theatrical communities at particular historical moments as sites for the negotiation, transmission and transformation of cultural values [... that are] productive of social and historical reification and change' (10). Theatre which engages with and challenges contemporary political and economic circumstances serves this sense of the medium as strongly influenced by the material circumstances of both its production and reception. In this essay I examine the effect of the contemporary Irish economic crisis, which began in 2008, on the development of contemporaneous drama by and for young adults in the Republic of Ireland, using two recent productions by Dublin-based theatre company Talking Shop Ensemble (TSE) as emblematic of theatrical responses to this crisis on the part of people in their early twenties.

Theatre by and for people at the life stage that Jeffrey Arnett terms 'emerging adulthood' offers a representation of an understudied but crucial period in the transition from youth to adulthood. Arnett calls this period 'neither adolescence nor young adulthood, but [...] theoretically and empirically distinct from them both' ('Emerging Adulthood' 469). Those in their late teens and early twenties bear the expectations of adult life, while still experiencing the uncertainty and emotional turbulence that are characteristic of the teenage years. To be young and rootless in a Western culture has been acknowledged, by Arnett and others, as a challenging and formative time period; to undergo these developments during a time of economic and social turmoil complicates the experience of developing from an adolescent to an adult. To explore the ramifications of Ireland's economic crisis on those currently in this stage of life, I use TSE as a case study of work being done by people in their early twenties; I focus specifically on two recent TSE works: *I am a Homebird (It's Very Hard)* (2011) and *Death of the Tradesmen* (2012). The company's work reflects the experience of young people in Ireland and the renegotiation of their personal and national identities in the wake of a severe change to their nation's – and their region's – economy. Knowles argues for the use of cultural materialism and material semiotics in considering theatrical productions in their specific material circumstances. I use Knowles' theory of the 'cultural politics of location' to analyse two TSE productions within their particular social, economic and political contexts in order to consider their utility as theatre by, for and about young people in Ireland (2).

Established in 2008, TSE is a theatre collective comprised of Shaun Dunne, Oonagh Murphy, Aisling Byrne and Lisa Walsh (as well as incorporating outside performers and dramaturges on a production-by-production basis). TSE produces original devised works that reflect the particular material conditions of urban Ireland in the early twenty-first century. The full ramifications of the experiences which TSE are depicting are strongly linked to contemporary Ireland. Previous TSE productions include *Do You Read Me?* (2011), *Fat* (2010), and *Ann and Barry: What Kind of Time Do You Call This?* (2009). Company member Shaun Dunne is given primary writing credit for both *I am a Homebird (It's Very Hard)* and *Death of the Tradesmen*, but both pieces are noted as being developed in collaboration with the other TSE members. In a 2013 interview, Dunne notes that:

> The ability to improvise and add to an idea as an ensemble is key to our artistic process. It also promotes a shared ownership of the piece – we all have different roles but we contribute to each other's input constantly. All the lines are not written by me, the staging or choreography is not solely the choreographer or director's responsibility – the process is rooted in the ability to discuss and change an idea on its feet as an ensemble.

Collaborative devising is thus key to TSE's work and to the community-centred nature of its performances. Dunne specifies that each TSE piece is 'led by conversation'.

> The initial development of a piece is geared around talking to as many people as possible who are affected by our subject matter. This benefits us in two ways; it lets people in on the work and it lets us have a better understanding of what the scope of the work

should be. It's all about talking initially; informal conversations with non theatre makers. This is why we're called Talking Shop! (Personal interview)

Their home base is Dublin, and the majority of their productions are staged in the city, but in the tradition of many Irish companies, TSE has toured its productions to other urban centres such as Galway and Cork. For this analysis I use the unpublished production scripts of both plays, provided by TSE; video clips from *Death of the Tradesmen* that are available to the public through TSE's Vimeo account; and interviews conducted with Dunne in July 2013. As a small theatre company, TSE material is relatively difficult to come by; none of its plays are published, and though there has been a good deal of media coverage of the company in the Dublin arts press, its web presence is limited to a blog, a Facebook page and a handful of short production videos posted by the company at sporadic intervals (though production videos are limited to *Death of the Tradesmen* alone).

TSE's works inform and are informed by the new realities of Irish life following the end of the Celtic Tiger era; that TSE was founded in the same year as the global contraction of markets and the collapse of the property bubble in many Western countries is significant. Crucial to any consideration of representations of the current economic crisis is an acknowledgment of the spectre of the Celtic Tiger economy. From the mid-1990s to the late 2000s, Ireland experienced its most affluent and economically productive period. Prior to the 1990s, Ireland's debt was 120 per cent of its gross domestic product and seventeen per cent of the country was unemployed (Emling). The government undertook massive economic stimulus programmes to attempt to counter this economic stagnation and to bring the country in line with European Union regulations on debt-to-GDP ratios (Emling). The corporate tax rate dropped to ten per cent and the government spent the equivalent of over four billion euro updating Ireland's technology infrastructure, which attracted investment from multinational tech companies such as Microsoft and Dell (Cowell). Unemployment fell to eight per cent on average, the economy doubled in size in the space of a decade, and the economic growth rate of Ireland was triple the EU average (Emling). The shift from poverty to affluence was not merely economic, however. The expectations and worldviews of the Irish people went through a profound transformation during this time. A nation long famous for emigration was suddenly a highly sought after destination for inward migration. The poorest country in Western Europe became, in the span of merely a decade, the second wealthiest. Those who grew up during this period, who are now in their early to late twenties, grew up in a nation of possibility. Jobs were plentiful; unemployment was low. To be Irish was to have options. As Lisa says in *I am a Homebird (It's Very Hard)*: 'Growing up we were always told how lucky we are to be living in a country like this. We were taught to be proud of where we're from' (3). She immediately follows this with an estimate of how many people had left Ireland that year. Given these circumstances, what did the Celtic Tiger promise a generation? How do the Irish children of the 1990s navigate the boom and bust nature of market capitalism?

TSE creates work on issues beyond political economics, but the pervasive issues of debt and unemployment in Ireland have been their main topic of interest since 2010. The current economic crisis in Ireland began in 2008 and occurred in conjunction with the Eurozone currency and debt troubles that have plagued the EU since roughly the same year. In 2008, Ireland became the first European country to fall into a recession during the global financial crisis, after having nationalized the failing Anglo Irish Bank and having established a federal guarantee of all Irish bank debt ('Ireland Profile'). Taoiseach Brian Cowen famously and prematurely called the rescue of Anglo 'the cheapest bailout in history' ('Ireland's Debt Crisis'). The spectacular success of Ireland's economy throughout the 1990s and 2000s perhaps clouded the judgment of those responsible for Ireland's fiscal future; the Celtic Tiger created an atmosphere of seemingly unending prosperity. By 2010, however, speculation in the property market led Irish banks to accrue more debt than the Irish government had financial reserves; the Irish economy quickly went into a tailspin because of their responsibility for Anglo's debt, with the significant gains of the Celtic Tiger period reversed in a staggeringly short period of time ('Ireland Profile'). By 2009, unemployment had reached double digits. In 2010, Ireland accepted a 67.5 billion euro bailout package from the European Union and the International Monetary Fund, leading to devastating austerity measures ('Ireland's Debt Crisis'). The destabilization of the Irish economy in tandem with the serious fiscal and debt woes suffered by the eurozone led to a protracted economic contraction. Young people have been disproportionately affected by this economic downturn with an average of thirty per cent unemployment of 'under twenty-fives' by 2013 ('Ireland Youth Unemployment Rose in February – Eurostat'). Both *Homebird* and *Tradesmen* address this downturn directly.

That TSE takes the ramifications of the debt crisis as one of its major topics of consideration since 2010 is significant for several reasons. Firstly, the company is representing on stage an experience common to thousands of young adults in Ireland. Between 2008 and 2012, 182,900 people between the ages of fifteen and twenty-nine left Ireland, from a country with a total population of only four million (Smyth). Secondly, this sense of dire economic circumstances from which it is difficult or impossible to emerge is one that has been felt not only by young people in Ireland, but by several generations who came of age before the massive economic boom of the 1990s and 2000s. Historically, affluence has been the exception in Ireland, not the rule. Prior to joining the European Union in 1971, Ireland was the poorest nation in Western Europe and had experienced over 100 years of continual net emigration out of the country (Emling). Thirdly, TSE is composed of artists who are themselves young adults living and working in Ireland. This is theatre about being young, created and produced by young people. The experience of being in one's twenties during the most serious financial crisis in the history of the European Union is one which is being represented by artists personally invested in and affected by it. TSE is representing their own contemporary material circumstances, often using the principles of postdramatic and other non-realist forms of theatre to embody their personal perspectives.

I am a Homebird (It's Very Hard) eschews traditional plot and character construction in favour of a conversational direct-address style to explore the re-emergence of emigration as an everyday aspect of Irish life. Shaun, Lisa and Lauren – TSE company members, who, in these two productions, use their real names rather than crafting character names – tell stories of friends and family members who have left Ireland since the 2008 financial collapse and discuss their conflicted feelings about staying behind. Shaun begins the play by immediately listing off his departed friends and family members: 'Davy, Carol and Aaron are in London. Niamh and Keira are in France. Sean is in Germany. Rochelle is in Scotland ... My twin sister Claire left for Australia two weeks ago' (1). The relationship between Shaun and Claire, and the difficulty in saying goodbye to each other, forms the bulk of Shaun's narrative in *Homebird*. Though Lisa, Lauren and Shaun try to see the benefits of emigration ('There are more people. You can meet someone new every day.'), emigration is, finally, presented as 'making the most of a bad situation' (3). *Homebird* is a thematic exploration of the personal effects of contemporary emigration from Ireland, rather than a traditional play with a narrative structure and a specific resolution. History is considered and questions are posed, but few answers are forthcoming. Performers repeat the phrase 'a lot of my friends have left already' at regular intervals, as though attempting to incorporate this new paradigm. TSE does not offer easy solutions for an intractable problem, though the end of the play does find Shaun encouraging others his age to stay in Ireland and improve the situation with him.

TSE's material circumstances are inextricably tied to their demographic circumstances. To consider the recalibration of national identity that young people in Ireland have had to undergo, it is necessary to consider the nature of identity during the phase of emergent adulthood in general and the significance of this life stage in Ireland in particular. Young adults between eighteen and twenty-eight years of age comprise twelve per cent of the Irish population, yet there is a lack of specific research devoted to the experience of this age group in Ireland during the contemporary period (Central Statistics Office). Arnett describes this life phase as 'emerging adulthood,' suggesting that the period from roughly eighteen through the mid-twenties comprises a separate and distinct stage of development for those living in Western countries. He coined this term in 2000, when American and European scholars were giving more attention to the idea of the colloquially-termed 'quarter life crisis,' particularly because the period of early adulthood in the twenty-first century looked radically different from the same period experienced by the 'Baby Boomers' and those older:

> As recently as 1970, the typical 21-year-old was married or about to be married, caring for a newborn child or expecting one soon, done with education or about to be done, and settled into a long-term job or a role as full-time mother. Today, the life of a typical 21-year-old could not look more different. Marriage is at least five years off, often more. Ditto parenthood. [...] For today's young people, the road to adulthood is a long one. [...] From their late teens to their late twenties, they explore the possibilities available to them in love and work, and move gradually towards making enduring decisions. (*Emerging Adulthood* 3)

Emerging adulthood as a stage implies a lack of fixed identity, geographical stability or financial establishment on the part of the young adult. Emerging adults are, so to speak, rootless, whether physically or psychically. Arnett notes that this stage is 'a time of frequent change as various possibilities [...] are explored' ('Emerging Adulthood' 469). The concept of 'possibility' is key to the consideration of these plays within the framework of emerging adulthood. Shaun, Lauren and Lisa are exploring various options for their lives, but finding few answers; the search and the confusion of one's late teens and early twenties are the focus of *Homebird*. As in other nations, a sense of rootlessness in regard to relationships and employment is pervasive in Ireland amongst people in this age group. Work is key to these theories of emerging adulthood, particularly through its absence or its inability to provide fulfilment. The relationship between work and self-identification in young Irish adults is highly significant, and the ability to find and keep gainful employment is a major theme that TSE explores in these two pieces.

While *Homebird* ends on an upbeat note of solidarity, *Death of the Tradesmen* offers a much bleaker picture of the possibilities inherent in twenty-first century Irish life. *Tradesmen* begins with Shaun describing his experience of reading *Death of a Salesman* in his literature class at school and being struck by how much Willy Loman reminded him of his own father. He notes that he sat down to write the play with two documents at hand: a copy of Arthur Miller's play and a letter from the Social Welfare Office addressed to his father, outlining the documentation he must provide within 14 days in order to continue receiving unemployment benefits. Shaun reads the letter in its entirety and then introduces himself:

> My name is Shaun Dunne.
> I'm a 21-year-old theatre maker.
> I'm a big talker and I've got a little bit of a temper.
> I'm the son of a carpet-fitter.
> I was born in 1989 ... and it's not time ... to make a change.
> (begins to sing 'Father and Son' by Cat Stevens) (4)

This song, 'Father and Son,' offers a similar split perspective between a father and son, the elder offering advice and the younger accepting it sceptically. 'It's not time to make a change,' Stevens sings, 'Just relax, take it easy/You're still young [...] There's so much you have to know.' In the video of an undated performance of the play, the audience laughs knowingly when Shaun begins to sing, a moment in which the experience of youth and family dynamics is shared across generations, particularly as the recorded version of the song used is by contemporary Irish pop band Boyzone. The song is a liminal moment, a bridge between their parents' generation and their own. Lauren then gives an account of her own family's situation, and remarks that she feels overwhelmed by these new dire circumstances:

> It was around four or five years ago that worked started to dry up for my father ... the tiler, the tradesman.
> And there was a whole new school of sentences being bandied around the house from the off-set.

Say for example, you might be in the kitchen making yourself something to eat and you might hear something like, 'You better get down to that Labour, I mean it.'
Or two seconds later, you might be sitting in the sitting room just having a cup of tea and you'd hear, 'I don't know what we're going to do. I haven't got a bleeding penny.'
And this was when I was about sixteen or seventeen ... in maybe fifth or sixth year... and this was all just coming at me. (5)

Shaun and Lauren then morph into Willy and Linda, performing a contemporary Irish take on *Death of a Salesman*. The script indicates that the play moves from a 'documentary format' to a more traditional dramatic format (2). Willy's introduction mirrors Shaun's, with the actor maintaining the same costume, same performance style, same vocal inflections:

WILLY: My name is Willy.
I'm a 54 year old tradesman.
I have a bad back and a short fuse
I like a pint of black and I tend to lose more than I win when it comes to gambling
I'm 54
My hands are sore.
They are calloused and dry and I'm sick of standing.
It's morning. (5-6)

Though middle-aged Willy and Linda are the focus of the dramatic portions of the play, the framing device of the 'documentary format' privileges the perspective of twenty-one-year-old Shaun and twenty-three-year-old Lauren. Willy and Linda are embodied on stage, but this is a tale of parents being observed by their young adult children, rather than one emerging directly from the parents' generation. *Death of the Tradesmen* questions whether the parents of Shaun and Lauren are living out a cautionary tale of sorts. *Tradesmen* speaks specifically to the experience of those affected by the downturn in the property and construction industries, carrying particular resonance within a country brought low by overzealous property speculation on the part of its major banks. As in *Homebird*, Shaun maintains a general air of optimism when playing himself. However, *Tradesmen* ends on a note of understated despair, as Linda attempts to unroll the now-useless carpet that her husband keeps as part of his floundering carpet-fitting business. She struggles with the unwieldy rug as Willy looks on, helpless. 'Can I show you?' he asks feebly. 'Can I show you?'

That TSE changed the singular 'salesman' to the plural 'tradesmen' for *Death of the Tradesmen* speaks to the deliberately collaborative production process used to create the piece and perhaps the intended reception. In *Death of a Salesman*, Miller sought to create an Everyman; TSE harken back to the iconic character of Loman by applying the framework of Miller's play to a highly specific context. Would this play be received differently if produced at a different place and in a different time? Certainly, and in fact Knowles dismisses the entire notion of 'universal' meaning as a possibility in theatrical production, stating 'cultural materialism [...] is explicitly concerned with resisting interpretive discourses of the universal' (13). *Homebird* and *Tradesmen* speak to a particular public, at a specific place and time; these two plays are so specific to post Celtic Tiger Ireland as to be difficult to translate to a different circumstance, even one that may be similar. While the specificity of *Death of the Tradesmen* may be contradictory to the often-assumed 'universality' of *Death of a Salesman*, it is perhaps a shrewd repurposing of the idea of an Everyman, particularly in a system of 'every man for himself' capitalism.

While *Salesman* is often lauded for its ability to resonate in various time periods and locations, there is also value in performance that is strongly tied to a specific era and place. Certainly TSE argue that the issues with which they engage cannot be understood outside of their local contexts; Dunne states:

> The work relates to the community and the country because it is out there amongst the situation from day one. We don't surmise or assume that we can understand a subject on our own. The opposite. We include the community in the construction of the art so to ensure its relativity and authenticity throughout (Personal interview).

TSE place community engagement at the forefront of their development process in order to honestly represent a community issue or experience on stage. Dunne continues, '[i]t's all about the sharing of the situation. We can't be specialists but we can try to promote something of an informed understanding' (Personal interview). Dunne notes that TSE worked closely with a Dublin unemployment centre called Jobcare in the development of *Tradesmen*; for *Homebird*, the 'specialists' consulted were young adults in Dublin who were living in similar circumstances to the artists of TSE.

Willy's sense of desperation and lack of utility mirrors that of Shaun's and Lauren's demographic. The sharp rise in unemployment levels in the Republic of Ireland is one of the most tangible and quantifiable effects of the debt crisis, but it is only one aspect of a more pervasive shift in Irish society. 2008 saw the constriction or near-collapse of many Western economies. Europe has been particularly hard hit, partly because of the unique nature of the Economic and Monetary Union. EMU links Eurozone economies through a shared currency but does not move the economies of these sovereign nations towards the optimal criteria that would protect a shared currency zone from regional shocks brought about by differences in each country's economic positions. In other words, Ireland, like all Eurozone countries, is not fully in control of its own economy. The Eurozone crisis, combined with Ireland's massive debt and bank restructuring issues, have created a sudden and precipitous drop in economic productivity in the Irish economy, and with it has come austerity measures that many Irish citizens feel are unliveable. As they have in decades and centuries past, many young Irish people have responded to this financial and emotional austerity by leaving their homeland.

Emigration is a fraught issue in Ireland, layered as it is throughout Irish history and carrying resonances of the mass emigration during the Famine period of 1845 to 1848. During this period, Ireland lost half of its population – a decimation from which the island has never recovered, demographically. With the exception of a brief period during the Celtic Tiger (when those who had previously left the country decades began to return), emigration in Ireland was typically on-going. One of the great successes of the Celtic Tiger was the fact that Ireland moved from net emigration to net immigration for the first time since the Great Famine. To reverse this trend, as the current status of Ireland's emigration statistics suggest is happening, is to admit that the idea of Ireland as a place of possibility for its young people was, at best, a fleeting exception to the longstanding rule. As Stephen Loyal writes:

> In September 2009, more people began to leave Ireland than to enter it for the first time in 15 years. The number of emigrants in the year leading up to April 2009 was estimated to have increased by over 40 per cent, and in 2009, Ireland had the highest rate of net emigration in the European Union, despite having had one of the highest net immigration rates during the 2000s boom. (87)

Outward migration quickly resumed after the end of the Celtic Tiger; what had been a standard reality for older Irish people was quite a bit more foreign to young adults, but the demographic trend towards emigration took root first and most significantly with young adults.

That TSE's personal perspectives are so thoroughly shaped by the economic and political circumstances in which they have created these works reflects Knowles' concept of 'the cultural politics of location' (2).

Knowles' argument for the use of material semiotics in addressing performance criticism and reception centres on the importance of the material circumstances surrounding the creation of a theatrical work, rather than privileging the aesthetics of the work alone. His recognition that these circumstances are vital to the consideration of how a work is received in its particular time and place is key to understanding how these two TSE works engage with the current economic landscape of the Republic of Ireland. TSE's work in theatricalizing contemporary economic realities fits well with Knowles' theory of 'historicizing the here and now' (Knowles 13), as opposed to the more remote historical understanding of previous incarnations of cultural materialism. Knowles writes, 'meaning [is] produced in the theatre as a negotiation at the intersection of three shifting and mutually constitutive poles' (3); specifically, performance, conditions of production and conditions of reception. His acknowledgement of these three poles as 'shifting and mutually constitutive' implies an equality of importance amongst the three – all are necessary to a complete understanding of a production in its contemporary circumstances, and all equally contribute to the ways in which the production creates meaning. Significantly, Knowles does not imply that these poles are always equally at work, however. The idea of meaning production as a 'negotiation' is central to his theory, suggesting that these poles do not always work perfectly in tandem, but instead are in a continual and perhaps dialectical struggle within and between each other.

The conditions of production and reception of *Homebird* and *Tradesmen* were crucial to the creation of the performance, but context is significant only insofar as the performances are effective in translating these contexts into a theatrical form. Both form and content offer a glimpse into the material world of early 2010s' Ireland. A focus on economic circumstances and the use of collaborative devising techniques are indicative of the current sociopolitical and artistic landscapes in which TSE are working. Ferdinand Lewis, writing in *Theatre Topics*, engages with cultural materialism to support the use of devising in creating and responding to local identities in a globalizing world.

> Professional theatre that is made for communities, in communities, and by communities contributes to its audience (and by extension the world) a theme of identity rooted in place. A commitment to devising new theatre, now, is in a real sense an investment in the meaning of place, and few things are more urgently needed. [...] At their best, the arts discover, recognize, and give voice. Devised theatre does this in the context of place,

where it will increasingly count the most. (23-24)

Despite regional differences and the urban/rural divide within Ireland, TSE is addressing their nation as a community. TSE is deeply invested in the maintenance of Ireland as a unique, valued and livable locale, supported by and supporting its upcoming young generations, as Lewis argues is 'urgently needed.'

Homebird ends with an impassioned monologue by Shaun called 'The Skype Plays' – a nod to the technology that keeps emigrants connected to home, in which he looks ahead to a more prosperous Ireland that will be created by today's young people. 'I'm sad to see them go,' he says of his departed friends and family, 'because they don't even know. They don't know about all the stuff we're starting' (26). He argues for a new perspective on contemporary Ireland:

> This isn't a derelict.
> This isn't a waste ground.
> There's room here.
> This is a fixer-upper.
> A project.
> We're workers. (27)

TSE's goal with these works appears to be the cultivation and maintenance of a strong local identity amongst people who may be likely, due to circumstances caused on a regional and global level, to seek new communities. Though Shaun is referring to the young people of Ireland generally, TSE is specifically engaged in the 'work' that he regards as so crucial to the revitalization of Ireland. Original performance here serves as a form of public service, in which TSE's commitment to its community is reified and through which the company advocates for such commitment on the part of others. Speaking on behalf of TSE, Dunne says that because of the local provenance of the work, the group feels that they 'have a better understanding of the city around [them].' He continues:

> I feel more involved, more politically and socially engaged in Ireland because that's where the work has taken me. I personally have a better understanding of my community because the work has provoked us into conversation with particular parties I would not have reached otherwise. Ireland can feel like a very angry place at times. Our process and methodology has led me to understand the anger in my community more. And hopefully the end result is a treatment of sorts. Or at least a tonic!

Devising original work, in this case, serves as both representation and activism; TSE reflects the experience of youth in Ireland while simultaneously arguing for a specific, locally-based response to these issues.

Shaun and Lauren of *Homebird* confront the new reality of emigration from the perspective of those who have chosen (or have been compelled) to stay behind. A continual question posed by the play is whether this emigration is necessary. Must young Irish people leave in order to make a life for themselves? Or is emigration a kneejerk reaction? As Shaun asks in *Homebird*, 'Are we really fucked? Or are we just fucking off?' (4). What Shaun really seems to be asking is whether the resumption of emigration is due to a genuine lack of economic possibilities, or due to the rootless, exploratory life phase in which they are living. Arnett has identified five features of emerging adulthood that make it distinct from adolescence or full adulthood. Emerging adulthood, according to Arnett, is 'an age of instability [...] and age of feeling in-between [...] a self-focused age [...] an age of identity explorations... [and] an age of possibilities' (*Emerging Adulthood* 69). This demographic has 'the highest rates of residential change of any age group' in developed countries, meaning that movement and instability are noted tendencies of people of Shaun, Lauren and Lisa's age (Arnett, 'Emerging Adulthood' 471). While it is possible that young adults from Ireland would be seeking experiences overseas regardless of their nation's economic circumstances, TSE suggest further on in the play that this migration is, in fact, highly correlated to economics.

> **LAUREN:** We can't care for kids –
> We can't look after the elderly –
> And there are no resources- sources or foreseeable ways out
> that don't involve
> a crippling/ debt –
> **LISA:** The IMF – The IMF – The IMF –
> **LAUREN:** So we're gonna take initiative We're gonna lighten the load.
> *They leave* (25).

In this way we can begin to see the limitations of Arnett's theories, which seem to reflect the realities of middle-class life in a stable economy. This is perhaps reflective of the fact that the majority of his work on the theory of emerging adulthood was done in the early 2000s. Leo B. Hendry and Marion Kloep are highly critical of Arnett on this point, writing 'We are now in danger of having a psychology of the affluent middle classes in Western societies, with other groups being seen as deviating from that norm' (76). Though I do not read Arnett's theories as entirely normative, Hendry and Kloep are right to place this theory within the context of class. Arnett's emphasis on possibility and flexibility are certainly not reflected in the stay-or-leave quandary in which the performer-characters of *Homebird* find themselves.

The emigration of these performer-character's family and friends causes a crisis of confidence for both Shaun and Lauren. Should they leave too? Will they have to? Can they resist the temptation to take the seemingly easy option of emigration? Is leaving, in fact, easier than staying? During a time of life that is defined by the inherent uncertainty and dislocation of those experiencing it, the question of emigration layers one more point of anxiety onto an already tumultuous psychosocial experience. How can Shaun and Lauren, and by extension other 'twenty-somethings' in Ireland, honour both their individual needs and their desire to remain committed to their nation and their communities? TSE leaves the answer to this question up to the audience; it is not the solving of the problem that is the point of *Homebird*, but rather the experience of being together in the questioning.

In *Homebird*, Shaun tells the audience:

> As a boy who feels like he has to leave, but wants to stay -
> This is very important to me.
> I hope we're representing.
> And I hope you feel represented.
> As a boy who feels like he has to leave but wants to stay -
> I have a lot to say. (5)

In its productions, TSE is endearingly heartfelt in its unselfconscious desire to create emotional connections between the performers and the audience, and to give voice to the specific experience of emerging adults in Ireland. Young people in the European Union, unlike Willy in *Death of the Tradesmen*, are not watching their livelihoods become obsolete; they are instead living in a region, and perhaps a world, in which they feel displaced, like Shaun, Lauren and Lisa of *I am a Homebird (It's Very Hard)*. Though 'emerging adulthood' is usually a period of uncertainty and rootlessness, those in their early twenties in Ireland face an even greater level of anxiety about their futures. High levels of unemployment coupled with struggling parents and the threat of emigration mean that Ireland is a challenging place in which to be a young adult in the 2010s. In addition, Ireland can be a challenging place in which to produce theatre in such dire economic circumstances. Dunne strikes a chord somewhere between frustration and resolve when he states:

> There is no money. What money there is, is not being stretched

wide enough. The community across the theatres in Ireland are defiant and working harder and faster to meet the needs of its audience despite the financial hardship of our country. It's impossible not to be encouraged and excited by this. It helps you make the work. It makes you work faster. The money and little security that once was present is now gone but the ambition and scope of the work is bigger than ever. (Personal interview)

Knowles argues for a view of theatre that considers the material circumstances in which productions are created and presented; in many ways *Homebird* and *Tradesmen* are indicative of theatre that cannot be understood outside of its socioeconomic circumstances and without the use of material semiotics. Certainly TSE argue that such issues cannot be understood outside of their local contexts. According to Dunne:

> The work relates to the community and the country because it is out there amongst the situation from day one. We don't surmise or assume that we can understand a subject on our own. The opposite. We include the community in the construction of the art so to ensure its relativity and authenticity throughout. (Personal interview)

TSE is responding to the challenges of life in contemporary Ireland by creating theatre by, for, and about the unique experience of young Irish adults, advocating for representation of these perspectives on stage, and for the utility of theatre to create community and, perhaps, a light at the end of the tunnel.

Works Cited

Arnett, Jeffrey Jansen. 'Emerging Adulthood: A Theory of Development From the Late Teens through the Twenties.' *American Psychologist* 55.5 (2000) 469-480. Print.

---. Emerging Adulthood : The Winding Road from the Late Teens through the Twenties. Oxford University Press: Oxford, 2004. Print.

Central Statistics Office. Preliminary Data, Census 2011. Dublin: Central Statistics Office, 2011. Web. 24 July 2013.

Cowell, Alan. 'From Backwater to Boom Town: Dublin is a Magnet for Technology and Young People.' *New York Times* 31 Oct 2000, Late Ed.: C1. Print.

Dunne, Shaun. *Death of the Tradesmen*. Talking Shop Ensemble. Dublin, Ireland. 2012. TS.

--- *I am a Homebird (It's Very Hard)*. Talking Shop Ensemble. Dublin, Ireland. 2011. TS.

--- Personal interview. 10 July 2013.

Emling, Shelley. '"Celtic Tiger" Prowling Anew for Tech Jobs.' *Cox News Service*. 26 Nov. 2003. Lexis-Nexis. Web. 24 July 2013.

Hendry, Leo B. and Marion Kloep. 'Conceptualizing Emerging Adulthood: Inspecting the Emperor's New Clothes?' *Child Development Perspectives*. 1.2 (2007): 74-79. Web. 24 July 2013.

'Ireland's Debt Crisis.' *Wall Street Journal* 24 Nov 2010. Web. 24 July 2013.

'Ireland Profile.' *BBC News* 24 Jul 2013. Web. 24 July 2013.

'Irish youth unemployment rose in February – Eurostat' *RTE News*. 02 Apr 2103. Web. 12 Aug2014.

Knowles, Ric. *Reading the Material Theatre*. Cambridge University Press: Cambridge, 2004. Print.

Loyal, Stephen. 'Migrants and Migration in Ireland: Adjusting to a New Reality?' Migration and Immigrants Two Years After the Financial Collapse: Where Do We Stand? *Report for the BBC World Service*. Migration Policy Institute: Washington, DC, 2010. 81-94. Print.

Smyth, Jamie. 'Ireland's Emigration Highest for 25 Years.' *Financial Times*. 30 Sep 2012. Web.24 July 2013.

7 | A Theatre of Truth? Negotiating Place, Politics and Policy in the Dublin Fringe Festival

Miriam Haughton

> For the least glimmer of truth is conditioned by politics. (Foucault 5).

Introduction: Institutional Collapse and Creative Response

When Róise Goan,[1] former Director of the Dublin Fringe Festival, spoke at a debate on 'The Futures of Irish Theatre' in 2012, she proclaimed 'it is about truth. Artists coming to us [the Fringe Festival] are interested in making work about truth and fact, yet these are not necessarily the same thing' ('The Future of Irish Theatre').[2] This public event included responses concerning Irish theatre's futures by a panel of theorists, theatre managers and practitioners including Róise Goan, Nicholas Grene, Declan Kiberd, Fiach MacConghail, Fintan O'Toole, and Willie White. Goan's declaration led to a flurry of concern regarding a perceived reduction of myth in contemporary Irish artwork – theatre, film, literature and dance, as well as visual, live and performance arts – and questions about why that might be. Commentary from the panel and the public was varied, but the concluding discourse seemed to

---

[1] Róise Goan has been the Director (the role comprises that of Artistic Director and CEO) of the Dublin Fringe Festival from 2008 to 2014. The Dublin Fringe Festival's mission statement declares 'Dublin Fringe Festival is a curated, multi-disciplinary festival and year-round organization focusing on new and innovative approaches to the arts' ('About Us').

[2] The Keough-Naughton Institute of Irish Studies at Notre Dame University hosted this event under the banner of the 2012 Madden-Rooney public debate at the Abbey, Ireland's national theatre.

support Goan's assertion. Reasons for this were also varied, but central to the discussion was a general acknowledgement that established Irish systems and myths had undeniably failed society in recent times and could no longer be turned to for support or meaning. Until faith could be restored in the integrity of national institutions, beliefs and ideas, theatre and performance were being led by a consideration of truth(s) – particularly, how society needs the notion of truth to be sought, questioned and valued. Perhaps in later years artistic focus would return to the creation of myth, some asserted, but not until some staple sense of truth(s) in relation to Irish life and experience had been voiced, witnessed, felt and acknowledged.

Yet as Michel Foucault rightly claims, truth cannot exist outside politics. Human beings are political animals according to Aristotle, and Foucault certainly agrees with this notion as his own hypothesis relates to the circulation of power which operates in society to manage society, as outlined theoretically in *Discipline and Punish*. While Goan's declaration signals that the call by artists at the present moment is for the enactment of truth, their search for truth and exposure of institutional hypocrisies and failures constitutes a querying of power economies. Truth can never be attained nor proven as the notion itself is a philosophical ideal, but power dynamics can be altered. Perhaps then this theatre of truth indicates another type of new economy taking place. This new economy is informed by a release from the dogmatic authority imbued in the fixed and unyielding laws, religions and even myths central to modern Irish social experience; but also, this new economy is one which converses as much with European and global partners and perspectives as it does with nationalist Irish history and cultural traditions.

This essay explores this milieu of 'truth' which Goan claims pervades the work proposed to and produced by the Dublin Fringe Festival (DFF) during her five-year directorship between 2008 and 2012. I employ the phrase 'milieu of truth' to acknowledge the general climate of exposure dominating contemporary Irish public and political life, rather than to insinuate that there is a 'truth' to be discovered or declared. Irish artists are responding to this climate through their attention to exploring critically and creatively notions of truth and fact, and how these notions operate in public and private experience. The timeframe of Goan's directorship coincides with the tumultuous fall of the so-called Celtic Tiger and the subsequent bailout imposed by the Troika (European Union, International Monetary Fund, European Central Bank), as well as the publication of the Ryan (2009) and Cloyne (2011) reports and the subsequent exposure of child abuse within the Roman Catholic Church in Ireland – a dominant political force in postcolonial Ireland and an organization which the Irish Constitution of 1937, Bunreacht na hÉireann, privileges. In light of such momentous scandals of corruption and collapse in Ireland's national structures, it may not seem so surprising that the DFF received in recent years a multitude of proposals relating directly to these events, or ones which investigate the very notions of truth, ethics, morality, community, nation and identity. These noticeable paradigm-shifts in theme are also matched in form. This essay explores the development of forms and practices inscribing the landscape of theatre and performance in contemporary Ireland which have emerged in tandem with seismic shifts in Irish national sovereignty and leadership. Indeed, the increasing footprint of collaborative practices and processes, the move from fixed and hierarchical roles of 'writer' 'director' 'performer' to more fluid and perhaps broad-ranging roles of 'theatre-makers,' 'auteurs' and 'performance artists,' and the notable rise of site-specific, documentary and verbatim performance has gathered pace alongside the overt focus on producing content which directly addresses the failures and fallouts of modern and Celtic Tiger Ireland. These trends reflect interventions in form and theme visible in recent Festivals, and the reasons for such shifts will be examined here.

Furthermore, terminology is being challenged as I write this essay and changing roles and hierachies are visible among contemporary Irish theatre and performance companies and artists. Often, the artists presenting work in the Fringe perform multiple roles, as Goan observes, 'Grace Dyas is a writer/director, Amy Conroy a writer/performer. Louise Lowe is a lot more than a director. Are Brokentalkers writers?' Goan notes that these artists are best referred to as 'auteurs' and 'theatre-artists,' though their European contemporaries may be more comfortable with such labels, 'where the crossover between theatre and performance [...] is very separate.'

This essay asserts that artists in Ireland are responding directly and urgently to these national crises, making work in which content and form reflect the wider public mood and movements. The DFF, thus, becomes an appropriate home for these works, as central to the organization's mandate is to showcase work that is new, eschews established traditions, and maintains a clear dialogue and relationship with the life of Dublin city. In summary, the DFF's multidisciplinary mandate offers a fluidity of conceptual and artistic space that supports the flux and development of emerging forms in contemporary Irish practice.

Beginning with an overview of Goan's reflections concerning the histories and identities of the DFF, I also consider DFF's relationship with other national and international festivals, the impact of funding on its creative aspirations and the quality of its productions, and the festival's particular role within the city of Dublin and its wider network base. A case study focusing on the production history of a Dublin-based company, ANU Productions, whose work has premiered at DFF delves further into the complex relationships between performance, power, politics and place – dynamics central to the roots of the DFF and its increasing footprint in Irish culture and society.

The Dublin Fringe Festival: Nuts and Bolts

The Dublin Fringe Festival curates a program of theatre, performance, performance art, live art, music, dance, and circus. Central to its mandate is engagement with Dublin city – its streets, people, beliefs, pride and problems. The work it supports is mostly new work from emerging artists, and the festival operates as an incubator from where the next new major company or artist will be nurtured and launched. Since Goan's tenure began in 2008, DFF has upped its belief in the artists it supports which simultaneously results in upping the risk level to the Fringe (Goan). The present attitude of 'we are all in this together' is directly embedded in DFF's economic model. For example, before 2009 a company/artist had to pay a registration fee, a portion of the venue rental, and a part of the insurance fee, and agree to a box-office split with the festival. Since 2009-2010, the festival has removed the registration and venue fee, maintaining only the box-office split. By sharing the risk, DFF reforged the dynamics of its relationship with the artists it programmed.

Goan's tenure in the directorial position was led by three key principles: producing a good quality programme; engaging with the city; and supporting emerging artists. These principles, she maintains, were at the forefront of the festival's roots when it was launched by Jimmy Fay in 1995, Artistic Director of Bedrock Theatre Company at the time. While DFF may appear in recent times as sturdy and successful an organization as the Dublin Theatre Festival (DTF), it was set up in response to the limitations the DTF programmes possessed in the eyes of emerging Irish companies and artists. Companies whose work fell more in line with European theatre-making at the time such as Pan Pan, Loose Canon, Corn Exchange, CoisCéim, Bedrock and others, felt themselves on the fringe of the professional industry approximately two decades ago. Establishing the Fringe to run in the same season as the DTF ensured not only theatre audiences were in target, but the theatre industry, and exposure to international companies, artists, directors and producers.

Goan shrewdly observes that while 'No festival can be all things to all people,' the Fringe was established as, and remains, a multidisciplinary curated festival programming cutting-edge work. Over forty presentations were proposed by companies and artists for the inaugural 1995 Festival. From those early years came significant successes, including Conor McPherson's *This Lime Tree Bower* (1995) and Enda Walsh's *Disco Pigs* (1996). Today, approximately 300 to 400 presentations are proposed, with sixty to eighty programmed. Recent notable successes include the premiering of work by Amy Conroy/Hot For Theatre, ANU Productions, Aoife McAtamney, Brokentalkers, Emma Martin Dance, junk ensemble, Shaun Dunne, THEATREclub, The Company and Veronica Dyas – artists and companies whose work has intervened, challenged, and reinvigorated the Irish performance landscape in recent years. Moreover, initiatives set up by the Fringe such as the Fringe Lab, a writers' room, and an artists' office contributes to the survival of emerging artists by facilitating a focused work structure, ensuring that artists have a place to work in an environment designed and managed to support such work. Locating emerging artists in this type of hub allows them to tap into an on-going dialogue about their work, the industry, and the future.

Of course, the sea-change in the Irish economy has impacted on DFF's resources. However, the innovative work the festival is producing is ensuring its survival. While the Fringe is working on a budget reduced by approximately one third since 2008, artistically, this period is considered by the Fringe as a time of growth. Audiences for the international work of this period have risen from thirty per cent to seventy per cent, and audiences for Irish work sprouted from forty per cent to eighty per cent. The 'milieu of truth' that is embedded in recent programmes is attracting audiences, and this box office support keeps the Fringe alive. It not only keeps the Fringe alive; it is redesigning and feeding the professional theatre and performance industry in Ireland. The artists and companies previously mentioned were premiered and supported by DFF. Today, they are multi-award winning, touring companies and artists building a tradition of theatre-making in Ireland of strength and acclaim to match the existing canon of twentieth-century Irish drama. The breeding ground the Fringe nurtures has not gone unnoticed by industry either. The 'Re-Viewed' element of DTF's programme (which concluded in 2012) was often packed with the most successful (in terms of critical reception and box-office revenue) and innovative works from the previous year's Fringe, and indeed, some major national and international theatre houses commissioned work from the artists responsible thereafter. For example, ANU's *World End's Lane* which had premiered at DFF 2010 was showcased as part of the DTF Re-Viewed programme in 2011 alongside their latest production at that time, *Laundry* (winner of 'Best Production,' *Irish Times* Theatre Awards 2012). ANU has since been awarded an International Artist residency at the Robert Wilson Watermill Centre in New York (2010), commissioned to produce work such as the 'Dublin Tenement Experience: Living the Lockout' (2013), and by Home Manchester, *Angel Meadow* (2014), which received a 'Best Director' nomination at the UK Theatre Awards (2014). Also, Hot for Theatre's production of *I Heart Alice Heart I*, written and directed by Amy Conroy, was first produced in the Fringe in 2010, after which it transferred to the 2011 DTF Re-Viewed Programme, followed by a run on the Peacock Stage at the Abbey Theatre (2012), an international tour spanning the Irish Arts Centre in New York (2012), the LOKAL Festival in Iceland (2012), the World Theatre Festival in Brisbane, Australia (2013), and a nationwide Irish tour (2013). Indeed, similar successes have also been achieved by the other artists and companies listed above.

Yet, while the population of innovative Irish artists and companies continues to multiply, gather pace, tour internationally, and win critical and popular acclaim, their presence and role in the contemporary Irish socio-cultural landscape is undervalued, both culturally and economically. The Fringe offers affordable events (the average ticket costs between ten and twenty euros) throughout the city every August/September, fostering a climate of celebration across Dublin for the enjoyment of and engagement with residents and visitors, stimulating both cultural and economic capital. However, does Dublin city nurture and protect its artists in turn? Often, in consideration of the remuneration and social protection of artists, the German economic model is called upon as a comparative tool, where artists receive state pensions in acknowledgement of their contributions to the state. Goan explains:

> The biggest problem is related to how artists are treated by social welfare. You can't compare how the arts are treated in Ireland versus how they are treated in Germany. The arts budget for a small municipal region in Germany would eclipse the entire arts budget for Ireland.

Perhaps a comparison between the social infrastructures for artists in Ireland cannot be usefully compared to Germany; nevertheless, there is an urgent and overdue need to begin a serious interrogation of the dialogical relationship between the contributions made by the arts to Irish culture and society, and the contributions made by Irish culture and society to the arts. If the festivals were cancelled, the theatres, cinemas, museums, and bookshops closed, the Irish exchequer would suffer the financial fallout,[3] and the major socio-cultural penalties that would occur are simply not possible to quantify or qualify. The 'truth' of the relationship between the arts and state support remains: the state does support the arts, but not in equal measure to the ways in which the arts support the state.

Staging Truths in Dublin City

Understanding the city, first, is immediately important as the world becomes predominantly urbanized: the United Nations Human Settlements Programme, UN – HABITAT, notes in its 2006-7 *State of the World's Cities* report that, since 2007, more than half of the world's population live in cities (p. viii). Theatre can help us understand how we live in cities. (Harvie 4)

If a visible drive dominating the emergence of contemporary Irish theatre and performance in the Fringe (and beyond it, but this essay is dedicated to the Dublin Fringe, and thus, the region of Dublin) is the exploration of notions and values of truth, the stage for this search is the landscape and history of Dublin city. Jen Harvie observes in her study *Theatre and the City* that more than half of the world population resides in cities, examining not only how the ever-changing material, aesthetic and social structures of the city are demonstrated in the

---

[3] While the wider effect of the arts in society cannot be wholly quantified, and is ever open to debate, due to the current economic recession in Ireland there is increasing pressure on arts and humanities industries to quantify their work. According to Arminta Wallace, recent efforts to note the economic impact of the arts have proven its significant economic contribution to the Irish economy. She details 'The arts sector contributed 306.8m in tax revenues, and a total of 21,378 jobs to the Irish economy last year, according to a report published by the Arts Council yesterday. Compiled by Indecon International Economic Consultants, the report – entitled "Assessment of the Economic Impact of the Arts in Ireland" – concludes that 'the arts continue to be a major employer and contributor to Irish economy output' (Wallace).

theatre, but that 'theatre is part of urban process, producing urban experience and thereby producing the city itself' (7).

In recent years, particularly throughout the Celtic Tiger economic boom, the representations or reflections of Dublin City in visual and print arts and media told a narrative dominated by myths fuelled by the ever-dangerous cocktail of insecurity and arrogance. Centuries of colonization result in the mark of otherness, shame and subjugation on a nation and these stains are not easily wiped away. A postcolonial hangover compounded by a poor and struggling Republic set the groundwork for a need and desire to do well, live well, and perform well on national and international stages. When the Celtic Tiger economic boom appeared centre stage, a new, shiny, neoliberal capitalist Dublin city persona became its key protagonist, and like many a hero, its tragic destiny was waiting in the wings. The extraordinary imbalance between these representations of Ireland, and Dublin city in particular, in visual and print media as well as in contemporary theatre and performance did not escape unnoticed, through perhaps, did not provoke the major disquiet in discourse one would expect from such wayward gaps between the life and art teleology. In mainstream news and visual representation, Dublin was akin to a mini New York; evidently, a gross overstatement. However, in contemporary Irish theatre and performance, Ireland's kitchen sinks in rural cottages remained predominant on the stages, though exceptions did occur; again, clearly, a gross overstatement. Some critics noted that Ireland was caught between the postcolonial and postmodern (O'Toole xi), and indeed, there could be substance in such claims. Regardless, both heightened tropes of representation were based on myths; a phantasmatic identity of glamour and glory emerging from centuries of struggle and sacrifice, and a romanticized pure past not tainted by industry, capitalism and their associate characteristics.

In 2000 Irish playwright Declan Hughes, rightly argued that contemporary Irish theatre and performance throughout contemporary Ireland was trading on totalizing postcolonial and pastoral identities, and not sufficiently engaging with seismic transformations in society, politics and culture. He declares:

> You don't live in Ireland; you know nothing of the country but the last thirty years or so of its literature [...] you arrive in Dublin in 1999 [...] Why didn't anyone warn you? The cranes, the plate glass, the extremes of wealth and poverty, the corruption, the vulgarity [...] What were those writers *doing*, obsessing about the Nineteen Fifties, stuck down the country being Irish with themselves? Who the hell do we still think we are? (8)

Thus, representations of contemporary Dublin (and Ireland) were either too much absent in contemporary Irish theatre or performance or fetishized in the name of desperate re-invention. However, to associate a lack of engagement with contemporary Dublin from established playwrights and theatre venues does not mean that a vital questioning of life in Dublin did not occur. As the Fringe has proven through its track record of identifying and nurturing major talent in Ireland, these shifts in society, politics, commerce, religion and culture were at the very nexus of the work of many, including this essay's case study, ANU Productions.

ANU Productions' *Monto Cycle*, directed by Louise Lowe, hit Dublin's north inner-city streets in 2010. This cycle unearths four time capsules, with each segment reflecting one of four periods of regeneration spanning 1925 to 2014. Lowe is the fourth generation of her family from this area and each phase of the site-specific cycle is directly connected to the histories of her family and community. Part one, *World End's Lane* (2010), thrust the spectator into the early 1900s at the exact location of the thriving 'Monto' red-light district, the largest of any in twentieth-century Europe. Part two, *Laundry* (2011), brought audiences into the former Convent and Magdalene Laundry, which had been run by the Sisters of Our Lady of Charity on Lower Seán McDermott Street (formerly Gloucester Street) until 1996. Both experiences were aesthetically and viscerally reliant on the isolation of the spectator from other spectators, the performative histories of the buildings and sites of performance, and evocation of all the senses – sight, sound, smell, touch, and taste. Part three, *The Boys of Foley Street* (2012) mapped the trajectory of the lives of four boys interviewed by RTÉ journalist Pat Kenny in 1975, a time when heroin was recently introduced to the area and part four, *Vardo*, premiered in late 2014.

According to Harvie, '[t]hrough observing changing representations of the city in drama over time we can better understand how cities have changed and what this change means for those who live and work in the city' (11). ANU reveals and probes both the transformations, and the apparent fixities, within Dublin's inner city. Through the mode of their viscerally and ideologically penetrative performance installations and aesthetics, they push audiences to critique their own habits and politics of visibility. Indeed, ANU's work highlights that it is the telling patterns of visibility, and invisibility, which ensures the discrimination and disempowerment of this part of the city throughout centuries.

The first segment, for example, *World End's Lane*, offers an explosive account of life for the hidden underclass in the 'Monto' during its height in the early twentieth century. Staging encounters between performers and single spectators in the exact location in which a brothel thrived almost a century earlier, *World End's Lane* not only shone a nuanced light on the daily experiences of these working-women, but exposed how this area of the city has been strategically subjugated throughout urban planning, politics and civic culture. Prostitution and poverty may not dominate these streets as they did then (though they remain in a worrying capacity), but the booming business of narcotics (demanded and consumed by inhabitants city-wide) ensures this area cannot escape a tarnished reputation marked by distress. Indeed, this is the 'milieu of truth' in which ANU performed, which in effect conveyed realities of past and present. Through encounters with each spectator, ANU ensured these experiences and social realities were witnessed by their audiences – who were thus made complicit. The geographical politics and consequences involved in the relationship between demand and supply is one embedded in neoliberal urban societies, 'showing how demand by the wealthy acting in their own self-interest makes the poor supply, even when to do so is ultimately self-destructive for the poor' (Harvie 21).

In terms of how Irish theatre stages difficult truths regarding Dublin city historically, one might refer to Seán O'Casey's Dublin Trilogy, and his deployment of tenement experience, civil war, and familial struggle. However, O'Casey's plays are often observed by audiences from comfortable (or uncomfortable) seats in the Abbey Theatre. One could hand one's coat into the cloakroom, enjoy a beverage pre and/or post show, and use the space between the stage and the audience to process and filter the images and dialogue in play on the stage. By staging *World End's Lane* in the exact location in which a brothel thrived almost a century ago, ANU intervenes not only in inner-city Dublin's local landscape but in how audiences and spectators receive and read performance, on stage and off, pushing them to consider the relationship between performance and culture in an urgent, visceral, and discomforting manner. Local children and passersby could interrupt and participate in the performances at will, and while the scenic space of The Dublin City Council Arts Office, 'The Lab,' may have been designed and dressed, the exterior moments of performance taking place on the streets did not undergo any major production design. Hence, the milieu of truth or sense of exposure that a spectator may realize could ring similar to Goan's mantra regarding the Fringe dynamic of 'we are all in this together.' As a society, 'we are all in this together,' or, we should be. Poverty, prostitution, and narcotics do not randomly enter the same locales and flourish for a century. They are strategically marginalized to certain locales for the benefit of some and to the detriment of others. Society becomes habitualized in 'not seeing' these places and not entering them, just as major commercial enterprises and infrastructures become strategically located in alternative locales.

Productions such as *World End's Lane* also intervene in the perceived 'truth(s)' of history. Ireland, both under the control of the British Empire and as a Republic, laid claim to strict Catholic beliefs and practices, manifest in constitutional law and government policy, education, healthcare, and social welfare. Catholic doctrine upholds the relations between man and wife as of sacred value with the family unit operating as the principle foundational structure of society. Surely, in such a Catholic country as Ireland, there would not be custom for brothels, or at the very least, not custom for the largest red-light district in early twentieth-century Europe? Yet, the evidence glaringly present on the city streets reveals that Irish society was sexually active outside of wedlock, though this perhaps entered the realm of public invisibility. Furthermore, the doctrine and dogma of Catholicism in modern Ireland was overtly visible, and thus, naturalized and normalized, masking the violence and devastation such sexual and religious politics engendered and facilitating the geographical politics that informed the daily life, business and experience of the Monto.

However, while *World End's Lane* offers a way to interrogate this recent theatrical culture of exploring notions of 'truth,' as stated at the beginning of this essay, truth is a philosophical ideal. This theatre and milieu of truth reflects a shift in influences informing the making of theatre and performance. The work of ANU, among many other companies and artists, is embroiled in this climate of immersive and politicized theatre and performance which delves directly into historical and contemporary lived experience, questioning the relationships between people, place, and politics. In this way, perhaps, these performance makers are filling a void left by mainstream spiritual and secular leadership in recent times, whose credibility and respectability are grossly tarnished by decades of revelations of widespread corruption and abuse. While many officials rely on the rhetoric of post-Celtic Tiger futures to skip past the multitude of political, economic, religious and socio-cultural crises of recent times, Ireland's artists are jumping into this hotbed of fear, anxiety, and discovery. By attracting established and new audiences to their work, previously naturalized and managed patterns of visibility and invisibility are being disrupted.

With ANU's delicately crafted 'moments of communion'[4] (Lowe) informing encounters between performers, place and spectators/participants, one is facilitated to look, and see, these staged and unstaged truths of Dublin city, past and present.

The current increase in immersive theatre and performance, site-specific theatre and performance, and verbatim theatre and performance so widespread in recent DFF programmes requires further critical attention. These forms of theatre and performance often result in under-critiqued affective experiences for audiences/-spectators/participants. As James Thompson argues in *Performance Affects* (2009), '[b]y failing to recognize affect – bodily responses, sensations and aesthetic pleasure – much of the power of performance can be missed' (7). Thompson outlines his theorization of performance affects, maintaining that '[p]erformance affects are, therefore, the sensory responses to both social and artistic processes' (8). In relation to the work of many of the companies and artists premiered by the Fringe, Thompson's consideration of the ideological and political role performance affect plays in reception is key to this analysis, as it promotes what I call a 'post-performance efficacy'[5] that continues to gather momentum following the end of the performance. Moreover, it may potentially provoke a transformative energy and agency amongst those who experience such 'moments of communion.' As Thompson outlines:

> It [the book] examines how the encounters between people in performance processes can become the site of felt individual responsibility and a moment through which universal claims to right or good can be made. Relationships created through an

---

[4] For further examples regarding ANU's 'moments of communion,' please see Haughton 65-93; Haughton 142-158.

[5] When I use the term 'efficacy' I do not intend this to be drawn from Richard Schechner's theory of the 'efficacy-entertainment braid' whereby 'If the performance's purpose is to effect transformations – to be efficacious – then the other qualities listed under the heading "efficacy" [results, linked to an absent Other, symbolic time, performer possessed/in trance, audience participates, audience believes, criticism discouraged, collective creativity] will most probably be present, and the performance is ritual'(130). Rather, I rely on the meaning of 'efficacy' to be considered similar to Baz Kershaw's theory where 'by efficacy I mean the potential the theatre may have to make the immediate effects of performance influence, however minutely, the general historical evolution of wider social and political realities' (1).

intense interpersonal encounter are presented as a vital place through which political commitment can be generated, and also through which politics retrieves its necessary ethical dimension. (10)

My argument does not intend to suggest that radical and immersive performances such as *World End's Lane* stem from motives within ANU Productions to provoke social or political change or that this or other productions maintain the capacity to incite such individual or collective responses. Rather, by considering the potential impact of a site-specific production embedded with intense personal and political encounters such as may result from ANU's focus on 'moments of communion,' where the present and past experience of the locale intertwine, there exists the potential for knowledge production and sensory reactions which can and do set the path for a personal reaction of discontent, frustration and resistance. As Thompson suggests, '[i]n a world of inequality, social injustice and endemic violence, they [forms of aesthetic expression] could be acts of resistance and redistribution, made in an intimate and sensory key' (11). By asking '[...] which show are we part of' (30), one may acknowledge that the performance encompasses not only the staged encounters, but the wider social and political performances which have informed this site and the surrounding community who live there, as well as far-removed communities who do not. These productions, indeed, include performances of social geography and urban planning, where the politics of staging (in terms of social geography) have been managed by various directors for over a century. The staging is reliant on the action in the Monto not spilling over its designated scenic space, away from its designated audience. ANU Productions, and the Fringe, disrupt these boundaries of performance, politics, space and society, as histories are excavated and presented by the city to the city.

Conclusion

> Theatre, in some respects, resembles a market [...] an exchange of all kinds of cultural goods and products goes on between theatre and other spheres of social life – other institutions, cultural performances, art forms, and elements of everyday life. (Fischer-Lichte 1)

Yes, the theatre resembles a marketplace – a bustling arena of passersby which facilitates the exchange of stories. These stories may have been sourced from history, literary and theatrical canons, cultural traditions, politics, religion, social concerns, psychological patterns, national and local interest or any other narrative, trope or event. These stories may be told in a style that one can easily relate to the outside world, or performed in such a way that an audience experiences distance and disorientation. Yet the classical consideration of theatre,[6] as a designated building or place for staging plays, cannot function as a fully competent term for the recent stories staged at DFF; these productions took place in venues, institutions, and streets throughout Dublin that were not always places strictly aligned with the presentation of plays. Whether drawn from local myth, inherited from times past, or imported from the furthest corners of the earth, these stories are imbued with the creative telling and retelling of human imagination and experience. They do not tell a 'truth,' or 'truths'; no artwork can. They are, however, particularly at the present moment, stimulating regional and national dialogue regarding events of false testimony from hegemonic civic and religious institutions, through staging encounters which critically question the performance of stories which claim to represent 'reality,' 'history' and 'society.' From engagement with these Fringe events, exchanges may occur between people whereby 'stories, rituals, ideas, concepts, perceptive modes, conventions, rules, techniques, actions, behavioural patterns, objects' (1) circulate to and fro. Fischer-Lichte concludes that these exchanges 'change the sphere they enter – sometimes slightly, sometimes considerably. And sometimes, in passing, they even change the sphere they leave behind' (1).

The Dublin Fringe Festival continues to pave the way for emerging, innovative and transdisciplinary arts events which engage with the city and its residents, visitors, and passing trade. Under Goan's directorship, it has not only survived, but grown, throughout the 'bailout' (naturally, I employ this term with heavy irony, as it implies 'help'), multiple austerity budgets, a change in national leadership (and a disappointing lack of change in national politics), and a multitude of international, national, and regional crises and conflicts resulting in the assassination of community and civic structures and supports. Companies and artists emerging from the Fringe are instigating a paradigm shift in the forms of theatre and performance making in contemporary Ireland, challenging their audiences to participate physically, politically, and personally in their performances; these

---

[6] According to the Oxford English Dictionary, the term 'theatre' (n) derived from Greek and Roman history refers to 'A place constructed in the open air, for viewing dramatic plays or other spectacles' ('Theatre').

performances participate physically 'on the streets,' and politically and personally in the histories and tensions of Irish society. The idea of 'a Theatre of Truth' reflects the mood behind the paradigm shift, not the expectations for any potential outcome of 'truth.' The work of the many artists and companies nurtured and premiered at DFF has honed increased attention on the site of performance, the script or testimony being performed, and the creation of diverse encounters between performers and audiences/spectators/participants. Essentially, this theatrical culture is disrupting traditional and tired ways of seeing, and thus, assumed ways of producing knowledge and meaning, thereby pushing for radical interventions in sensory and intellectual reactions of sight and interpretation, analysis and reaction. Perhaps then, this 'Theatre of Truth' will be followed by new questions, new conversations and new interventions, on stage and off. Indeed, the 2013 Dublin Fringe Festival Call for Applications declares:

> In 2013 the Dublin Fringe Festival will further endeavour to reveal new truths about Dublin city; its landscape, its citizens, its past, future and present preoccupations. The festival will serve as a meeting point between brave and talented artists and an adventurous audience willing to take risks and looking to be inspired. ('Fringe Submissions')

Works Cited

Dublin Fringe Festival. 'About Us.' *Dublin Fringe Festival*. N.d. Web. 2 August 2012.

---. 'Fringe Submissions.' *Dublin Fringe Festival*. N.d. Web. 5 August 2013.

Fischer-Lichte, Erika. *The Show and the Gaze of Theatre: A European Perspective*. Iowa: University of Iowa Press, 1997. Print.

Foucault, Michel. *The History of Sexuality 1: The Will to Knowledge*. Trans. Robert Hurley. London: Penguin, 1998. Print.

Goan, Róise. Personal Interview. 11 June 2013.

Haughton, Miriam. 'From Laundries to Labour Camps.' *Modern Drama*, 57:1 (2014), 65-93. Print.

---. 'Mirror Mirror on the Wall.' *Masculinity and Irish Popular Culture: Tiger's Tales*. Ed. Conn Holohan and Tony Tracy. Basingstoke: Palgrave Macmillan, 2014. 142-158. Print.

Harvie, Jen. *Theatre and the City*. Basingstoke: Palgrave Macmillan, 2009. Print.

Hughes, Declan. 'Who the Hell Do We Still Think We Are' in *Theatre Stuff: Critical Essays on Contemporary Irish Theatre*. Ed. Eamonn Jordan. Dublin: Carysfort Press, 2000. 8-15. Print.

Kershaw, Baz. *The Politics of Performance: Radical Theatre as Cultural Intervention*. London: Routledge, 1992. Print.

Lowe, Louise. Personal Interview. 15 May 2012.

O'Toole, Fintan. 'Introduction.' *Martin McDonagh Plays: 1*. London: Bloomsbury, 2003. Print.

Oxford English Dictionary. 'Theatre.' *Oxford English Dictionary Online*. n.d. Web. 25 April 2012.

Schechner, Richard. *Performance Theory*. New York: Routledge, 2008. Print.

'The Futures of Irish Theatre.' Madden-Rooney Public Debate. Peacock Theatre. Dublin, Ireland. 21 June 2012.

Thompson, James. *Performance Affects: Applied Theatre and the End of Effect*. Basingstoke: Palgrave, 2009. Print.

Wallace, Arminta. 'Arts Sector Raised 306.8m in Tax Revenues Last Year.' *The Irish Times*. 17 November 2011. Web. 26 April 2012.

'*World End's Lane*.' ANU Productions. Wordpress, n.d. Web. 5 Aug 2013

8 | Mapping Contemporary European Theatre(s): Reconsidering Notions of Devised and Postdramatic Theatres through Pan Pan Theatre

Noelia Ruiz

Introduction

Labelling and categorizing are elusive tasks for Gavin Quinn, co-artistic director of Pan Pan Theatre, when it comes to defining his own work (see my interview with Quinn, which follows in this section). Pan Pan, from its inception in 1991, has regularly engaged in what could be seen as collaborative theatre making, and the aesthetics of the company's work might be located within the postdramatic paradigm. International touring has been key in the aesthetics and evolution of the company, and participating in different European Arts Festivals led Pan Pan to create the Dublin International Theatre Symposium (1997-2003), aiming to showcase international experimental work in Ireland. Through an interdisciplinary methodology, Pan Pan's aim is to examine and interrogate the nature of theatre as an experiential art. For Quinn, however, the term 'devised' has negative connotations – as do other culturally-bounded terminologies that classify contemporary theatre making.

Indeed, different socio-cultural contexts comprehend and conceptualize similar realities idiosyncratically. This is reflected in language and is the reason why translators face many obstacles when attempting to translate meaning from one set of cultural conventions to another, a process we may consider as adaptation. Certainly, meaning is embedded in history, traditions, genealogies, socio-political and economic realities, and in performative processes of socio-cultural validation. Consequently, upon inspection, current debates on terms such as postdramatic theatre, collaborative and collective creation, and devised theatre, clearly illustrate that those meanings – and the academic discourses they generate – belong to specific environments, and need to be contextualized in their cultural spaces. For instance, Liz Tomlin's deconstruction of the ontology of the postdramatic exposes an inherent dichotomy between text-based and non-text based theatre. For Tomlin this dichotomy problematizes the analysis and categorization of new playwriting that does not abide by dramatic conventions, such as the work of Tim Crouch. By extension, if we follow Tomlin's logic, it also renders certain adaptations of canonical dramatic texts outside of the postdramatic frame, regardless of whether they are deconstructions and/or radical contemporizations. Therefore, the work of companies such as Pan Pan Theatre and Forced Entertainment could not be strictly classified as postdramatic.

However, Duška Radosavljevic observes that the same dichotomy operates in the UK with regards to devised theatre, where this practice is largely identified with non-text-based performance. Radosavljevic further argues that the 'power-dynamic between text and performance [...] has to be understood as being specifically characteristic of the English speaking world and may not find easy equivalents in some of the other European cultures' (65). Therefore, in other contexts, the postdramatic may not imply a friction between text and non-text-based performance because there is a different understanding of notions of text, authorship, playwright's *intention* and director's *interpretation*. Furthermore, the processes of staging a dramatic text also defy classification when it comes to methodologies and techniques used in the rehearsal room (including workshops prior to the rehearsal phase). Consequently, it is worth reconsidering the academic tenets of devised and postdramatic theatres, their genealogies, their strategies and modes of production within their respective cultural spaces. These reconsiderations also reveal categorization as bounded to processes of creation and their aesthetics, making possible a defiance of hierarchical notions of authorship. They reveal, for example, theatre making as a collaborative process – often interdisciplinary – that challenges the conception of the director as *auteur*, and issues of fidelity in adaptation as an aesthetic dramaturgical choice. Finally, also at the centre of all these approaches to contemporary theatre making, there is a reconsideration of the role of the audience as a participant co-author in the meaning-making process, being affected by a reconfiguration of the relationship between text and performance.

Reconsidering Notions of Devised Theatre

It is observable that many theatre practitioners and scholars seem reluctant to adopt the term 'devising.' On one hand, as Radosavljevic argues in *Theatre-Making: Interplay Between Text and Performance in the 21st Century* (2013), the term is largely identified with ideological practices that emerged in the UK during the post-Second World War period, as Deirdre Heddon and Jane Milling also maintain in *Devising Performance: A Critical History* (2006). At the time, a politically aware atmosphere led artists to adopt devised methodologies as a reaction against mercantile theatre as well as a way of expressing 'political and ideological commitment' (13). Thus, the ideal of a participatory democracy in opposition to hierarchical structures henceforth steered many theatre artists to use collaborative/collective devising as an alternative to mainstream praxis and its modes of production. Consequently, devised theatre had a strong emphasis on ensemble process, shared roles and responsibilities, and actor's training through labs and workshops. In England, the first significant company to apply these political ideals and methodologies was Joan Littlewood's Theatre Workshop, founded in 1953. This contextual specificity, as Radosavljevic argues, explains why

> On balance, a departure from the term 'devising' in contemporary theatre and performance discourse may well be wise, not least because of the fact that its apparent inflation in the United Kingdom has led to a number of misconceptions (71).

On the other hand, this reluctance can also be explained by the term's inadequacy to convey similar practices in other cultural contexts. As Radosavljevic points out, in France (and similarly in Spain, Latin America and Italy) devising practices such as those of Arianne Mnouchkine (whose political stance is similar to that of Littlewood) are called 'collective creation' while in the US they are referred to as 'collaborative creation.' These terms are gaining prominence as evidenced by recent publications such as *Collective Creation in Contemporary Performance* (2013) edited by Kathryn Syssoyeva and Scott Proudfit, and Barton Bruce's *Collective Creation, Collaboration and Devising* (2008). They refer to a broader understanding of theatre making as 'an all-inclusive collaborative process whether the outcome is a solo show or an ensemble piece, a new play or a performance installation' (Radosavljevic 23). These models share a processual approach in which all the agents are considered co-authors to different extents: playwrights, designers, actors, dramaturgs, composers, directors and other collaborators such as videographers and visual artists. In this light, Radosavljevic proposes a genealogical differentiation between devising as an 'aesthetic-methodological' strategy that infuses much contemporary theatre making, prominent in Europe, and devising as a political response that was generated in the UK, even if currently 'devised' theatre in the UK has departed from its ideological genesis. In that regard, Radosavljevic stresses how gradually 'scholars are willing to subsume the notion of "devising" into postdramatic theatre or, simply, theatre-making' (61).

A further argument she makes is that in the UK devised theatre has come to be associated with non-text-based theatre and this 'implied binary opposition to text-based theatre tends to create confusion among continental Europeans, as work on any pre-written text in many European mainstream theatres customarily involves a collective and an improvisational approach in the process of rehearsal' (62). Certainly, in Europe the ensemble approach and the use of improvisation techniques as a creative tool to explore characterization and generate dramaturgical material around a given text can be traced back to Konstantin Stanislavski. Consequently, the binary proves unhelpful when considering contemporary intra-adaptations or deconstructions of canonical plays in which 'devising techniques' are used; that is, improvisational techniques which inherently involve a collaborative mode of creation. For, once the actors are improvising, they are shaping the dramaturgical material and, consequently, they become co-authors in the process. For instance, Quinn often uses such approaches to deconstruct the text; in *Everybody is King Lear in his own home* (2012) the dialogue shifted from Shakespearean verse to text that had been improvised by the actors around the themes of the play, based on their personal experiences. Pan Pan's last project, *Americanitis Presents The Seagull and Other Birds,* combined a series of intertextual strategies in which five texts were commissioned to respond to the meta-theatrical themes in Anton Chekhov's play, *The Seagull.* In addition, the actors generated text from improvisations around approximately thirty texts, including plays such as *Who's afraid of Virginia Woolf?* by Edward Albee and *Histrionics* by Thomas Bernhard. All of these texts, whether 'commissioned' plays or texts generated from improvising with existing texts, shaped the final performance script which used *The Seagull* as a dramaturgical spine that allowed for this splicing of texts.

However, for Quinn, labelling his work as devised seems inaccurate, despite the use of devising strategies in the process of rehearsal to *find* the performance text. His methodologies are rather in line with European 'aesthetic-methodological' models. Hence, as Radosavljevic argues,

> Due to the fact that this creative methodology grew to represent a non-text-based theatre genre in the United Kingdom, the term 'devising' can sometimes create confusion in continental Europe where the same methodology is customarily used in text-based theatre (82).

However, Syssoyeva identifies an equivalent ideological turn to that of devised theatre in the UK in the context of the utopian movements of the 1960s in North America, Australia, parts of Latin America and Europe.

Collective creation – the practice of collaboratively devising works of performance – rose to prominence, not simply as a performance-making method, but as an institutional model. This was the heyday of The Living Theatre, years that saw the nascence of France's Théâtre du Soleil, The Agit Prop Street Players in England, El Teatro Campesino in the fields of Southern California, English Canada's Théâtre Passe-Muraille, and Quebec's Théâtre Euh!— companies associated, variously, with collective performance creation, egalitarian labor distribution, consensual decision making, and socio-political revolt. (1)

Thus, these collectives shared the ideological and utopian commitments of devised theatre in the UK. However, in their different cultural contexts, these practices are perceived as dissociated from mainstream theatre rather than from the dramatic text or the text per se. In fact, their methodologies can often be used to explore a given text, but also to *create* a play-text as in the case of Joan Littlewood who collaborated with playwrights such as Brendan Behan. Contemporarily, many 'devising' companies use this model to create a performance-text or a dramatic play. Thus, Syssoyeva rather than dismissing these terms given their ideological genesis, advocates

> broadening our understanding of collective creation [...] better historicize a confluence of relationships and practices, drawing into the historical map companies whose influence on international devising practice has been considerable and yet – as a result of apparently apolitical or non-egalitarian practices – have been marginalized or even written out of the conversation. (6-7)

Syssoyeva's recalibration makes it also possible to include in the category figures associated with 'authoritarian auterism' that do not fit the egalitarian model, such as the influential Jerzy Grotowski. His anthropological, collective and phenomenological perspective had a seminal influence in the intercultural ensemble practices of Peter Brook and Ariane Mnouchkine. These practitioners use a combination of physical acting techniques – particularly Eastern methods – as a means of improvisation to explore possible meanings in dramatic texts. Grotowski's legacy was also felt in many European countries and in mainstream practices that use different acting techniques to explore characterization and dramaturgical possibilities in dramatic texts. These physical approaches, along with Jacques Lecoq's methodologies, eventually had an impact in the UK in the 1990s, when a shift took place towards what was labelled as 'devised physical theatre' through the work of companies including DV8 and Théâtre de Complicité. Heddon and Milling link the trend of physical theatre to funding cuts in the arts and a consequently more competitive market for actors who had to acquire new skills to broaden their employability opportunities. However, devised physical theatre is posited still further at the end of the non-text-based theatre spectrum associated with devised theatre in the UK, whereas the work of Grotowski, Brook and Mnouchkine is embedded in a methodological approach to the dramatic text.

In light of this milieu it is understandable why Quinn, as many other practitioners and scholars, finds the term 'devised' problematic, especially when the use of text is inherent to their practices. This is also the case for Kneehigh Theatre, a UK company that adapts dramatic or non-dramatic texts creating highly visual and physical performances, responding to ideas or themes rather than to the text as a literary artefact. The company has created a strong methodology through ensemble and training, with methods learnt by Emma Rice (joint artistic director along with Mike Shepherd) through working with Polish company Gardzienice, which was created by one of Grotowski's pupils in the late 1970s. Interestingly, Radosavljevic argues that 'Rice's most significant formative experience as a theatre artist seems to have been gained outside of the Anglophone context' (75). Thus, Kneehigh Theatre seems to fit better within the European 'aesthetic-methodological' model.

In Ireland, however, we find a paradigmatic case within the Anglophone context, as there is little lineage of either devised theatre or aesthetic-methodological models visible within the existing discourses of theatre practitioners, scholars and critics. This can be explained by the country's strong dramatic tradition in mainstream institutionalized theatre (and its modes of production), which until the early 1990s was largely unchallenged as experimental practices remained mostly at the margins. And, indeed, it also might be explained by Ireland's historical, socio-political, geographic, economic and demographic contexts, characterized by mass outward migration. There is no space here to analyse in depth such milieu, but it is no coincidence that when economic recovery started in the 1990s, a phenomenon known as the Celtic-Tiger, a proliferation of independent theatre-makers and companies took place. In 1991 three companies were created with the aim of offering an alternative to the dramatic tradition that dominated the Irish institutional theatrical landscape. Corcadorca (Cork), long-term collaborators with playwright Enda Walsh, was born with the purpose to explore plays out of traditional venues. Blue Raincoat (Sligo) aimed to focus on investigating plays through physical theatre, following Etienne Decroux's techniques. Finally, Pan Pan Theatre (Dublin) was committed to explore the language of theatre itself and considered itself inspired initially by the modernist avant-garde movement. To different degrees, these companies all share a collaborative approach to process and were inspired by different European schools of theatre-making. Within their differing aesthetics, we can partially locate Corcadorca, Blue Raincoat and Pan Pan within the aesthetic-methodological model in their approach to the dramatic text, in which improvisations and other creative techniques taken from different disciplines are used to scrutinize the play in order to deconstruct it and contemporize it or, rather, adapt it.

However, it is probably Pan Pan that fits best Radosavljevic's classification of the aesthetic-methodological. The European avant-garde inspired the company from its inception. This influence not only had an impact on its aesthetics but also in its modes of creation and on Quinn's rehearsal methods. Furthermore, since it was formed, Pan Pan has been touring around Europe and beyond, especially on the festival circuit, which has had a considerable influence in the company's aesthetic evolution. In that sense, Pan Pan was also a paradigmatic case in Ireland in using from its early years interdisciplinary collaboration as a creative method, key to its scenographic, conceptual and dramaturgical approach. The company was formed by Quinn and scenographer, Aedín Cosgrove. They also work with long-term collaborators such as sound designer Jimmy Eadie, sculptor Andrew Clancy, and photographer and videographer Ros Kavanagh. This methodology defies to a certain extent the 'theatre of the director' or 'auteur theatre' model. However, Quinn's direction is a clear drive behind the company's oeuvre and in that sense one must agree with Syssoyeva's proposal to broaden notions of collaboration: 'For just as we may find authoritarianism lurking beneath the surface of an egalitarian rhetoric, we may find ample examples of collaborative devising lurking beneath the surface of directorial dominance' (7).

Reconsidering Notions of Postdramatic Theatre

Beyond Radosavljevic's argument that scholars are adopting the term postdramatic as an alternative to devised theatre, we may contemplate other factors in the equation. I would argue that the rapid assimilation of the postdramatic as a paradigm by scholars worldwide, especially since Hans-Thies Lehmann's *Postdramatic Theatre* was translated into English in 2006, may be explained by the limitations that postmodern discourses and performance studies presented, eventually, to the specificity of theatre as a medium, especially in relation to the analysis of new forms and approaches to contemporary theatre-making. Until *Postdramatic Theatre* was translated academic discourses borrowed terminologies, theoretical frameworks and conceptualizations from critical theory, gender studies, poststructuralism, psychoanalysis, anthropology, ethnography and, indeed, performance studies. In contrast, Lehmann's thesis provided a much-needed new critical framework, corpus of concepts and vocabularies specific to the medium, to critically analyse contemporary theatre and performance forms in all their variety and complexity. Moreover, its impact is countable for a number of rich critical debates that have revitalized academic discussions when the equally considerable impact of performance studies was starting to weaken. For instance, many questioned and dismissed the choice of term in relation to 'postmodern'; however, the postdramatic refers specifically to theatre as a medium whereas, as Mark Fortier argues, 'if post-modernism is the condition of contemporary culture, then all culture produced in our time is by definition postmodern' (175).

One of the recent debates has been postulated by Tomlin, who has addressed the same dichotomy Radosavljevic identifies between devised and text-based theatre in the UK, with regards to the binary dramatic/postdramatic:

> While Lehmann never explicitly aligns dramatic with text-based practice and post-dramatic with non-text-based practice, I will argue that his conclusions, inconclusive as they are, are ultimately more likely to consolidate than to fracture the existing binary. ('"And their stories"' 58)

For Tomlin this division problematizes the analysis and categorization of contemporary writing for the stage given that 'there is no easy recalibration of the playwright as postdramatic' ('Foreword' ix).

Tomlin reasons that if a pre-exiting text dictates the mise-en-scène 'must remain, within Lemann's thesis, under the dramatic rubric and consequently bear the ideological weight of his analysis' (*ibid*). It is worth considering that Lehmann and Tomlin engage with two opposed schools of thinking, the former belonging to German idealism and the latter to materialism. Thus, Tomlin reconsiders the ontology of Lehmann's thesis from a Marxist standpoint, proposing through a poststructuralist lens a dialectical synthesis from the thesis of the dramatic and the antithesis of the postdramatic. A similar stance is held by Stephen Bottoms for whom Crouch's *An Oak Tree* 'offers a powerful reinvigoration of dramatic traditions rather than a step "beyond" them' ('Authorizing the Audience' 67). Arguably, following Radosavljevic's observations, perhaps we are also faced with different layers of understanding what the 'dramatic' and the 'postdramatic' may mean in different cultural contexts. For example, Bottoms' assertion that Crouch 'challenges the widespread assumption that "drama" belongs to a literary theatrical tradition that remains quite separate from, even hostile to, a "performance tradition"' ('Authorizing the Audience' 67), may be located within the power-dynamic between text and performance identified by Radosavljevic as characteristic of the Anglophone world. Radosavljevic further argues that the oppositional dichotomy between what is understood as 'text' (dramatic-text-based) and what is understood as 'performance' (non-dramatic/non-text-based) is not new: 'Throughout the twentieth century, theatre scholars and historians tended to view the turn of the century split between text and performance through the mutually opposed categories of text-based theatre and the avant-garde' (8). Furthermore, in the context of the avant-garde the figure of the director emerged as an artist experimenting with form by exploring the potential languages of the stage and the possibilities of a given (dramatic)-text. Thus, following Lehmann, Radosavljevic asserts that within this context many directors in Europe sought to revitalize and re-discover canonical texts, rescuing them from the dusty frames of realist and naturalist traditions. The director emerged as the new authorial voice, replacing the playwright's authority, engaging in a process of adaptation or translatability from one set of theatre conventions to a new understanding of the stage as purely theatrical, rather than just a device or medium at the service of the literary. Consequently, in Europe 'dramatic theatre is largely director's theatre' (Radosavljevic 15). Therefore, she identifies as a key factor in the troubled relationship between text and performance in the English-speaking world: 'the fact that the profile of the director never really developed in the same way in the United Kingdom and the United States as it did in Europe in the early twentieth century' (10).

Additionally, following Dwight Conquergood's identification of drama as holding intellectual value, and performance as associated with manual labour, Radosavljevic also ascertains that UK and US educational systems traditionally favoured the training of playwrights (and posteriorly directors) in university departments, whereas skills-based training took place in drama schools (actors, stage managers and technicians). Thus, in these cultural contexts there was an inherent class-value system operating, which positioned the 'dramatic text' as intellectually superior in opposition to the craft of theatre-making. Radosavljevic explains that in the cultural spaces of Eastern Europe this positioning never occurred and:

> theatre professionals within much of the former Eastern Bloc were regularly perceived in their own contexts as both artists and intellectuals – often responsible for ideological subversion [...] the communist context did represent a very different scope not only for the interplay between text and performance, but also for the relationship of theatre artists (and their teachers) to notions of cultural and economical capital. (14-15)

Thus, in light of these arguments, the 'postdramatic' may be better comprehended in European contexts as an understanding of the text beyond the dramatic conventions of neoclassicism and its re-interpretation of the Aristotelian units, which includes its associated aesthetics, particularly in terms of acting style and scenography. Thus, the postdramatic may be considered as a departure from the mise-en-scène as 'subordinated to the primacy of the text. In the theatre of modern times, the staging largely consisted of the declamation and illustration of written drama' (Lehmann 21). Consequently, Bottoms' interrogation of the status of representation proposed by Lehmann, for whom it is anchored in the 'logocentric logic of drama,' might not be in a clear-cut opposition to the postdramatic beyond the ontological argument. For instance, Bottoms highlights the meta-theatrical strategies of much contemporary performance, which plays with multiple layers of signification including an illusionism that may function as an enhancer of the performance's liveness and actuality, a strategy used by Pan Pan in its dramaturgy and acting approach. This is not dissimilar from Lehmann's assertion that:

> In postdramatic theatre, the theatre situation is not simply added to the autonomous reality of the dramatic fiction to animate it. Rather, the theatre situation as such becomes a matrix within whose energy lines the elements of the scenic fictions inscribe

themselves. Theatre is emphasized as a situation, not as a fiction. (128)

Furthermore, contesting postmodern notions of presence, for Bottoms, theatre is 'placed within the frame of art, the "real" is always already representational, and the "self" always already a characterization' ('Authorizing' 74). However, Lehmann's reflections on self and presence as opposed to characterization must be understood within Michael Kirby's acting/not-acting continuum, as well as an enhancement of the inherent qualities of performance: 'For performance, just as for postdramatic theatre, "liveness" comes to the fore, highlighting the provocative presence of the human being rather than the embodiment of a figure' (135). In that regard, Tomlin explores characterization and self by making use of Derrida's citational theory, providing useful vocabularies to analyse contemporary acting approaches:

> Read through the lens of Derrida's analysis, the inadequate characterizations produced by the Forced Entertainment surrogates can be seen to be clearly citational. Not only should such characterizations be read, as is more commonly the case, as intentionally failed attempts to meet the demands of dramatic theatre, but also as productive expositions of citational, rather than essential, readings of identity, as they are demonstrably representations without referent; ostensibly refusing to point to any semblance of an originary reality as would be anticipated within more realistic, or psychologically-rounded, modes of characterization. ('Acts & Apparitions' 87)

To further illustrate these arguments, we can again use Pan Pan's performance style as an example. Quinn's approach plays with layered understandings of character as interpretation, identity and performance persona. His multifaceted approach seeks a specific quality that normally undulates between the poles of Michael Kirby's acting/not-acting continuum, creating a certain undecidability that subtly destabilizes the triad character/actor/performer. This layering of acting styles blends the real and the representational, the self with characterization, ultimately demonstrating the interplay of these categories. As described earlier, Pan Pan's 2014 project, *Americanitis presents The Seagull and Other Birds*, responded to the meta-theatrical and self-reflexive themes in Chekhov's play, expanding intertextuality through working with multiple source texts. Through this method, the characters and their relationships were explored in diverse (con)texts. Thus, if for Michael Frayn the lack of an authorial voice in Chekhov's plays, or what Frayn calls Chekhov's 'elusiveness,' forces us not to see

'Chekhov's world but the world of his characters' (xiii), Pan Pan's own 'elusive' response makes us see these characters in different worlds and scenarios, becoming citations of citations or iterations with no reference to the original, only to their situation. In *The Seagull and Other Birds*, this situation was explored through a web of contemporary cultural referents, from TV shows to street-gang culture. To reinforce situation over characterization the actors called each other by their real names but maintained their relational characterization. The performers were acting as 'citations of figures whose drama has already taken place' (Fischer-Lichte 342) bringing their roles in *The Seagull* into a web of contemporary scenarios.

On the other hand, Quinn's approach might be understood within Robert Gordon's classification of acting techniques, in particular the idea of the actor as 'scenographic' element as fostered by Edward Gordon Craig and Meyerhold:

> Directly opposed to the naturalistic conception of the actor as imitator of human behaviour was the notion of the actor as an instrument [...] mode of acting in which a more aesthetically controlled vocal and bodily expression might be fully integrated within a unified artwork. (89)

Thus, we can locate Pan Pan's work within the frame of postdramatic aesthetics and use these new critical recalibrations to analyse the company's aesthetics beyond unhelpful binaries and their consequent limitations towards text, representation and characterization.[1]

Pan Pan productions are mostly text-based, albeit understood as what Anne Bogart calls a '*source*, whether it is a question, an image, a historical event, etc.' (163). Thus, Pan Pan takes the play-text as a point of departure, which is usually treated as a pre-text that is bent, contemporized and/or deconstructed during the creative process, both

---

[1] We must also consider the festival circuit and the subsequent dramaturgical, aesthetic and production choices they endorse. As Jen Harvie and Andy Lavender state, internationally tourable work has to be 'marketable, distinct and artistically and economically viable.' Hence, 'its design aesthetics are frequently marked by an apparent fluidity and quasi-minimalism, which reflect materially what the work also means to represent thematically as its (international) fluency and adaptability' (10-11). That is, when shows are conceived for touring in different cultures and languages it implies that they must have an international appeal, without losing its cultural specificity.

in the pre-rehearsal and rehearsal phases. Thus we might consider Pan Pan's work under the frame of adaptation theory, understood in Margherita Laera's terms:

> Evidently, there are several types of adaptation, depending on the nature of the adapted work, the kind of engagement with it and the product resulting from this process. In this intertextual sense, the process of adaptation implies negotiations of numerous kinds, such as interlingual, intercultural, intersemiotic, intermedial, but also ideological, ethical, aesthetic and political (4-5).

With regard to terminology, Quinn uses the term 'response' to refer to Pan Pan's processes. Pan Pan's adaptations of the Bard – *Mac-Beth 7* (2004), *The Rehearsal, Playing the Dane* (2010), *Everybody is King Lear in his own home* (2012) – heavily deconstructed the core themes of the plays in order to contemporize them. Laera classifies contemporization as 'intertemporal adaptation' or 'actualization' in which an 'old source' is relocated 'into more recent times' (7). In contrast, Pan Pan's contemporization of *A Doll's House* (2012) did not deconstruct the text, it just repositioned it in a contemporary setting, working with several layers of adaptability: 'intraideological transpositions retain the ideological landscape of their source [...] the shift in language, culture, or medium always entails a refocusing and repositioning of the adapted work, and consequently of its emphasis on specific issues' (Laera 7-8). Issues of translation also arose in this particular production. Pan Pan used four different translations of Ibsen's masterpiece and created its own performance text in a collaborative approach; that is, the actors' input was crucial in finding the 'right' contemporary expressions and terms, finding a balance between Irish localisms and international English. This process is called 'domestication' in Translation Studies, in which the text is bent in order to make it familiar to target audiences. This involved adopting idiomatic Irish expressions and cultural references, while keeping a balance between the local and the global. Another example is *Americanitis Presents The Seagull and Other Birds,* which can be understood within Tomlin's application of citational aesthetics to adaptation:

> not only can the adaptation no longer find an originary authority in the text it cites, as we have discussed, but that text itself can now be seen to be drawing from a 'real' which is no less another text, consisting of an infinite multiplicity of citations.' (2013, 98).

Pan Pan's allegiance to exploring and investigating the theatrical text – using what we might call scenographic adaptation – is epitomized in their two productions of Beckett's radio plays *All That Fall* (2012), and *Embers* (2013), winner of the Herald Angel Award at the Edinburgh International Festival 2013. The approach to scenography borrowed installational art aesthetics, which we can trace back to the avant-garde and Edward Gordon Craig's modernist idea of 'total theatre.' Pan Pan's aesthetics put the emphasis in creating an atmosphere that fosters an experience for the audience interweaving scenography, dramaturgy and performance style. In general, these atmospheres are associative rather than symbolic, although both Cosgrove and Quinn play with manifold signifying levels. In both *All That Fall* and *Embers* they created a communal effect through the act of listening: 'a social sculpture' of light and sound. Pan Pan's visual dramaturgy partially responds to Lehmann's assertion 'that theatre is not subordinated to the text and can therefore freely develop its own logic' (93); however the company's scenographies respond to an overall concept of the piece understood as a work of art.

Scenographically, *The Seagull and Other Birds* responded to its rehearsal environment: a dance studio. The actors, director, stage manager and assistant director were all present on stage dressed in ballet attire. The stage re-enacted the rehearsal space and it was bare except for a wooden floor and a few props, creating the sense of a space in process that responded to the performance dramaturgy: every night the show used different inter-texts, which were decided on the day. The concept of scenography as a space in process also responded to a new methodological approach: an open rehearsal process in which audiences could pop in at any time and, on occasion, were asked to actively participate in the rehearsal, and eventually during the performance. For instance, when Masha is looking for a husband, ten male spectators were picked from the audience and brought onstage for her to choose a candidate.

Conclusion

To conclude, the new reconsiderations of the keywords such as 'devised performance' and 'postdramatic theatre' enrich the critical frameworks and expand the terminologies necessary to analyse contemporary forms and their aesthetics. However, they are not exclusive or unreservedly oppositional as Tomlin's argument seems to assert following a genealogy of scholarly discourses. As she ultimately argues, 'all attempts to conclusively categorize artistic forms, in any case, will inevitably be defeated by the vital and necessary resistance of artistic forms to totalizing categorization' ('Foreword' x). Yet, it is of course vital and necessary to engage with critical and theoretical frameworks that allow us to understand and examine new theatre and performance practices and their methodologies. Thus, categorization is inevitable even if no artist is going to fit rigorously any given framework. However, as it has been exposed, these categorizations and its debates must be contextualized within cultural contexts, traditions and genealogies, in order to resist being limited by some forms of hegemonic academic discourse. Radosavljevic, for example, critiques Martin Puchner in this regard:

> Puchner is seemingly more radical in his insistence that only by a simultaneous emancipation of dramatic text as literature and theatre performance as art – and a subsequent idea of staging as a process of adaptation – would it be possible to transcend the polemic between text and performance which has dominated twentieth-century criticism in the Anglophone world.' (81)

All these debates are more than necessary in order to self-reflect on our contextual academic frameworks and to evolve and enrich our critical and analytical tools even if they will only ever be partial in their coverage. Thus, as it has been explored through Pan Pan's work as a representative case study, we can locate the company within the frame of European postdramatic aesthetics in which visual dramaturgy is fundamental to the overall conceptualization of the work. At the same time, Pan Pan's use of devised methodologies is in line with the European aesthetic-methodological model, which is collaborative without being in opposition with auteurism. Finally, we can also productively analyse Quinn's approach to text, acting, and performance strategies from the viewpoint of citational aesthetics and adaptation theory. These diverse critical frameworks provide a viable and ample set of tools to analyse and comprehend contemporary theatre and performance forms and their aesthetics in Pan Pan's work and beyond.

Works Cited

Albee, Edward. *Who's Afraid of Virginia Woolf?*. Richmond Hill, Ont.: Pocket of Canada,1962. Print.

Barton, Bruce. *Collective Creation, Collaboration and Devising*. Toronto: Playwrights Canada, 2008. Print.

Bogart, Anne, and Tina Landau. *The Viewpoints Book: A Practical Guide to Viewpoints and Composition*. New York: Theatre Communications Group, 2005. Print.

Bernhard, Thomas. *Histrionics: Three Plays*. Chicago: U of Chicago, 1990. Print.

Bottoms, Stephen. 'Authorizing the Audience: The Conceptual Drama of Tim Crouch.' *Performance Research: A Journal of the Performing Arts* 14.1 (2010): 65-76. Web. 10 Dec. 2012.

Chekhov, Anton Pavlovich, and Michael Frayn. *Plays*. London: Methuen, 1988. Print.

Fischer-Lichte, Erika. *History of European Drama and Theatre*. London: Routledge, 2002.Print.

Fortier, Mark. *Theory/Theatre: An Introduction*. London: Routledge, 2002. Print.

Gordon, Robert. *The Purpose of Playing: Modern Acting Theories in Perspective*. U of Michigan P, 2006. Print.

Harvie, Jen, and Andy Lavender, eds. *Making Contemporary Theatre*. Manchester UP, 2010. Print

Heddon, Deirdre, and Jane Milling. *Devising Performance: A Critical History*. Basingstoke: Palgrave Macmillan, 2006. Print.

Laera, Margherita. *Theatre and Adaptation: Return, Rewrite, Repeat*. London: Bloomsbury, 2014. Print.

Lehmann, Hans-Thies. *Postdramatic Theatre*. Trans. Karen Jürs-Munby. Oxon: Routledge, 2006. Print.

Radosavljevic, Duška. *Theatre-making: Interplay between Text and Performance in the 21st Century*. Houndmills, Basingstoke, Hampshire and New York: Palgrave Macmillan, 2013. Print.

Syssoyeva, Kathryn Mederos, and Scott Proudfit. *Collective Creation in Contemporary Performance*. New York: Palgrave Macmillan, 2013. Print.

---. 'Introduction: Toward a New History of Collective Creation.' *Collective Creation in Contemporary Performance*. Ed. Kathryn Mederos Syssoyeva and Scott Proudfit. New York: Palgrave Macmillan, 2013. 1-12. Print

Tomlin, Liz. *Acts and Apparitions: Discourses on the Real in Performance Practice and Theory, 1990 2010*. Manchester University Press. 2013. Print

---."'And their stories fell apart even as I was telling them": Poststructuralist performance and the no-longer-dramatic text.' *Performance Research: A Journal of the Performing Arts* 14.1 (2010): 57-64. Web. 10 Dec. 2012.

---. 'Foreword: Dramatic Developments.' *Contemporary British Theatre: Breaking New Ground*. Ed. Vicky Angelaki. Hampshire: Palgrave MacMillan, 2013. Print.

9 | An Interview with Gavin Quinn

Noelia Ruiz

Scenographer Aedín Cosgrove and director Gavin Quinn met in DU Players, the Trinity College Drama Society, where their first collaboration took place in 1990. They staged *The Vampire* by British dramatist J. R. Planché (an adaptation of Charles Nodier's *Le Vampire*, which was a dramatization of John Polidori's novel by the same title). The following year they premiered *Negative Act*, written and directed by Quinn and designed by Cosgrove, at the Lombard Street Studio Theatre (now Green on Red Galleries). The production was inspired by The Futurist Synthetic Theatre manifesto written in 1915 by F. T. Marinetti, Emilio Settimelli and Bruno Colla, and toured to the Lyon International Student Festival, France (1991). It was then that Cosgrove and Quinn decided to form Pan Pan Theatre. The company made a name for itself very quickly and in 1995 it was awarded Best Overall Production in the first Dublin Theatre Fringe Festival with *A Bronze Twist of Your Serpent Muscles*. The piece had been created for the Brouhaha International Arts Festival in Liverpool (1994), and was also presented at the Imaginaire Irlandais Festival in Marseille, France.

Both the European avant-garde and international touring have remained key in the aesthetics and evolution of the company. Furthermore, participating in different European Arts Festivals led Pan Pan to create the Dublin International Theatre Symposium (1997-2003), aiming to showcase international experimental work in Ireland. The Symposia consisted of a dynamic programme of talks, workshops, demonstration-performances and full productions. They gave Irish audiences the chance to engage with a variety of styles, approaches and viewpoints in experimental theatre from Europe and further afield. The Symposia were a seminal influence on the surge of new Irish experimental theatre-makers and was nominated for the Special Jury Award in the Irish Times Theatre Awards 2001. It also served as a springboard for the International Mentorship and Bursary Programme (2012-present), which this year has engaged Tim Crouch as a mentor to five selected participants.

Since it was formed Pan Pan Theatre has created twenty-eight theatre and performance pieces, toured worldwide, and received multiple national and international awards, including the Herald Angel Award at the Edinburgh International Festival 2013 for *All That Fall* and *Embers* by Samuel Beckett. The aesthetics of the company can be located within the postdramatic paradigm. Through an interdisciplinary methodology, Pan Pan's aim is to examine and interrogate the nature of theatre as an experiential art. Their last project, *Americanitis Presents The Seagull and Other Birds*, reflects the company's aim to examine and challenge its own work in order to resist well tried formulas. Quinn defines *Americanitis* as a frame to create an aesthetic onstage: work that is simple, precise and open to possibilities. Within this conceptual aim, *The Seagull* operates as a dramaturgical spine that allows for an investigation of form and content, in line with Chekhov's own experimentations with the dramatic conventions of his time. At the same time, the piece is a self-reflective research project that led the company to rehearsals which were open to spectators in order to explore a different relationship with the audience. It premiered in September at the Dublin Theatre Festival 2014. This interview took place after their first developmental phase, which was shown as a work-in-progress at the Dublin Theatre Festival 2013.

Noelia Ruiz: How would you define 'devised performance'?

Gavin Quinn: Well, devised performance is not a term that I would use for my own work. I find it has a sort of negative connotation for me, personally, that it suggests that people get in a room and randomly try out ideas and at the end of it they have a performance. I would consider the shows I work on as having a text. Whether there are words, actions, or simply ideas, they are texts, so in one sense they are for the theatre, so they are plays, even though they may not have dialogue or monologue on every aspect of every page. 'Devised' is, for me, a problematic word. It is a word that was used a lot in the UK, and it reminds me of when they use words like, 'cultural industry.' Words are important, but sometimes you can get too caught up on labelling work, and I think that the word, 'devised,' is not helpful.

N: So do you think there is another label to define the whole spectrum of contemporary theatre making? How would you define your work?

G: Every country has different labels. In Germany, they might say, 'progressive theatre;' they don't say, 'contemporary,' because that's just an arts movement. 'Avant-garde' is a hundred years old. In America, they still use 'avant-garde' and 'experimental.' 'Experimental' could be interesting. In Europe they use 'experimental' a lot. They have 'classical' and 'experimental' theatre so they can both coexist under those titles. Canadians would call the work we do *auteur*, because they have a tradition of that in the French-speaking Canadian world, with *auteur*-directors like Robert Lepage. I would describe our work as mostly 'idiosyncratic,' and that's the crux of it. It's definitely theatre, it's idiosyncratic, and it's contemporary dramaturgy, it's contemporary work and seen as contemporary work. But experimental is problematic, because it suggests that you're always trying things out, whereas after a while you tend to learn from your experiments and put that into practice. There are a couple of different characteristics of our work. There's certain work that's more installation-based, and other work which is very pure, very theatrical, very simple, so it's difficult to describe.

N: What led you to make work in this way?

G: When we started off with the company, there were only 4 or 5 companies in Ireland at the time, and they all existed pretty much in the literary tradition, so from the work that we saw, and we're not criticizing it, we thought it was good, but we didn't want to work for anybody else. We didn't want to work for the neck-down theatre, so we decided that we wanted to start our own company and make work that we wanted to see ourselves, and that develops into your own personality, your own company personality, or work personality.

N: Are there any artists who have inspired you or models of best practice?

G: Not really in terms of artists of best practice. I'm interested in everything, so of course, I admire work that I see, that has a specific atmosphere that you enjoy. In the past I have liked the work and atmosphere of some of the companies we brought over when we used to run the international symposium. I liked the atmosphere of some of Rodrigo García's pieces from La Carnicería in Madrid; they're rigorous, they have a certain intensity. I like some of the work of the Wooster Group in terms of the deconstructionism and of what they were willing to do, and how they evolved. And you can admire some of the work of

Castelluci, because he's trying to make the artwork on stage, but again, it's more the atmosphere than the influence. And in terms of other theatre-makers, going back in time, there's the importance of people like Artaud, and the idea of connecting the nervous energy he had to his work. I admire some of the work of Tadeusz Kantor. So it goes on and on, all those people who were pioneers and decided to experiment with form, and bring a real rigour to what they were trying to achieve. But in terms of model practices, I don't think so. You tend to think up the way you want to work.

N: Do you think there are any challenges or benefits to working in this way?

G: The benefit of working the way you want to work is that there's a freedom to what you're making, in terms of how you organize the workplace, of what you're doing, and choose your own programme. You choose your own programme not in a naïve way, but in a way that allows you to develop a work with audiences, because theatre works only when there is an audience, when it's concrete. The most important thing is the idea and the execution of the idea, so you can get rid of other political distractions, like if you're working in a bigger venue, or you had to work in a certain way that's prescriptive. So the advantages are the freedom and being able to follow a clear course between imagination, idea, carrying out of the idea, and the realization of it on stage, so you can follow a path which will get you somewhere, whereas if you probably worked it somewhere else, or if you worked for somebody else, then perhaps that path could be interrupted regularly, and it becomes muddy, and pretty soon it's no longer your own work, because people are interfering.

N: Do you consider that Irish theatre is still playwright's theatre nowadays?

G: By and large, Irish theatre is a playwright's theatre. I would agree with that. I mean, most of the work that is put on in the Abbey, the Gate, Druid, Rough Magic, Blue Raincoat, Corcadorca – all the companies primarily put on plays by new or else old [writers] ... but the main focus is to make the play work. Theatre is made up of different elements, so it's always a question of where the emphasis is. And you could see that in any production of a work. You could see where the emphasis lies. But if you do anything different it's very difficult in a small place because it's much easier to repeat what you've done before, so mostly it's playwriting still.

N: So what do you think is the role of 'devised' or 'contemporary' performance in Ireland?

G: There are a number of young people who are experimenting and making work, but it's all linked to theatre, the relationship to content, the relationship to form, it's all the same thing whether it's a play, a story, a piece without words, a dance piece, it's all in the same vein. I suppose their goal is to make good work. It's not a navel-gazing exercise. The role is to build an audience for their work and to make work which will have some energy behind it and will resonate with audiences either here or internationally. But the first thing they have to do is make good work, as opposed to being in love with the notion of making exciting new contemporary theatre, or whatever way you want to describe it, but the most important thing is that you have to earn your artistic stripes and make the work first, and make it have a certain quality, integrity and rigour, and put in the work to make it work, so that's the most important thing.

N: How do you compare contemporary Irish work to international work?

G: Hard to say without specific comparisons. I would say that a lot of the young companies make good contemporary work. It's quite young work. It has a certain atmosphere because they are trying to make it work in Ireland, make it work abroad, make it work for a local audience, and make it work for an international audience. It can be tricky negotiating what you're trying to do. But mostly it has a good feel to it, a lot of the young work that's coming out. It's quite authentic. Some of it has a feel of being half-finished, but I suppose that's because of the experience, or money, funding, or their attitude towards their work, and how much effort they want to put in.

N: In terms of Aedín being co-artistic director, how is that relationship? How does it work when you plan a new project?

G: Because we've worked together a long time, it works almost instinctively or through osmosis. We always have five or six things we want to do, and some things we'll keep in the private collection that we never need to do because perhaps we're not ready to do them or feel that it's not appropriate to do them. So we generally come up with what we'd like to do next. So it happens almost without thinking, and then eventually the idea comes out. You can't force the idea. You have to let the piece happen. You have to find out what it's really about, and then you can go forward in steps. But the commercial model of having it all … well in some cases things are very well thought-out beforehand and they can all be pre-planned. But mostly it's better to do it in steps. The commercial model is that it has to be ready at this particular time.

There's a four-week rehearsal period, there's a model block showing for their idea, and what you get is exactly the same as what you've seen.

N: When I joined you in the rehearsal room in 2011, you were workshopping the idea of staging *Exiles* by James Joyce and doing at the same time *All That Fall*; then in 2012 came *A Doll's House* and *Everybody is King Lear in his own home*, and in 2013 *Embers* and *Americanitis*. This is quite prolific and varied work: what is the impulse behind these different choices?

G: In our terms we want to attack different subject matters, different ideas in order to keep exploring. But they all feed into each other, although we always try to change course. Obviously, in the last while we have worked on quite robust material, such as *A Doll's House* and *King Lear*, as a way to investigate the doing of these pieces as well as their ideological impact. Why would you put on these pieces again? How? What does that mean? So that is mostly the reason. We can see it as a clear development of our work.

N: How do you approach the work?

G: Well, you find a way in, you find your own response to the piece and you formulate it, and that is what is contemporary about it. You are formulating your own response and you allow that to happen, you do not cut off that response. You are allowing yourself that sort of freedom to let it unfold, and therefore it suddenly becomes a very live event because it really connects to you, to the people who are doing it, and what you are trying to achieve. Therefore it is actually about allowing the expression to unfold and to be responsive to how you react, almost how you riff, to the piece.

N: In your adaptation of *A Doll's House* you respected the structure of the original play, whereas *King* was very deconstructed. Can you tell me more about this?

G: *King Lear* is a different performance and a different concept. The space becomes a found space, which is Andrew Bennett's flat, the actor's own space; but that found space gets moved to being on stage as an exact replica. It is a transient space, a sort of odd equation. That is the most important thing about that piece: it is the guy in his real flat presented onstage. So that is an installation, if you like, of Andrew Bennett's flat, along with a photography project and all his items listed. And then it is perceived as a theatre show because it is about a woman and a man essentially. She is a sort of carer/daughter/friend/neighbour who is looking after this older man, so that is the real story. And then through text, using some of the *King Lear* text in certain points it becomes a kind of *Lear* but it is a presentation of a certain kind of reality.

A Doll's House was a theatrical exercise, showing how this is the first modern play and it was questioning the whole notion of modernism, realism and naturalism. What is interesting about that play is that it really gets thought-provoking in the last act where it is just a conversation between a man and a woman sitting at a table – in the original – and discussing their life. We kind of did the piece for the last scene but also we wanted to examine Ibsen's innovation in terms of the purpose of doing it now.

N: What about Beckett's two radio plays, *All That Fall* and *Embers*?

G: They are very much about creating a world, and specifically with *All That Fall* it was the idea of making a social sculpture where we come and listen to a radio-play. So the first thing was to create an environment, a chamber, whereby people would come and watch each other listening, having a communal effect and that in a sense is like an event. The second piece is different because *Embers* was front-done, proscenium, live-actors inside a skull, an example of sculpture and light. But they both have this very deep investigation of inner voices, subconscious, memory and story. *All That Fall* was written for the minimal radio and the mechanical elements Beckett was bringing out are very obvious. In *Embers* he is going much deeper into the whole idea of the psyche and the superpower of voices and how a voice becomes more than just a person, it becomes something else, it becomes sound waves, it becomes an artistic creation: the voice becomes a creation itself. Henry is a character that is not even a human being; he is like a sort of proton being, almost transliminal. So the idea was trying to connect with sound, with voice, with words, becoming partly musical, partly supernatural almost. They are very particular investigations and we were looking at presenting Beckett's radio work for a live audience and to create a space for these elements to come out.

N: As an audience member it was a great experience because the text is very dense and your production clarified it, making it accessible. I am guessing it was also a great experience for you to dissect it.

G: It was a great experience to really hear the text moment by moment and this worked best with *Embers* because you don't try to join up the dots, as it's not written that way. You just experience it sentence by sentence, moment by moment, so it does feel like a brain thinking, whether that's story or whether that's memory or whether it gyrates between the two. The clarity of the text is quite extraordinary and it is an amazing and powerful experience to follow a text like that and to be really immersed in it when you are hearing it every day in rehearsals and it becomes ingrained in some way. *Embers* is like a snake that wraps itself around you, coils itself around you; and it goes back to what Beckett said specifically about *Endgame* that the text should claw you; it's not too light, it's not too soft, it's not too dark, but the idea of the text coming out and clawing you like a living being that gets under your skin, in your skin, that actually causes you harm almost. And I think that is a very interesting concept, the text clawing you.

N: What is *Americanitis*?

G: I'm still trying to answer that question. I have written a little bit about it. What I hoped it would be is the atmosphere, and a piece we can do in any room, a theatre, a rehearsal space or a town hall. But that doesn't really matter, it's not like it's meant to be easily moved. It's more that you walk in and you realize that the rules of this performance are that anything can happen, it can go anywhere, and putting all the emphasis on the content and in the simplicity of just doing it in a room without all the other elements that are kind of pre-decided. *Americanitis* is really a frame to make new work, it could be perceived as a kind of festival, so one could imagine putting up a poster on the day in the room and saying 'we are now doing this performance.' And this performance is meant to show, I suppose, how a world can be so flexible, how our minds can be so flexible. *Americanitis* is a slang word for neurasthenia, which is this urban anxiety you have from living in the city, and it's meant to mean that you have an alive nervous system. What we are trying to do with the piece is to travel through different texts and experience different stories so we are able to respond and evolve the piece to where it should go, and we don't know where it's going yet. If you had to describe it you could describe it as a mash-up of different texts. But it's not even that. You could describe it as a post-poor theatre, asking the classic question: what can theatre do without? But maybe that's too loaded. It's more an expression of what it is trying to create, a mood and an atmosphere in a theatre performance whereby there is genuine mystery but at the same time there is a charm to it, there is a lightness of touch. The worst part of *Americanitis* is how you can describe it and that's gonna be problematic because people don't want to hear that the piece is mysterious. We had to describe it a few times to people and it's proving very difficult. But it is about this flexibility we have, about our minds changing, about how we can take on new things. My hope is that we'd be able to perform different pieces on different nights, like Monday could be all new work, Tuesday could be *The Seagull* plus new work, Wednesday could be nothing. The most extreme thing is to do nothing, obviously.

N: You also told me that *Americanitis* was also a sort of self-reflexive research project.

G: It is a sort of research project too, yes. There is a sort of quasi-scientific element to it in terms of art as research as a total project, so part of the idea is that all of the rehearsal notebooks that I have for the last twenty years directing plays are going to be part of the show: as part of the exhibition of the show, or as part of the material of the show, or actively used live or talked about or spoken or influencing the way the event goes. In a way you can say that *Americanitis* could be like a happening or an event, but I'm trying to search for a couple of things: one is a very particular relationship with the audience, and secondly a way of dealing with complex issues or themes in a very simple way. It's pretty much an idealistic spirit because you are trying to discover new things, you are open to it, and at the same time you are looking at the notion of entertainment in theatre, what that means. We had an audience from the very beginning, so it's looking at that connection that makes for a particular energy and developing certain skills that you hone along the way in terms of how you communicate with an audience, with people. It's an experiment on how many types of plays there are, how many types of theatre and performances there are, how many types of caveats there are, so it's that idea of open discovery. But it would probably end up being something quite simple, I would imagine.

N: How has the experience been of having an audience in rehearsal, or more specifically, a pop-in audience? And did that feedback influence or shape the piece?

G: Yes. It was wonderful coming at five to ten and finding people waiting for you in the rehearsal room. That was interesting; it was a turn on its head. You are immediately on and turned on by having an audience there; it allows you to move forward and do and make, and not get obsessed with talking, which I don't think really helps in the rehearsal space. We also did once-off performances with the audience, which will never be done again. We got them to perform some of the pieces, mixing up the audience on the stage and in the audience, and that created a very interesting dynamic. The audience sometimes were sort of just part of the space and sometimes they were speaking or moving, so they become part of the material and you become accustomed to the audience, they are not just this odd surprise at the end of the rehearsal process. So far it's informing the work and it's of benefit and I'll continue that.

N: This approach brings many interesting questions to the very nature of theatre, of what Paul Woodruff calls 'The Art of Watching and Being Watched,' and the relationship with an audience, as well as opening the hidden world of the rehearsal room (paraphrasing Susan Letzer Cole).

G: It brings a lot of questions about growing and nurturing as well. The actor normally doesn't have a chance to respond to the audience until the first preview, so in this sense the actor is responding to an audience and it's like a new form of light, a new form of energy almost, a completely different attitude. You can see how it may have negatives and positives towards that: people might get too used to an audience, they could take it for granted, you might end up fighting for an audience. But it doesn't really matter. I'm not abandoning the actors onstage, it's very much a fluid space where things happen and you can tell it is charming and not offensive; it has a good atmosphere and not an oppressive atmosphere.

N: Why did you choose the specific texts that were used during the process, such as *The Seagull* by Chekhov, *Boy in a Boat* by Rob de Graaf, Who's afraid of Virginia Woolf? by Albee, *Histrionics* by Thomas Bernhard or the short story *Godigums* by Keith Ridgway?

G: We explored about thirty to thirty-five plays, a couple of short films, a couple of ideas and about thirty or forty concepts, so I created a whole wealth of material for this piece. They fitted together well, the notion of the actor on tour morphing into the story of the man on tour, which is the individual who emigrates, lives abroad, and comes back, but in that really strange sense of coming back and then lying about this life that no one's ever seen, lying with that risk of being caught out, but then lying literally to yourself. So there is the notion of inscribing your own stories upon yourself and then the lies become inscribed and you are wondering who is who and what you are. So it's similar to the notion of 'theatrical lying' and of being on tour doing plays and then ending with the notion of the chamber play, which is the classic situation of entering and exiting. So they went together for a number of reasons and we made the decision because you have to make a decision. There were other pieces that we would have done.

N: I really enjoyed *Histrionics*, which is almost an anti-theatrical manifesto.

G: It's interesting to begin with that because it sets up a proposition for the audience. It kind of designates what's meant to happen in a sense, and you see everything through that lens to an extent, as you do in any situation where you come in and the mood starts, or there is an atmosphere in the room. You begin propositions, they can be theatrical propositions or more intellectual propositions, and then you see how they come and go, and die, and get legs, and filter, and go through, and how they all intertwine. And then you add a second proposition to that and then the first proposition comes back later on and the second one disappears. So it's how you build a response from the audience through the layering of your material but also through the different propositions that you make throughout the piece and the answers that you give, and the questions that you give, and the questions you don't answer and the ones you do answer; all that sort of interplay is what makes the world, the room, the performance quite rich, making clarity out of disparate parts; there is a link, you are not quite sure but it seems to have a flow. Because one of the aims of *Americanitis* is the attentive suicide of non-representational theatre, so the idea is what does theatre represent? But also when theatre represents things it doesn't really represent anything because it's not reality.

Works Cited

Woodruff, Paul. *The Necessity of Theater: The Art of Watching and Being Watched.* Oxford University Press, 2008. Print.

Fig.1 Sorcha Kenny in ANU Productions' *Laundry*.
Photo: Pat Redmond

Fig.2 Lloyd Cooney and Caitirona Ennis in ANU Productions' *Boys of Foley Street*. **Photo: Pat Redmond**

Fig.3 John Finegan as Desmond O'Prey and Ciaran Kenny as Teddy O'Sullivan in Upstate's 2006 revival of *Hades*

Fig. 4 A Scene from Upstate's *The Mango Tree* (2011). Photo by Matt Dillon

Fig.5 (L to R) Andrew Bennett, Gina Moxley, Daniel Reardon, Samantha Pearl, Dick Walsh and Una McKevitt in Pan Pan's *Americanitis* presents *The Seagull & Other Birds* (Dublin Theatre Festival 2014). Photo by Ros Kavanagh

**Fig.6 Zita Monahan in Martin Sharry's *King Alfred: A Mystery Play*.
Photo by Jaesin Yu, JS Photographic**

Fig.7 (L to R) Kate Murray, Jarlath Tivnan, Seamus O'Donnell, Teresa Brennan, Oísín Robbins and Maria Tivnan in Fregoli's *Home*, Nun's Island Theatre, Galway (2012). Photo by Rob McFeely

Fig.8 Blue Raincoat's *At the Hawk's Well* (2010) with John Carty, Sandra O'Malley, Fiona McGeown (Chorus), Marketa Formanova (Hawk Woman), Ciaran McCauley and Niall Henry (Old Man and Young Man) at The Factory, Sligo. Image by kind permission of Joe Hunt and Blue Raincoat

Fig.9 Blue Raincoat's *The Cat and the Moon* (2009) with Ciarán McCauley, Fiona McGeown, Sandra O'Malley as the Chorus. Image (2010) by kind permission of Joe Hunt and Blue Raincoat

Fig.10 Patrick McCabe's *Frank Pig Says Hello* with Jarlath Tivnan as Piglet. Photo by Jane Talbot

Fig.11 The Reliables teach Pius Mulvey (Zita Monahan) a lesson in Moonfish's devised stage adaptation of Joseph O'Connor's novel *Star of the Sea*. Galway Arts Festival, 2014. Photo by Marta Barcikowska

Fig.12 Grace Kiely as Grantley Dixon in Moonfish's devised stage adaptation of Joseph O'Connor's novel *Star of the Sea*. Galway Arts Festival, 2014. Photo by Marta Barcikowska

Fig.13 Actor Fran Gunn as Barney in Kabosh Theatre's *Belfast Bred* (2010).
Image courtesy of the Northern Ireland Tourist Board

Fig.14 Antoinette Morelli and Gerard Jordan in Kabosh Theatre's *The West Awakes* (2010). Photo by Aidan Monaghan

Fig.15 Poster image for TheatreofplucK's first incarnation of *Divided, Radical and Gorgeous*. D.R.A.G. was first performed as part of the OUTburst Queer Arts Festival in 2011. Performed by Gordon Crawford. Photo by Simon Crawford

Fig.16 Karl Schappell in TheatreofplucK's *Automatic Bastard* (2005). Photo by Niall Rea

Fig.17 *Urban Circus*, the 2004 Belfast Community Circus Youth Circus show. Photo by Will Chamberlain

Fig.18 *PaperDolls* (Elaine McCague, Emily Aoibheann and Karen Anderson) at the Festival of Fools, Belfast, 2012.
Photo by kind permission of Belfast Community Circus

Fig.19 Image of *Decadence* by St Petersburg group Mr Pejo's Wandering Dolls. Belfast festival of fools 2010. Photo by Grant Goldie

Section Three: Regional Practices

10 | Staging Blue Raincoat's production of W.B. Yeats's *The Cat and the Moon* (2009) and *At the Hawk's Well* (2010)

Rhona Trench

Introduction

Two of Yeats's one-act dramas, *At the Hawk's Well* and *The Cat and the Moon* are the plays; Kellie Hughes is the director; Jo Conway is the guest set and costume designer; Joe Hunt, the sound designer; Michael Cummings, the lighting designer. Blue Raincoat Theatre Company will stage the play in the company's resident space, the Factory, in Sligo. All involved in the realization of the productions have been sent the texts to read before they meet for workshops and rehearsals. There are definite scripts, a director, designers, a cast and a rehearsal space.

But the director does not know how these productions will take shape, though she is likely to have an imagined vision of it. The set and costume designer does not know what the world of the plays will look like or what the actors will wear though she may have some concepts in mind. The lighting designer does not know what he is lighting other than the kind of plays to be lit and the space where they will be staged. The performers may have their viewpoints on characterization, how they will deliver their lines, what they will wear and how they will move in a space, but without the collaborative input of the other creative artists. How then does devising feature in this situation, particularly when the works to be realized are authored by Yeats? And how is this different from a traditional rehearsal process?

Devised theatre is often considered as having no script as the starting point for making a performance. In this understanding of devised theatre, the 'script' emerges instead from concepts and ideas shared collaboratively by all participants in the rehearsal room which may (or may not) be written down by any of the people in the room. A director, if there is one, might shape the overall concept that arises from this process, as well as generally sequencing the performance; s/he is not necessarily considered the leading creative artist in the process. Alex Mermikides and Jackie Smart state: 'Devising work involves practitioners in articulating their private thoughts to each other, explaining their intentions and their reactions to ideas, improvisations and other proto-performances' (2). In doing so, what would have been carried out in the traditional rehearsal process (the director would meet the designers in private and they would work in isolation, presenting their work to the cast and crew before rehearsals begin) becomes a shared venture with everyone present from the beginning of the realization process.

This chapter examines Blue Raincoat Theatre Company's realization process of Yeats's *At the Hawk's Well* and *The Cat and the Moon* arguing that devising approaches were adopted within the process of making these productions. The plays were rehearsed in a similar manner to a devised show. The approach to theatre-making not only utilized the performers' creative potential but harnessed the creativity of all those involved in realizing the works, inspiring each other and collaborating on ideas, discussions, plans, research and praxis.

This interpretation follows a reading of Blue Raincoat's process through Pierre Bourdieu's concept of *habitus* as defined in *The Logic of Practice* (1980). *Habitus* shares similar principles with devising in terms of discovery and integration. Like the individual's sense of play, *habitus* frees the performer to engage in invention and improvisation within the demands of the performance. For Bourdieu, *habitus* is not a group of actions, but rather a set of systems of productive principles for determining actions, 'functioning like a conductorless orchestra' (53). Objectively 'regulated' and 'regular' without being in any way the product of obedience to rules, they can be 'collectively orchestrated without being the product of the organizing action of a conductor'(53). Within this framework, this chapter considers the paradox inherent in the notion of Blue Raincoat's collaborative work. On the one hand, the social and cultural systems of hierarchy within the company determine how power and status operate. On the other, the objectives of these productions brought about by the creative process (which included devising), and the forms of the plays themselves, demanded the realization of the works as a shared experience.

A Visual Impetus

Blue Raincoat is known for its proficiency in physical theatre, influenced by the company members' training in Étienne Decroux's method of performance, a technique of devising that encourages the creative potential of the performer in accessing the imagination through the body, and in considering spoken and written text as elements of performance within a wider performance idiom. Decroux preferred to veil the face to give emphasis to the body, and promoted slower movements (an Eastern influence) to help with body awareness and attune a disciplined mind. He encouraged improvisation and games to help liberate the imagination, which frees the actor from being tied into particulars and allows her/him to work with a *feeling* or *idea* and not a literal aspect of the text (Bicât and Baldwin 9). Performers get to respond to one another in the context of the visual tapestry of the performance, and do not react to something specific in the story or portrayal of characters. Yet Heddon and Milling are mindful of the limits of self-expression through improvisation:

> [S]elf expression is paradoxical, since at the same moment as the performance is made more authentic or truthful by seeming to arise directly from the actor's 'self,' it is simultaneously a display of their technical virtuosity and artistry, facilitated by training and exercises (30).

Thus, the conditions in which improvisation takes place shape the already established set of experiences shared by the group's training.

Blue Raincoat's physical discipline is corporeal mime, espoused in the practices and ideologies of Decroux, who was inspired by earlier performance traditions and experiments, principally the work of Jacques Copeau. Copeau demanded that actors commit to strict timetables of rigorous daily exercise, including athletics, dance, games, movement, improvisation, slowness and silence. Copeau wanted his actors to access a more instinctual creativity, and a simplicity of movement in which external action is matched by state of mind. Copeau was Decroux's teacher 'who himself was inspired by circus artists and the traditions of commedia dell'arte and Japanese Noh theatre' (Callery 8).

Yeats's *At the Hawk's Well* and *The Cat and the Moon* are Noh-inspired dramas which advocate a non-literal, non-realistic theatre – a physical theatre of fantasy, dream and metaphor. Interestingly, Edward Gordon Craig was a significant influence on Yeats. Craig's principles of unity for the stage are a devising method where line, colour, sound and movement work together in dramatic form, exploiting the holistic power of theatre as a medium. Additionally, Craig, an admirer of Decroux's work, sought the actor to achieve the ideal performer, conceived in his *übermarionette* concept; this was a masked actor-puppet which he felt was a more 'pure' character, with a reduced sense of the actor's presence. Again, Craig's ambition for actors shares what devising seeks to accomplish, that is, placing the imaginative responsibility on the actor as a central resource.

James Flannery describes Yeats's ambition for the stage as follows:

> The convention of the Noh – including masks, ritual, dance and symbolic posture, all exercised within a vividly concentrated stage environment emphasizing the human being as the primary expressive instrument – are what Yeats employs to carry the audience into the phantasmagorical reaches of the imaginal. Always as an audience member experiencing a Yeats production, one is conscious of existing in the same time and place as the performers as well as others in the audience. Always the possibility of passing over into an altered state of consciousness is present ('Staging the Phantasmagorical' 95).

What Flannery describes is Yeats' desire to produce work which can be seen as akin to the aesthetics of devised theatre, work in which fluid imagery and contrast serves to punctuate a loose narrative, unified by a ritual style that carries an ideological message. The demands of Yeats' dramas then require physically skilled actors, who are proficient in ritualized movement and mask work, as a way of striving for the poetic possibilities of the stage in ways that might achieve a theatre of heightened consciousness.

For Blue Raincoat, devising is common practice in rehearsals. These rehearsals are informed by the company performers' training in Decroux's style of physical theatre in which devising is a regular part of the work. The company has a resident performance/rehearsal space called The Factory in Sligo town, which also informs the company's practice and the scenographic aesthetics of its work. The performance space, where the actors also rehearse, is fully enclosed and its configuration (size and shape) impacts on what is going on onstage as well as in the audience. The space is rectangular in shape, and the performers and audience use the same entrance. Its raked seating flanks the entrance doors and provides good sight-lines for the audience. The raked seating is four metres (approximately) from the performance area. The space has no wings or open scene docks above for flying in backdrops. There are exits stage left, one a fire exit and the other one at the back wall used by the performers. The ceiling height is six meters, and from the floor to the lighting grid is five-and-a-half metres. The width of the space is eleven metres, ten centimetres. The raised seating bay when there is a full house helps to soak the various frequencies of sound and, in doing so, reduces the 'bounce' or 'reflections' off the back wall. The space does not require monitors for the actors to hear sound cues. Thus, the dimensions of the space no matter where an audience member sits provoke intimacy between the performers and the audience, which contributes to the overall experience of the production.

Significantly too, the company boasts that it is a venue-based ensemble theatre company. The word 'ensemble' is worth exploring because while it yields ideas about something 'shared' or 'brought together,' what exactly is being shared, who is sharing it and how it is being shared is called into question. According to the Oxford English Dictionary, the word 'ensemble' is a French word for 'group,' but it holds different meanings about the group depending on what that group is and in what context it works. Its roots lie in the Latin word '*insimul*' meaning 'at the same time.' In a theatre context, the meaning emphasizes the roles of all performers as a whole rather than singling out principal performers. In general, however, the term refers to all parts of something considered together.

Ensemble for Blue Raincoat means that as a permanent group (most of the cast and crew have been working together for over ten years and some have been with the company since its foundation) with a resident performance/rehearsal space, the company's practice stems from a shared language and aesthetic. Over the duration of such a long period working together, the talents and skills of company members have developed in tandem with one another. Trust and familiarity are part of the ensemble. The longevity of the membership, together with the performers' Decroux-style training, allows the collaborative practice to rid itself of the traditional division of labour typically associated with theatre in Ireland and elsewhere in the West. While this has the possible disadvantage of the group getting tired of one another, Blue Raincoat often try to alleviate potential lethargy by employing guest member(s) and/or changing the roles within the ensemble; this alters the dynamic and brings new challenges and provocations to the group. The devised and collaborative process, therefore, draws on what ensemble theatre means specifically to Blue Raincoat.

Typically, of course, it is only at the curtain-up stage of a production that an audience will get to see the completed work by the group. Details about what to share, what to keep and what to discard, what to refine, attune and adjust are difficult to measure because in devising, the creative moments can happen suddenly and by the time they are developed, the original idea may get lost or forgotten. What can be said about Blue Raincoat's ensemble is that all ideas that are shared get tried and tested through the physical manipulation of the body in the space and with all designers present from the beginning of the process. However, despite the shared aesthetic, (as with any group) the company members come to the rehearsal space with different levels of skills, abilities and talents on which to draw. As Alison Oddey writes:

> Devized theatre offers the performer the chance to explore and express personal politics and beliefs in the formation and shaping of the piece. [...] A performer/deviser has a personal input and commitment to the making of the product from the start, which consequently means that the needs for the performer/deviser are recognized, and therefore different for the actor in the text-based theatre (11).

Unlike the roles and responsibilities defined by text-based theatre, which might restrict the actor to a specific job, in devised theatre the performer might draw on a wider spectrum of talents including administration and developmental research work. Claiming that Blue Raincoat employs devising is not to say that company members do not have designated roles. Nor do they ignore the different skills, abilities, qualifications, and training between members within the group. What it does suggest is that some roles are more fluid than others.

Bourdieu reminds us that our *habitus* or the 'common sense' way we interpret the world is massively affected by the very specific structures of gender, class, age, ethnicity, industry, politics and culture which defines who we are and how we think 'because the *habitus* has an infinite capacity for generating thoughts, perceptions, expressions and actions but within the limits set by the historically and socially situated conditions of its production' (Bourdieu 55). Considered in this context, the way in which Blue Raincoat operates can be seen as constantly evolving, shaped by the group from within – while from outside, factors such as the economy, society and technology also impact on their working processes. Thus, the economic pressure of the recession, advances in technology and the changing face of communication are some of the factors affecting the company. Currently, for instance, budgetary constraints have placed pressure on members to work in other areas depending on the needs of the particular production, including Box Office, PR, prop sourcing and the general day-to-day maintenance of the space.

Other *'habitus'* factors include Hughes's position as the youngest and most recent member of the company (Hughes joined in 2004); her third level qualifications in addition to her training at The Theatre de l'Ange Fou and the International School of Corporeal Mime in London; the fact that she is the company's first female director; the company's geographical position in the North-West of Ireland; that Blue Raincoat is one of a handful of professional companies to be regularly funded by the Arts Council; each member's personality; how long they have known each other; and so on. To hone in on the impact of funding, as one of only seven regularly funded organizations in Irish theatre, Blue Raincoat has been able to develop and evolve its physical style through productions, teaching, seminars and workshops. However, with cuts in state funding for the arts across the board since 2007, the impact on Blue Raincoat means that planning, programming, touring, remuneration, staffing and marketing have all been affected. This has had a knock on effect on budgets for each production, affecting in the case of these Yeats' plays the devising methods employed.

A Cursory Glance at the Style of the Productions

In *At the Hawk's Well*, the Old Man and Young Man (played in Blue Raincoat's production by Ciaran McCauley and Niall Henry respectively) are looking to drink the waters of immortality and both are deceived by the hawk woman (played in Blue Raincoat's production by Marketa Formanova) who guards the dried up well on the desolate mountain top. For Blue Raincoat's 2010 production of the play in The Factory, the lights slowly came up to reveal a wide circle of scattered stone designating the performance area. In the dim light, an Old Man and Young Man bent to the ground to take their masks and put them on. Two high pitched sounds from a triangle initiated the three-member chorus who sat upstage right to the audience and who began singing: 'I call to the eye of the mind/A well long choked and dry/ And boughs long stripped by the wind/And I call to the mind's eye ...' (899).

A similar ritualized scene opened Blue Raincoat's *The Cat and the Moon* (2009), also performed in 2010 in The Factory, revealing a circular space demarcated by reeds and lit in a soft yellow hue. A low rumble drumming created the rhythm for the three-member chorus and the two performers, a Blind Man (John Carty) and Lame Man (Niall Henry) to enter. They entered where the audience had come in and followed outside the path of reeds to the right. The chorus went through the break in the circle upstage centre and came to sit on the reeds upstage right, face the audience and set up their instruments. The

Old Man and Young Man took their masks from the upright canes which were positioned upstage and slightly to the left. They put the masks on and remained by the canes until the chorus had sung the opening phrase of the production. A chorus member began by making a four-note rhythm with a zither. Another joined in using a brush banged against the wooden box on which she was sitting. The last made the rhythm beating sticks. The rhythm sounds then stopped. The singing began:

> The cat went here and there
> And the Moon spun round like a top,
> And the nearest kin of the moon
> The creeping cat, looked up.
> Black Minaloushe stared at the Moon,
> For, wander and wail as he would.
> The pure cold light in the sky
> Troubled his animal blood. (Yeats 792-793)

When the singing stopped, the performers entered the circular space taking up the opening dialogue of the play: 'One thousand and six, one thousand and seven, one thousand and nine. Look well now for we should be in sight of the holy well of Saint Coleman' (Yeats 793). In *The Cat and the Moon*, a Blind man and Lame man search for the holy well that might cure their afflictions. Dependent on each other (the Blind man carries the Lame man on his back/the Lame man acts as Blind Man's guide) yet increasingly frustrated by that dependence, they set off in search of transformation.

Devising Sound, Set and Costume

The process involved in realizing Blue Raincoat's productions of *At the Hawk's Well* and *The Cat and the Moon* took the company two intense weeks each, where the five performers together with the lighting designer, sound designer and a guest set and costume designer worked collaboratively on these texts in the Factory for the duration of the rehearsals. Rather than delve into the complexity of the written text, broad ideas about both plays were introduced by Hughes in her role as director. Ritual became the starting point for the productions with everyone responding to the concept of ritual from her/his area of expertise. On stage, it became apparent that the range of forms called on by ritual demanded rhythm, song, movement (also involving an interaction with costumes and masks) and dance supported by lighting, sound, set and costume design. Ritual was examined through performance but imaginative ideas and concepts were developed collectively through research and life experiences. A layering of ideas around ritual happened daily through exploratory physical, mask and vocal work using impulse reaction, interaction and improvisation which became movement and sound.

The role of the chorus, for Hughes, is at the poetic heart of these works. Playing a pivotal role in the plays, the chorus acts as a guide for the audience, underscoring the action, setting and tone for the entire creative process and resulting production. Rather than have three performers play individual musicians as indicated in both scripts, Hughes merged the musicians together, placing their differences into one body and strengthening their power. In *The Cat and the Moon*, the musicians also played the role of the Saint; the connection between the chorus and the Saint enhanced the moment of transformation in the text. The ritual tone of the chorus literally and metaphorically helped the actors to find pathways in the space to journey from degeneration to spiritual renewal, struggling between action and contemplation, between blind faith and active discovery. These themes emerged through devising, in the development of the concept of ritual, by keeping ideas about ritual influenced by the text, in a loose framework.

Sound designer Hunt created the original scores for the pieces, devising a choral song inspired by what he was seeing in front of him during rehearsals. In the evenings he would work on his ideas and share these with the ensemble the following day. Initially, Hunt worked on a sean-nós air – an unaccompanied, highly ornamented, stylized form of Gaelic singing which is usually used to express loss, the sadness of daily existence, nature, or to record a historical and/or political event. However, the air was abandoned after being tested out because its ornamentation distracted from the movement in performance. Hughes felt it detracted from the slow ritualized imagery emerging from devised movement patterns, disrupting the sense of unity inherent in the dramatic composition.

Subsequently, other sound ideas were tried and tested, which came to evolve into a simple four-note tune, sung slowly in a minor key. The song set the ritualistic atmosphere and mood of the plays in motion, and the processional hymn-like chant which resonated in the brick-walled space of The Factory offered some of the inspiration for Hughes' direction, as well as Cummings's lighting and Conway's scenography. There was always something circular concerning ritual that resonated with these collaborators; this, together with broad ideas about the natural world, offered ways in for creating the set, costume and lighting designs for the productions. Cummings's lighting, for example, designated the ritual space, giving emphasis to its circular shape and flooding the circle with different whites, ambers, yellow and reds, depending on the action. He operated the lighting cues live with the performances (not just in rehearsal but for the run of the productions), allowing fluid devising methods to change as the pieces developed.

Designing the set for *The Cat and the Moon*, Conway found herself drawn to the work of sculptor and land artist Richard Long, particularly for his use of materials like stone, mud and driftwood. Long is renowned for his walks through the world's landscapes, where he leaves marks or pathways on the world. The circle for *The Cat and the Moon* was initially going to be demarcated by upright reeds, giving emphasis to Blind Man and Lame Man's disabilities as they negotiated the natural rugged landscape. However, financial constraints contributed towards the decision to lay the reeds flat in the circle, because the amount of reeds needed and the structures necessary to support the upright reeds proved too costly.

In *At the Hawk's Well*, Conway felt the chorus/musicians had an earthier role to play in the telling of the story, bearing witness to the central events embodied by the Old Man/Young Man in the circle. While Conway was observing the performers working amidst the stones, the stones reminded her of the barren landscapes of work camps, particularly of photographs by August Sander, who recorded ordinary German people between and during the First and Second World Wars. Conway also looked at images of Jewish people in ghettos, observing how people were becoming almost spectral before her eyes. She sought to have the set design reflect a shallow crater, echoing something like a river bed and/or a shattered graveyard, something earthy and grounded. The stone she collected came from a building that had been demolished. Conway recollects:

> I felt that the roughness and subtlety of the stones spoke of the parchedness and tragedy of the story. We tried out various arrangements on the Factory floor, but with the tired nature of the Old Man and Young Man's physical efforts, and the cyclical nature of the play, quite soon the circle emerged. (6 July 2010)

The visual design was simple and came about from being in the rehearsal space, watching the scenes unfold. Haibo Yu reminds us that in devised work, a humble budget will force the designer to be economical and efficient: 'Minimalism and simplicity should be seriously considered as valuable design principles for low-budget theatre productions' (Yu qtd. in Bicât and Baldwin, 33). Watching, listening and hearing in the rehearsal space, Conway recalls how the space for the pieces came about quite quickly using stone (*Hawk's Well*) and reeds (*Cat and Moon*) in a broken circle, which she felt gave a timeless quality to the work: 'It formed a performance space that was ritualistic and particularly sensitive to the fabric of the Factory space itself, with its exposed brickwork. And it also offered a diverse range of movement possibilities for the bodies that would be working within it' (4 July 2013).

The costumes too were inspired by watching and listening to the scenes unfolding in the space. Conway looked to the work of Mexican artist/muralist Diego Rivera, whose monumental figures came to mind when the actors started to inhabit the reed arena. Rivera's figures were slow and ritualistic, offering a sense of other worldliness. Without wanting to lose the nomadic narrative in the Old Man/Young Man characters, or making the Musicians look the same as them, Conway opted for a tight palette of colours so that the distinctive physicalities of the performers were clearly defined, yet captured in the overall ritualistic spell of the production. The Hawk woman (dancer) too was clothed in natural bleached fabric and, like the beggars, the material allowed her to move freely, revealing the sculpted nature of her body and limbs. Like most devised work, changes can happen up until the final day of rehearsal, and in this production all performers came to be covered late in the process with Fuller's Earth powder so that everyone looked hot, dusty and bleached, reflecting the sombre nature inherent in the work.

Devising Movement: A Micro-Scene Process

A close examination of Blue Raincoat's *The Cat and the Moon* reveals a devised form of theatre, which dramaturgically places the image as equal to the spoken text and which therefore pays close attention to the visual potentials of stage pictures. To choose one scene from potentially many, the fight scene in *The Cat and the Moon* illuminates the ways in which the company used devising methods to realize the action. Carty and Henry as Lame Man and Blind Man worked on rhythm first through the technique of action/reaction. They based their movements on the reason for their fight. Blind Man, suspicious that people 'are always stealing [his] things and telling [him] lies' (799), accuses Lame Man of stealing his black sheepskin coat which Lame Man wears. Lame Man insists that his sheepskin coat is white and 'made of the most lovely white wool [...] that would dazzle you' (801). The Blind Man's and Lame Man's physical disabilities can be healed by the Saint but they each cannot be both blessed and healed. Lame Man elects to be blessed instead of getting the power of his legs. Blind Man chooses to have his sight restored and when this happens, he sees that Lame Man is wearing his black sheepskin coat. That moment stirs old vengeful thoughts into physical action:

> I have a long arm and a strong arm and a weighty arm, and when I get my own two eyes I shall know where to hit... I shall know where to hit and how to hit and who to hit (802).

In Blue Raincoat's production, the chorus alerted the audience to the fight with a special kind of expectancy. Increased percussive noises marked the tension between Blind Man and Lame Man, and monotonic rhythms from all instruments denoted the change of mood which culminated in the physical attack. Hughes explains her vision for the Chorus:

> The Chorus is a constant presence in the play. They are a watching presence in the frame. They need to be seen as continually active in creating the presented drama. They underpin the action with the sounds they create.

The fight scene, carried out in the form of a 'dance' and bathed in a soft red light, was broken by a rhythm change performed by drum beats by a chorus member, and demonstrated what Decroux terms 'dynamo rhythms [...] a way of describing the weight, speed and path of a movement' (qtd. in Leabhart 82). Decroux's 'dynamo rhythms' gave emphasis to sharpened senses, as well as contributing to the performers' abilities to observe and receive impressions and situations as if they were second nature.

During the first three days of rehearsals for *The Cat and the Moon*, the actors were working with natural forms of movement loosely inspired by the text. Hughes wanted to simplify certain gestures and movements. Rather than give sterility to movements, Hughes asked Carty and Henry to amplify (not exaggerate) their hostile/protective gestures. By doing this, the underlying antagonism/defence motivations involved in the action/reaction movements were given a sense of proportion. The anger expressed through the body emerged alongside a style that communicated the deepest meditations.

For ritualizing the fight scene, Henry and Carty were asked to expand the thought(s) that provoked the movements. They then slowed down the movements, making each specific movement consciously representational rather than realistic. This formalization of form is directly influenced by the performers' training in the Decroux style. Remembering his training under Copeau, Decroux states: 'The manner of playing resembled the slow motion film. But while that is the slowing down of fragments of reality, ours was the slow production of one gesture in which many others were synthesized' (qtd. in Leabhart 112). The idea of producing gestures that integrate complex thoughts is the foundation of Decroux's physical theatre and serves to illuminate for the audience expression beyond words. However, this is not to say that physical theatre is devoid of words. Bicât and Baldwin's statement on the benefits of devising can be applied to Blue Raincoat's integration of physical theatre within the devising process: '[Devising] uses the text as a baseline. As all company members bring their creative potential to the table, ideas will continue to evolve as the play process develops' (7). As this exploration of Blue Raincoat's process shows, such an approach is also applicable to the performative and scenographic interpretation of an existing play text.

The use of mask in the rehearsal process was introduced on the fourth day. The chorus wore white make-up on their faces which elevated them from humanity to a more primal force. When the actors put on their bone coloured masks, their body techniques were revealed. Though devising and mask improvisation, the psychophysical beings of the characters were released, permitting the archetypal images of the masks to do their work. Carty and Henry used a more stylized form of movement when the masks were worn. The actors played loosely with passive and aggressive physicalities working across a spectrum of those ideas, but the power of the mask brought the fighting bodies to another level, charging them with the symbolism of opposition. According to Flannery, '[m]asking is the very essence of imaginative perception in the theatre' ('Staging the Phantasmagorical' 103). Through the mask, Flannery writes, 'the dramatist is provided with a flexible creative tool to embody ideas analogically' (ibid).

The masks were made of latex which allowed the actors to animate the material with their faces. The masks were not completely indeterminate, retaining a fixed type of personality, but not detailed enough to suggest an aspect of character. They enhanced the artifice essential to the work, 'gradually drawing the audience out of its own historicity, away from familiar themes and into the 'strange' world of the play' (Putzell 113). The use of mask openly acknowledges the consciously theatrical nature of the play, producing what Flannery has observed as a Brechtian 'alienation-effect,' forcing distance between the character and the audience. The outcome provoked an intellectual and experiential transaction with the audience.

In the actual fight, Blind Man enacted a blow with his cane at Lame Man who was on the ground clutching his. The canes did not physically connect (instead the Chorus provide the sound) but the technique of action and reaction was gestured. The act of hitting and being hit was timed with the Chorus's use of instruments. A finger piano, wooden sticks and brush combined to create the intensity of rhythm and drama in the fight. The pace continued to increase as Blind Man jabbed the cane at Lame Man, with Lame Man retaliating. Sometimes their movements mirrored one another as they turned, charged, repelled, crossed over and jumped at one another. A whistle sound added to the tension of the fight as it reached crisis point when Lame Man finally fell to the ground. The rhythm slowed as Blind Man carried on hitting him until his movements came to a near stop. The final part of the fight sees Blind Man retrieve his sheepskin coat in slow motion and exit the circular space, his exit marked by red light fading back to the original yellow hue.

At the moment of Blind Man's exit, the lighting and sound changed, and the space flowed in from Blind Man to Lame Man to a moment in dark silence. Then the final scene change occurred, achieved by bathing Lame Man, who was centre stage, in a white light against a yellow circle of light on reeds. The configuration of the space now changed; the chorus expanded it by filling it with different sounds. With the increased level of music, Lame Man discovered his power of movement and took possession of the stage. The invisible Saint (performed by the Chorus) was carried on Lame Man's back who, according to the text, 'doesn't weigh more than a grasshopper' (Yeats 803). The movement continued to expand the space until it filled the circle, moving it from the realm of the cerebral to spiritual recognition. Through a simple change in lighting, music and movement, Yeats' arrangement of alternating cycles in the play shifted from the one established at the beginning (the un-regenerating nature of the Blind Man/Lame Man pairing, signifying the body/soul dependency) to the one at the end when Blind Man and Lame Man, now independent people, mark a transformation, reaching the zenith of their spiritual journey.

In the production, the connection between physical deprivation and spiritual wisdom was realized. The development could be described by what Ross Brown refers to as transitional rites, that is, rites that 'contain internally a number of distinct changes: those of separation, the marginal state, aggregation and the return to secular time' (Brown 87). Blind Man acknowledged his humanity in recognizing the solitary existence for the life of the Saint. Lame Man's sacred event is dramatized the moment the Saint mounts his back. The Blind Man/Lame Man (body/soul) pairing questions whether they are each contained within the other and by implication within all people. Their pairing advocates Yeats' discernment for opposite psychological principles where each wins dominance in turn.

Conclusion

The process involved in Blue Raincoat's realization of *At the Hawk's Well* and *The Cat and the Moon* drew on many international influences. Decroux for his meticulous technique in modern mime; Yeats for his unwavering efforts to turn his incantatory verse and archetypal themes into a theatre of poetry; Craig for the provocative stance in giving emphasis to the director whose role it is to ensure a fully integrated approach to theatre. Arguably, all three aim for a transcendental art for the theatre that might be interpreted by symbol.

All participants involved in Blue Raincoat's productions brought with them their own influences and training, their *habitus* forming 'an acquired system of generative schemes objectively adjusted to the particular conditions in which it is constituted' (Bourdieu 95). As a venue-based ensemble theatre company, Blue Raincoat's physical, visual and aural signature is observable in various ways: physical agility, mask work, choral work, ensemble acting, mime, movement, and the expressive possibilities of the human body. In the company's productions of *At the Hawk's Well* and *The Cat and the Moon*, the natural elements on the stage, the intimate setting, the distancing devices, the methodical movement, the devised performance and improvisations, the stylized music and symbolic dance, all resulted in an abstract spiritual experience, but in a way that made it very much a Blue Raincoat production.

Works Cited

Bicât, Tina and Chris Baldwin, eds. *Devised and Collaborative Theatre: A Practical Guide*.Wiltshire: Crowood, 2002. Print.

Bourdieu, Pierre. *Outline of a Theory in Practice*. Cambridge: Cambridge UP, 1977. Print.

Bourdieu, Pierre. *The Logic of Practice* 1980. Trans. Richard Nice. California:Stanford University Press, 1990. Print.

Brown, Ross. *Sound: A Reader in Theatre Practice*. Basingstoke: Palgrave Macmillan, 2010. Print.

Callery, Dymphna. *Through the Body: A Practical Guide to Physical Theatre*. New York, Routedge 2009. Print.

Conway, Jo. Personal interview, 4 July 2013.

---. Personal interview, 6 July 2010.

Craig, Edward Gordon. *On the Art of Theatre*. Chicago: Browne's Bookstore, 1911.Print.

Decroux, Etienne. 'Étienne Decroux.' Trans. Mark Piper. *Words on Mime Journal* 11 (1985): 9-23. Print.

Flannery, James W. 'Staging the Phantasmagorical: The Theatrical Challenges and Rewards of W.B. Yeats.' *Irish University Review* 26.1 (1996): 92-106. Print.

Flannery, James W. 'W.B. Yeats's Poetry is "A Dialogue of Self and the Soul"' Web. http://simplycharly.com/yeats/james-_flannery_interview.htm. Accessed 6 May 2011.

Heddon, Deirdre and Jane Milling. *Devising Performance: A Critical History*. Basingstoke: Palgrave MacMillan, 2006. Print.

Hughes, Kellie. Personal interview, 21 August 2010.

Leabhart, Thomas. 'Words on Decroux 1.' *Mime Journal*. Ed. Thomas Leabhart. Claremont, California: Pomona College Theatre Department, 1993-1994. 110-124. Print.

Mermikides, Alex and Jackie Smart, eds. *Devising in Process*. Basingstoke: Palgrave Macmillan, 2010. Print.

Oddey, Alison. *Devised Theatre: A Practical and Theoretical Handbook*. London:Routledge, 1994. Print.

Pound, Ezra and Ernest Fenollosa. *Certain Noble Plays of Japan*. Dublin: Cuala Press, 1916. Print.

Putzel, Steven. 'Poetic Ritual and Audience Response, Yeats and the No.' *Yeats and Postmodernism*. Ed. Leonard Orr. New York: Syracuse UP, 1991. Print.

Walton, J. Michael. 'Edward Gordon Craig.' *Craig on Theatre*. London: Methuen, 1999. Print.

Walton, J. Michael. 'Edward Gordon Craig.' Introduction. *Craig on Theatre*. By Edward Gordon Craig. Ed. J. Michael Walton. London: Methuen, 1983. 15-38. Print.

Yeats, W.B. *The Collected Plays of W.B. Yeats*. London: Papermac, 1982. Print.

Yu, Haibo. 'Set Design.' *Devised and Collaborative Theatre: A Practical Guide*. Eds.Tina Bicât and Chris Baldwin. Wiltshire: Crowood, 2002. 30-45. Print.

11 | Repeating, Revising and Devising: Communities in Contemporary Galway Theatre

Siobhán O'Gorman

Introduction

This exploration focuses on devised performance in Galway theatre that premiered in 2012. One of the companies I discuss, Side-Show Productions, cites Pulitzer-winning American dramatist Suzan-Lori Parks as a key influence on its work (Sharry). The title of this essay draws on terminology that Parks uses to explain her style:

> 'Repetition and Revision' is a concept integral to the Jazz esthetic in which the composer or performer will write or play a musical phrase once and again and again; etc. – with each revisit the phrase is slightly revised. 'Rep & Rev' as I call it is a central element in my work; through its use I'm working to create a dramatic text that departs from traditional linear narrative style to look and sound more like a musical score. ('From Elements of Style' 9)

While scholars often locate Parks' plays within the more experimental and multidisciplinary genre of postdramatic theatre[1] the playwright usually employs conventional writing practices to create her dramatic texts. However, the terms repeating and revising can also be applied to devising and can extend our understanding of its processes.

---

[1] In Karen Jürs-Munby's introduction to her English translation of Hans-Thies Lehman's *Postdramatic Theatre*, Jürs-Munby specifically locates Parks within the genre of the 'postdramatic,' referencing in particular Parks' *The America Play* and *Imperceptible Mutabilities in the Third Kingdom* (6). These plays are published in *The America Play and Other Works*, where Parks' notes on 'Rep & Rev' appear in her essay 'From Elements of Style' (8-10).

Although some theorists seek to circumscribe devising as a method 'in which no script – neither play text nor performance score – exists prior to the work's creation by the company' (Heddon and Milling 3), devised work regularly begins with pre-existing materials – be they stories, recollections, interviews, documents, significant spaces, common objects or historical artefacts. From those seeds often grow the workshops or rehearsals that create, repeat and revise the performance until it is ready to be staged. Indeed, Tim Etchells, reflecting on devising performance with British company Forced Entertainment, sees their theatre-making as 'collecting, sifting and using bits of other people's stuff' (101). A combination of 'repetition' and 'revision' seems key to these productively parasitic activities.

I will examine three productions that employed devising, investigating the theatre-makers' aims, working processes, and engagement with issues of sociocultural stratification pertinent to Ireland's histories and contemporary moment. Side-Show's *King Alfred: A Mystery Play* was penned by one of the company's founding members, Martin Sharry, but it was initially inspired by workshops incorporating Parks' dramaturgical techniques. The play collates, merges, repeats and revises moments from MGM's *Alfred the Great* (1969) and local stories about its 1968 filming in Co. Galway. Fregoli's *Home* meditates on the meaning of 'home' in contemporary Ireland; drawing on group work and interviews, its performers devised, interwove and enacted fictional narratives concerning the central theme of home. Finally, Galway Youth Theatre (GYT) and Galway Arts Centre Community Drama's *Frank Pig Says Hello*, under Andrew Flynn's direction, revised Pat McCabe's two-hander of the same name to create a visually arresting, widely-inclusive ensemble piece. Although the makers of *Home* and the Galway production of *Frank Pig* did not draw on Parks' work (as did the creators of *King Alfred*), the American dramatist's appropriated phrase 'repetition and revision' also can illuminate the working processes that imbued the inception of these works.

King Alfred, *Home* and the Galway production of *Frank Pig* could – or could not – be described as devised, depending on how this terminology is understood in the context of theatre-making. Since the 1990s, the implications of the term 'devised' have been, perhaps productively, in flux. For example, in Alison Oddey's 1994 volume *Devising Theatre: A Practical and Theoretical Handbook*, the author admits that no classification of devising is definitive. However, she sees devised performance in general as a 'reaction' to 'text-based theatre,' to 'the prevailing ideology of one person's text under another person's direction' (4). More recently, in 2005, Deirdre Heddon and Jane Milling view devising as work that takes place without any pre-existing script, play text or performance score (3). My case studies do not fit easily within some of these criteria. The Galway production of *Frank Pig*, for example, employed (however flexibly) a pre-existing play. Oddey sees devising as a *reaction to* literary theatre, but the collaboration that underpinned the making of *Home* and to a lesser extent *King Alfred* resulted in play texts that produce meaning through poetic language and wordplay (as much as other theatrical languages). Moreover, the 2012 productions of *Frank Pig* and *King Alfred*, if considered as devised, move beyond Oddey's general theory in that these works were presented as one person's text under another person's direction. In the 2007 volume *Making a Performance: Devising Histories and Contemporary Practice*, Emma Govan, Helen Nicholson and Katie Normington acknowledge the shifting applications of the term 'devising,' seeing it in a much more permissive way as 'a process of generating a performative or theatrical event often but not always in collaboration with others,' and admitting that 'it would be misleading to suggest that this umbrella term signifies any particular dramatic genre or style of performance' (4). Similarly, I delineate devising to encompass a wider range of practices. Drawing on Etchells' reflections cited above, I see devising as working processes that often openly draw on and, ideally, acknowledge diverse contributions to create a new performance piece, which might involve sampling (to apply another musical term) pre-existing texts. In addition to the improvised, inventive and collaborative work that remains central to perceptions of what constitutes devising, this wider definition embraces methods such as adaptation, appropriation and, either in the process of making the work or in its stage production, community participation. The recent productions of *King Alfred*, *Home* and *Frank Pig* can all be located within these broader parameters.

Devising in contemporary Irish performance has found artistic innovation in its emergence from urban and regional geographies, its engagement with local communities and histories, and its relationship with broader national and international movements in theatre and culture. Internationally, a range of interdisciplinary performance practices have flourished since the latter half of the twentieth century. As outlined in the introduction to this volume, such diversity also has been a longstanding feature of theatrical activity in Ireland. However, Irish devised and interdisciplinary performance practices seem only since the 1990s to have proliferated more widely, and progressively garnered increasing acclaim, with recently established companies such as ANU and Brokentalkers quickly rising to prominence. Here, I explore how devising relates to community – as source, participator and subject matter – in the 2012 productions of *Home*, *King Alfred* and *Frank Pig*. These works also showcase how recent theatre in Galway negotiates broader shifts in the working processes of theatre-makers. *Home*, *King Alfred* and *Frank Pig* draw creatively on national concerns and local communities, but often challenge cultural hierarchies linked to traditional concentric models of community that eddy outwards from the patriarchal family. These productions allow us to explore how devising and the theatre that emerges as a result function to interrogate the workings of privilege and exclusion within a post-Celtic Tiger Ireland that remains highly stratified in its social and cultural values. Illuminated by Jill Dolan's theories on utopia and performance, this essay proposes that devised performance can work to illuminate the restrictions of the present while non-coercively suggesting more inclusive, communal and radically democratic ways of living and organizing society (*Utopia* 13).

Side-Show's *King Alfred: A Mystery Play*

Side-Show evolved out of an earlier company, Waterdonkey, which was established by graduates of NUI Galway's MA in Drama and Theatre. Two of Waterdonkey's members, Zita Monahan and Martin Sharry, went on to found Side-Show with Dick Walsh, a graduate of NUI Galway's MA in Film Studies (Walsh). Sharry's *King Alfred* was staged at the Town Hall Studio in March 2012, where each performance was accompanied by a showing of Walsh's video installation, *Witnesses to 1968*. The latter was composed of a series of interviews with local people who remembered or were employed in the making of MGM's *Alfred the Great*. Walsh's film offers a more clearly defined 'history' than Sharry's mystery play. The play is a highly experimental work set in the here and now (Galway, 2012). The relationship between its title and its content seems tenuous until fragments of the MGM movie that partly inspired it are enacted by the cast. Since Sharry began working in the theatre, he had aimed to produce material that explodes the conventions of naturalism, and *King Alfred* certainly achieves this. The production, under Walsh's direction, gradually became more bizarre and disjointed through an eclectic mix of role-play, music, song and projections. Yet, arguably, the power of *King Alfred* lies in its status as an unfulfilled search for meaning.

The inception of the play occurred when Sharry and Walsh ran workshops in Galway in 2011. These focused on comparing two different approaches to the history play: that of Shakespeare and that of Parks.[2] Side-Show had wanted for some time to make a history play, but the company proceeded first with another work that it had in the pipeline, *Dreams of Love*. However, the subject matter of the proposed history play emerged by accident during rehearsals for *Dreams of Love* when Sharry and Walsh went to buy props in a fishing tackle shop in Galway city. As they were about to pay, the man serving them held on to the goods – as if he was, Sharry recalls, holding them at ransom. The server began to relay a story from his youth: the remarkable summer of 1968 when he, like thousands of Galway locals, worked as an extra on MGM's production of *Alfred the Great*. He told of how members of the community benefitted from this massive event in which MGM (or 'Money Gone Mad,' as he called it) paid those involved up to three times the average industrial wage. Yet, the weather conditions were often not dreary enough to satisfy director Clive Donner's vision for the film and, during the scorching summer that endured, the local extras frequently ended up sunbathing rather than working (Sharry). This image seemed to Sharry like 'a joke' depicting a 'flagrant Irish contradiction,' especially when considered in the context of the year 1968 internationally.[3] He and Walsh decided to use the story as a starting

---

[2] Lee A. Jacobus offers a broad definition for the history play, describing it as a 'drama set in a time other than that in which it was written.' However, he qualifies this by adding that the term 'usually refers to late Elizabethan dramas, such as Shakespeare's *Henry* plays, that draw their plots from English historical materials such as Holinshed's *Chronicles*' (1102). History plays, which often chronicle the lives and deaths of their central historical figures, are regularly positioned within a subset of tragedy. Parks can be seen to move the history play into the postmodern realm by using formal innovation to question the validity of her own historical sources.

[3] 1968 saw several important developments internationally. For example, the UK introduced a new wide-ranging race relations act and in the United States – following the assassination of Martin Luther King Jr. – President Lyndon Johnson signed the Civil Rights Act. Many key battles took place as part of the Vietnam War, meeting continuing protests from the Peace Movement. The Soviet Union invaded Czechoslovakia and arrested President Dubcek. May 1968 saw the biggest general strike ever attempted in France. In Mexico, students protesting the military occupation of the National Polytechnic Institute threatened the Mexican Olympics, while China celebrated 20 years of communist rule under Mao Tse-tung.

point for the history play that they had been eager to make. Indeed the quote, 'Money Gone Mad,' from the shopkeeper who initially inspired the subject of *King Alfred* appears repeatedly in the final play text. Both Sharry and Walsh ended up writing versions of the play, but it was Sharry's draft that was eventually staged at the Town Hall Studio in Galway. Having struggled with the anarchy that Sharry claims had sometimes characterized the collaborative work behind other productions in which he had been involved (including *Dreams of Love*), the duo decided that Walsh (whose academic background is in film) would be the named director and Sharry the named writer (Sharry). This allowed each to hone his individual strengths while continuing to share resources.

MGM's *Alfred the Great* was a high budget production. Its filming had significant (though fleeting) social and economic impacts both within and beyond Co. Galway at the time. A studio complex built in the village of Kilchreest, situated roughly halfway between the towns of Gort and Loughrea, was the focal point for 'a dozen other locations within 20 to 30 miles' (Grehan). In a 1968 *Irish Times* article on the subject, Ida Grehan reveals that, while film industry professionals of international renown rented local castles (for example, star David Hemmings took over Anita Leslie's castle and director Clive Donner was housed at Kilcolgan Castle, both in the town of Oranmore near Galway city), the hotel and catering industry throughout Co. Galway profited from the vast team of actors and production assistants drafted in to make the film. Emigrants returned from Britain with the promise of work, and production designer Michael Stringer 'found in the craft grades of carpenters, plumbers, painters, props etc. that the Irish labour was extremely keen, adaptable and fast, supervised by very experienced MGM studio supervisors' (qtd. in Grehan). Yet, while 'Irish craftsmanship was given a very stimulating shot in the arm,' a local dissident group protested that students were being underpaid. These campaigners were 'rebuked from the pulpit at Moycullen for their "rapacious avarice"' (Grehan). Such scenarios and their coverage within national newspapers such as the *The Irish Times* reveal the hype surrounding the advent of MGM in Co. Galway, as well as the local and national significance of the event at the time.

Yet, the fact that a high budget MGM production was filmed in Galway, impacting on the lives of thousands, is not necessarily widely

---

Meanwhile, in Galway, film extras were sunbathing and, with the arrival of MGM, 'Money' seemed to have 'Gone Mad.'

known today. Sharry puts this down to the fact that the film was a box office flop. He suggests that, had *Alfred the Great* been commercially successful, spaces significant in the making of the film would have become tourist attractions, like Cong, Co Mayo, which entices visitors because *The Quiet Man* was filmed there. Sharry is fascinated by the way in which certain histories are marked out and preserved, while others are in danger of being forgotten, as well as the role economics have to play in this. Here, Sharry's comments reveal Parks' influence: Parks' plays have exhibited an enduring concern with how histories that serve in the interest of dominant power become mythologized and commodified while much of Black American history remains 'unrecorded, dismembered, washed out' (Parks, 'Possession' 4). The Galway filming of *Alfred the Great*, and its absence in much of today's public memory, points to the way in which 'profitable' histories – such as those with the power to attract tourists through global recognition – are transformed into local and national heritage commodities, while past events that have had individual or collective significance for the people who inhabit that locale are often allowed to slip away from the wider public consciousness. And yet, the traces of these more marginal histories become manifest in somewhat random ways, like Walsh and Sharry's chance encounter with the story, or local men who still maintain the beards that they were required to grow when they worked as extras for the film – according to such a bearded interviewee in Walsh's video installation.

Sharry and Walsh felt that the material garnered from research on this fascinating portion of local history might take on added significance if publicized and explored within a post-Celtic tiger context. MGM was present in Galway for the 'best part of the year,' including its preparation time for the filming of *Alfred the Great*, with units scattered 'all over Galway from Barna to Loughrea' (Grehan). Yet when MGM's work concluded, it left an economic vacuum in its wake. In Grehan's *Irish Times* article, which was published in late October after filming had ended, she quotes a Galway accountant: 'It's upsetting to the employment structure [...]. Students earning £24 a week find it difficult to adjust to the £7 a week they'd earn in a hotel.' Sharry maintains that this boom and bust scenario can be viewed retrospectively as a microcosm for Ireland's Celtic Tiger years. Grehan's article ends on the following note:

> And at Kilchreest, the general verdict was that the unique, self-contained studio complex which worked well for MGM, could well be acquired to form the nucleus of an Irish film industry. It may

not long be idle. David Lean's men are scouting around for locations for the next Galway picture.

The hope for the studio complex, which remained unfulfilled, was not informed by any specific plan from local or national perspectives, but reliant on international professionals working for the English film director and screen-writer David Lean, who had by 1968 achieved global acclaim for big screen epics with Colombia, Sam Spiegel and MGM. Indeed, this calls to mind the overdependence on foreign investment, lack of precise forward planning and naïve hopes that a period of affluence will continue indefinitely which characterized the so-called Celtic Tiger era. Considering this, Sharry is perceptive in his apparent belief that even the most obscure histories can help to illuminate present conditions.

Side-Show's King Alfred project pieced together stories about the filming of MGM's *Alfred* obtained from Galway individuals old enough to remember vividly the events concerned. In doing so, Side-Show aimed to draw attention to this specific portion of local history, while exploring more broadly the fabrication of public memory. While Walsh's film presents details in a documentary format, the play fragments narratives and quoted material, juxtaposing these with re-enacted moments from MGM's *Alfred*. The production began with two moderators leading four volunteers in a focus group concerning 'the mystery of history' and 'the history of mystery.' These opening moments set the tone for a work replete with clever wordplays and metatheatre. Before the focus-group participants enter, the moderators remind the audience to 'act as normal as possible.' After some farcical preliminary questions, the volunteers are left alone to ponder the function of the experiment – until a caricature figure called the Irish Man bursts in to tell them the 'whole story,' before recalling the summer of 1968. Ironically, though, his rendition is full of gaps and repetitions: the character personifies the amnesia of public consciousness. Left with little else to do, the characters begin to enact a variety of scenarios, including scenes from *Alfred the Great*. Throughout, hollow clichés are exchanged along with clever contradictions and insights. Like Parks in her 'Rep & Rev' plays (some of which are published, with the essays that explain this style, in *The America Play and Other Works* (1995)), Sharry resists forcing a history that can never be whole into a manageable, easily-marketable format.

Sharry appropriated Parks' idea of 'Rep & Rev,' applying it to the process of creating *King Alfred* (by exploring the concept in preliminary workshops, then repeating and revising moments from the MGM film and the interviews conducted with locals). However, 'Rep & Rev' also emerges as a stylistic feature of the final play. *King Alfred* transcends its own defining labels through the cumulative creation of what I describe in my *Irish Theatre Magazine* review of the production as an 'echoing, pulsating madness' (O'Gorman). The play's 'Rep & Rev' style was instrumental in achieving this effect. Parks is interested in 'how the structure of Rep & Rev and the stories inherent to it – a structure which creates a drama of accumulation – can be accommodated under the rubric of dramatic literature where, traditionally, all elements lead audiences towards some single explosive moment' ('Elements of Style' 9). The 'echoing, pulsating madness' of *King Alfred* similarly resulted from a more multiplicitous 'drama of accumulation,' which involves the characters repeating, with subtle alterations, sets of actions and words. Under Walsh's direction, this evolved into a rhythmic pace and went on long enough for audience members to perhaps push beyond possible confusion and to become captivated by the strange cyclical activities taking place on stage (which often skipped progression and recurred like the sound from a corrupted CD). Many spectators responded by embracing this strangeness through laughter. As such, the combined energy of stage action and audience helped to produce what might be considered, from the perspective of Dolan's work, as a utopian performative – a shared affective moment that is productively elusive, both palpable and just beyond our grasp (7-8). This kind of performative moment, in Dolan's view, has the potential to move us into a limitless, fantasy space in which we can critically assess the present and imagine an improved future. While *King Alfred*'s unconventional qualities might initially have been frustrating for those clinging to expectations inscribed by the play's title and opening, embracing the work's liberation from these slippery markers led to an exhilarating theatrical experience. Karen Jürs-Munby's comments regarding the postdramatic work of Forced Entertainment (in her introduction to Hans-Thies Lehmann's *Postdramatic Theatre*) are also applicable here. *King Alfred* can equally be described as 'a theatre that cannot be taken in "at once", that is not easily "surveyable", and thus a theatre that does not make the world "manageable" for us – fundamentally because the world we live in, globalized and multiply mediatized as it is, *is* less "surveyable" and manageable than ever' (11). Sharry's play interrogates the commodification of history by showcasing, in a variety of ways, a resistance to dominant signifying systems, including money, the written word, realistic representation and linear narrative.

Side-Show's *King Alfred* was produced independently at the Town Hall Theatre's sixty-seat studio, which was less than half-full on the night I attended. It missed out on the publicity it might have garnered had it been staged as part of the many festivals that take place in Galway, and the production ran for only three performances. Sharry reveals that, with a work such as this, the members of Side-Show were comfortable in sacrificing commercial success for their ideals of artistic integrity: this was the kind of work that the company had sought to make since some of its members had taken Thomas Conway's module on postdramatic theatre as part of NUI Galway's MA in Drama and Theatre. Sharry also contends that financial limitations have at times stimulated the company's inventiveness. Avoiding having to pay for script rights often leads theatre groups to work innovatively to devise original work. It is unfortunate that Side-Show was unable to risk touring the dual production of *Witnesses to '68* and *King Alfred* (at the very least within the regions where work for *Alfred the Great* had taken place decades earlier). The project as a whole resurrected a significant portion of local history, explored directly within the interviews in its film installation; the multi-layered theatre production promoted a heightened awareness of self in the moment, and worked to question historiography itself. As such, Side-Show's King Alfred project has the potential to affectively illuminate the gaps between intimate memories and public histories, and between felt experience and commodifiable cultures.

Fregoli's *Home*

Fregoli's *Home* premiered at Nuns' Island Theatre as part of the 2012 Galway Theatre Festival. The auditorium was full on the night I attended and, following its initial success, the production was later revived on the main stage of the Town Hall Theatre. Through *Home*'s style, themes and production forums, Fregoli sought to achieve its stated aim to produce 'plays that appeal to a large cross-section of the public, which deal with issues of a changing society and its attitudes' ('About Fregoli'). *Home* – initially and fruitfully marketed as part of a festival programme – was more popular than Side-Show's *King Alfred*. It was also easier to digest: although the play jumps between, and sometimes fuses, a variety of monologues and vignettes, these offer recognizable scenarios that progress logically and hang together in quite a coherent way. Each cast member scripted her/his own characters' lines, but the writing showcases continuity in style with lyrical rhythms of varying, but structured, pace balancing vigour with pathos throughout.

Fregoli was established in 2007, originating from NUI Galway's Drama Society (DramSoc). The company maintains strong connections with DramSoc which has since served Fregoli in sourcing burgeoning new theatre artists for professional work. Fregoli's style is characterized by rhythmic pacing, along with quick shifts in character and emotion, and its production repertoire includes apt works by Irish playwrights, such as Enda Walsh's *Disco Pigs* in 2010 and Raymond Scannell's *Breathing Water* in 2011. In recent years, the company has also begun to produce original plays, including *The Secret Life of Me* (2011), collectively created by Maria Tivnan, Rebecca Ryan and Tracy Bruen under the direction of Rob McFeely (the company's four founding members), as well as Tivnan's own plays, *The Sweet Shop* (2012), *Let Me Be* (2013) and a selection of shorts under the composite title *Shur I'll be Alright Here on Me Own* (2014). Making *Home* allowed Fregoli to extend its collaborative work by including in the devising process a larger cast of actors with whom the company had chosen to work for the purpose of the project. Tivnan explains the drive to devise that underpinned *Home* as follows:

> It seemed to us [that] to gain entry to a lot of festivals in Ireland e.g. Dublin Fringe, Midsummer etc. work needed to be original/devised, and to be honest it seemed to be the way to get attention in the media and 'on the scene,' [sic] I also felt we had a group of really strong, creative, energetic actors who we knew and worked with really well and that it was our time to try this [.... It] would both develop us as a company and as a working group. We also felt there were many issues and themes in today's Ireland that we would like to tackle and have our take on through theatrical performance.

Tivnan's response reveals that Fregoli's motivations were firstly strategic, then practical and finally driven by a desire to respond to current issues in today's Ireland. The above reflection also showcases the ways in which the repertoires and application procedures of festivals can, on the one hand, stimulate resourceful, collaborative strategies to create original theatre and, on the other hand, initiate within theatre companies a pressure to adopt particular modes of working.

Ideas of repetition and revision also illuminate the processes involved in creating *Home*, which encompassed cyclical but progressively more honed actions of deliberation, improvisation, research, reflection and writing. Having established the preliminary objectives outlined by Tivnan above, the six writer/performers involved in the project that became *Home*, in addition to Rob McFeely who would go on to direct the production, proceeded with a group discussion of possible ideas. After some initial improvisations and play, the group created a large chart containing 'everything and anything people felt relevant' to Fregoli's aims (Tivnan). They then sorted these ideas into the following thematic categories: 'the passing of time, growing up, identity (specifically Irish identity) [...] the feeling of entrapment and the desire to express' (Tivnan). Tivnan then considered these themes in relation to the performative imagery that had emerged in the improvisations and at the next meeting she suggested the concept of 'home' as a way of bringing these different strands of interest together. At this time, Fregoli was considering the Dublin Fringe Festival as a possible forum for its new work. As such, the company used the application process to guide its development of the piece. The group considered different spatial and visual possibilities, for example a promenade piece in which actors would each carry a suitcase of props that would aid them in performing the characters' stories along the way. The company also consulted with Irish contacts living abroad, garnering feedback on possible titles, structure and content for their project. These activities brought to the fore the following driving questions: 'Why would you stay in Ireland? Why would you leave?' Tivnan extracted from these developments emigration as a key focus for the planned work, and the company decided for both promotional and research purposes to ask people on the streets of Galway and Dublin about home and Ireland, and why they might stay or leave. Reflecting on the information reaped from research, using further improvisational work, the creative team agreed on six characters that both suited the actors and would give the company the scope its members felt it needed: Australian wanderer, young Irish farmer, agoraphobic city writer, homeless youth, and a young Irish couple trapped by negative equity and duty.

Certain characters satisfy Fregoli's stated focus: the relationship between emigration and contemporary Ireland. The young Irish couple, Oisín Robbins's Daithí and Teresa Brennan's Karen, as well as Seamus O'Donnell's Australian wanderer, serve to complicate romanticized visions of home through this framework. Daithí, a labourer, has had to emigrate to Australia in order to continue paying Celtic Tiger prices for a house in Ireland now worth much less. The couple's tense telephone conversations and their individual, regretful monologues successfully conjure the strain felt by many young people in similar situations.

O'Donnell's Australian wanderer envisions his trip to Ireland as a kind of homecoming and a tribute to his late, Irish-born father. Seeking out the idyllic home of his father's childhood, his expectations are shattered when he meets a shell of a cottage in an Ireland vastly different from his father's stories. The ideals of these characters are crushed by transnational journeys motivated by economic or psychological strain.

Yet characters such as Ellie (Maria Tivnan) and Amy (Kate Murray) broaden the scope of *Home*, moving it beyond the context of emigration and towards an exploration of privilege, class and what home might mean for different people living in contemporary Ireland. Murray and Tivnan worked together to flesh out Ellie, Amy and their interconnected stories. The tentative exchanges between the two performers offered some of the most moving moments in the production. Ellie, a novelist, was the primary caregiver for her mother who had a long-term illness. Consumed by grief, she has not left the house since her mother's death. Amy, born into an environment of urban crime, has ended up on the streets. When Ellie finds out that Amy has been sleeping in her garage, she begins to share meals with Amy, and the two gradually start to talk through the traumatic personal experiences that have brought each to their current, contrasting situations: Ellie, housebound and Amy, homeless. In performance, these actors' interactions exemplified the production's imaginative use of minimal props within a relatively bare set. During the moments in which the characters converse through the wall dividing the house and the garage, Murray and Tivnan placed a white rectangular frame between them. This was effective in evoking the actual wall, as well as the wider social structures, that separate these characters. Their burgeoning friendship allows us to imagine them transcending those structures and accessing psychological healing through shared love and support.

The development of Murray's and Tivnan's interlinked contributions extended *Home*'s focus to a consideration of what home means, or could potentially mean, for diverse individuals currently residing in Ireland. However, the final play as a whole missed out on important possibilities offered by this wider framework. A more thorough interrogation of contemporary Ireland as 'home' might have been achieved had Fregoli sought in its research and in the final production to explore immigrants' experiences of living in Ireland. An ERSI report published in June 2013 'highlights Ireland's high foreign-born population at 17 per cent, compared with other high income countries in the OECD' (Crosbie). Fregoli is based in Galway city and could have drawn contributions from the city's sizable immigrant community, largely from Poland and other Central European and Baltic states. In 2011, twenty-five per cent of Galway city's population and almost fifteen per cent of the county's population as a whole consisted of non-Irish born people (Central Statistics Office 4). The inclusion of the Australian wanderer figure goes some way towards investigating non-Irish-born experiences of Ireland as 'home.' Yet the final play overlooks some of the scope suggested by its title – specifically by not offering for consideration what might constitute 'home' for those from abroad who have relocated to Ireland, whether immigrants feel at home here, and how such perspectives might add to broader understandings of 'home' in contemporary Ireland.

Home, as it stands, does offer some productive engagement with Irish constructions of community, and this lies in its interrogation of traditional Irish family models. Characters such as Jarlath Tivnan's Brendan the farmer showcase how overinvesting in an isolated, family-run industry can stunt an individual's personal growth. Following his parents' death, this character is left alone with his tractor, reliving the past and his family's mundane habits (like watching *Fair City*), afraid to move forward due to a lack of life experience. The young couple dramatize the devastation caused by that frantic fusion of tradition and modernity that characterized Celtic Tiger Ireland, when – influenced by the clever marketing strategies of banks in particular – young people sought to have it all: getting married, having children and getting on that property ladder, often with ill-fated urgency. Finally, the hopeful development of a shared living space and friendship between a homeless youth (Amy) and a writer (Ellie), in addition to prompting the audience to imagine empathy transcending class boundaries and a healing of trauma through sharing, gestured towards new ways of constructing families, of making a 'home.' This showcases the play's potential to achieve, through performance, Dolan's conception of the 'utopian performative:'

> The utopian performative leaves us melancholy yet cheered, because for however brief a moment, we feel something of what redemption might be like, of what humanism could really mean, of how powerful might be a world in which our commonalities hail over our differences. (8)

Home takes us on six, interlinked emotional journeys, gradually delving more poignantly into each character's home-related neurosis. It calls to mind current issues in Ireland, a country littered with vacant houses and families divided by increasing emigration, reminding us that 'home' might be defined by shared love, compassion and support rather than abstract structures of cultural convention or concrete structures of bricks and mortar.

GYT and Galway Arts Centre Community Drama's *Frank Pig Says Hello*

In director Andrew Flynn's work with community groups such as GYT and Galway Arts Centre Community Drama, he often revises existing plays by both Irish and international dramatists to suit a large ensemble, aiming to involve as many local participants as possible. In 2010, for example, he directed GYT in *Yellow Moon*, the group's version of Scottish playwright David Greig's *Yellow Moon: The Ballad of Leila and Lee* (2006); the original play requires only four performers, but Flynn collaborated with his team in redeveloping the work to include thirteen actors. That year he also extended Conall Morrison's *Tarry Flynn* (1996) to include a cast of more than forty actors, none of them professional, for a well-attended production at the Town Hall Theatre. For GYT in 2011, he directed German playwright Marius Von Mayenburg's *The Ugly One* (2007), which normally requires four actors who can play a variety of roles. Flynn's production incorporated nine GYT performers, a chorus and a live pianist, and was re-envisioned to appropriate elements of Brechtian epic theatre such as singing, dancing, placards and strobe-lighting – blending high entertainment with unsettling provocation. Flynn's mission is inclusion and community engagement, facilitating a sharing of resources amongst diverse performers, stage designers, visual artists and musicians of varying professional levels. The work that emerges as a result is highly proficient and sensually stimulating, supported by attention to detail and harmonized collaborations. For Flynn's theatre work with the community, pre-exiting texts become fluid and his practice as director often necessitates aspects of devising.

Flynn's goal for *Frank Pig* was similar to his objectives for the works mentioned above: to blend a variety of diverse creative perspectives by bringing together a range of community and professional artists. *Frank Pig Says Hello*, originally a two-hander, is Pat McCabe's stage version of his acclaimed novel *The Butcher Boy* (1992) and it first appeared as part of the 1992 Dublin Theatre Festival. Yet, overshadowed by Neil Jordan's 1997 film adaptation of the novel, *Frank Pig* has rarely been revived since its premiere. In the aftermath of the film's success, Flynn wanted to offer a new take on McCabe's overlooked play by expanding it to include a wider range of characters and increased stage action. Working between the play and the book, he collaborated with his team to redevelop the drama for a cast of 30, featuring a blend of GYT's young performers, more mature actors from Galway's Community Theatre Network, and exquisite visual and spatial design from Ger Sweeney (scenic painting) and Owen McCarthaigh (set). The scope of this collective effort led to a show filled with variety, but also served a promotional function. Word of mouth spreads quickly in a small city such as Galway and, with so many locals involved, I kept hearing about the show before and after I saw it. Nuns' Island Theatre was packed when *Frank Pig* was staged as part of the 2012 Galway Arts Festival; the production received a standing ovation on the night that I attended.

When I asked Flynn about his motivation for reimagining McCabe's two-hander as a more densely populated ensemble piece, he explained that he wanted to find a way to maximize the potential offered by his access to a wide range of theatre people through his work in community networks. For Flynn, there is also 'something very theatrically striking' about putting such a large group on stage and, working with a blend of amateur and professional artists afforded him the opportunity to achieve this. He told of how, in his work with professional theatre companies such as Decadent, the necessity to acquire payment for all full-time personnel involved prevents the development of material on such a large scale. Flynn had recently attended several stripped back, one-man shows, as well as a rare production of McCabe's original *Frank Pig*. Although he had adored *Frank Pig* when it premiered, its style now seemed to him 'dated,' as in, it 'didn't seem to resonate' in a contemporary context; Flynn explains, considering this, that he wanted to work together with a group to expand upon the existing material. He went about doing so through his determination to flesh out *Frank Pig*, heartened by how well similar projects including *Tarry Flynn* and *The Ugly One* had worked for him in the past. Ultimately, Flynn aimed to achieve a highly entertaining show that would be 'epic' and of 'big scale.' He wanted to move 'as far away as possible from the minimalist style of the original.'

Flynn admits that preparations for the Galway production of *Frank Pig* were a 'logistical nightmare' (in that, for example, it was difficult to have everyone present at once with such a large team, including amateurs with other commitments) but he also found the experience to be full of rewarding, organic developments. Having discovered early on that McCabe's original script would not accommodate his vision without significant alteration, he collaborated with the cast for two weeks of workshopping using both the play and McCabe's novel, *The Butcher Boy*. Going back to the novel gave the team a much broader scope with which to work, allowing for several key additions. In the original play, for example, the character of Uncle Alo has only three lines, while the book offers significant detail on his visit to the Brady family: Francie's excited anticipation, his mother's obsessive preparations and the party filled with neighbours, music, song and Alo's stories, which turns sour when Francie's alcoholic father starts a row. Flynn and his team could see the theatrical potential of material such as this, and so they worked it into their version of *Frank Pig*. During these moments of the production, viewers were made to feel like attendees at Alo's welcome party through a combination of the cast's live performance of songs, Nuns' Island Theatre's intimate spatial qualities, and the arrangement of non-tiered audience seating around two perpendicular sides with the action taking place on the same level, giving spectators a clear view of each other as well as the stage action ahead. Returning to the novel also facilitated the inclusion of more performers. The original script allowed for one actor to play Piglet (Francie as a child) and another to play Frank (the adult Francie), with the latter also enacting fragmented personas from Francie's locale. In the Galway production, Frank was revised only to narrate, rather than join, the action, and his lines were fleshed out with narrative from the novel. Meanwhile, the members of Francie's community became a chorus, incorporating actors with varying levels of expertise. In the production, the chorus members often moved and spoke in unison, which was surreal and stylized, but some also stepped out of this mass to play individual characters. After two weeks of workshopping, the team had a script, but this was continually edited and revised throughout the six-week rehearsal period (Flynn).

Flynn describes the process behind Galway's *Frank Pig* as 'collaboratively infusing' the production with dialogue, narrative and iconic images from *The Butcher Boy*. The visual and sound design also emerged from working with the novel; the artists involved attended and drew on the work-shops and rehearsals in an effort to evoke sensually striking moments from *The Butcher Boy*. It is important to Flynn that the community groups with which he works are given productions of professional quality, and so he enlisted the services of expert designers to work on *Frank Pig*. The final production was visually intricate and made admirable use of the small space. Mike O'Halloran's lighting contributed to the story's unfolding, bathing in golden hues nostalgic scenes of playing in the countryside and using more artificial, bluish tones for the Dublin night. McCarthaigh's set, painted colourfully by Sweeney, consisted of a selection of tall, rectangular pieces representing such settings as the corner shop, the interior of Francie's home, the exterior of another house, a train and an abattoir. The latter featured a realistic pig carcass which visually encapsulated the novel's grotesque elements. The set pieces were placed close to the audience and to each other, remaining as a backdrop throughout the performance. This had the effect of condensing into one all the scenes from Francie's youth; they appeared garish, surreal and larger than life. Hence, the audience was invited to experience Francie's tormented psyche through the scenographic landscape. Flynn achieved his goal in that the final production, in its artistic detail and scale, *was* vastly different from the stripped-back original.

Returning to the book to revise the script of *Frank Pig* allowed those working on the Galway production to harness and elucidate the novel's moving consideration of persistent issues in Ireland, for example child protection, taboos surrounding mental illness and addiction, and the pernicious impacts of social stratification even within small communities. The Brady family of *The Butcher Boy* are the underclass within a small Irish town, labelled 'pigs' by Mrs Nugent who occupies the upper echelons of the town's social hierarchy. In Flynn's production, the audience was bombarded by the term 'pigs,' which carried further weight in a post-Celtic Tiger context: it reminded spectators of larger European hierarchies and derogatory systems of labelling following Ireland's amalgamation as the second I in the acronym PIIGS. This abbreviation has been used in financial discourse after the European sovereign debt crisis to designate countries availing of Troika assistance in managing government debt and keeping national economies afloat. In *The Butcher Boy*, however, Francie receives little support, economic or otherwise. With a mother oscillating between suicidal and manic behaviours, and an abusive, alcoholic father, the young Francie is starved of nurture at home, seeking warmth instead through his friendship with Joe Purcell. Yet Joe's burgeoning camaraderie with Philip, the son of the condescending Mrs Nugent, compromises Francie's only support system. The conventional, 'respectable' Nugent family becomes the focus of the protagonist's adolescent rage. The Nugents come to represent everything that Francie has missed out on growing up, and he blames them for his alienation. Revising the *Frank Pig* script to include more of this rich and challenging material allowed Flynn not only to include more members of the local community as part of his cast, but to offer a critique of hierarchical constructions of community pertinent to Ireland's history and contemporary moment.

In *The Butcher Boy*, Mrs Nugent dubs the Bradys 'pigs' because they are not a 'functional' family of means, and we see Francie throughout the novel developing various coping mechanisms to deal with the shame of being different. Flynn's production of *Frank Pig* drew heavily on the novel to expand the play's critique of how conventional, patriarchal families – particularly within small towns and rural communities – continue to be valorized in Ireland. This was achieved through Flynn's devising work with Galway's community theatre networks, leading to a production that widely dispersed the disparaging voices within Francie's locale. The novel's first person narrative calls into question the legitimacy of Francie's memories because the story is communicated from Francie's disturbed perspective. McCabe's original stage version – though it is a two-hander – still takes a singular viewpoint by offering only an older and younger version of the same Francie: Frank and Piglet. Hence, in both the novel and the original play, we might understand the suspicion and fear with which Francie is viewed as a product of the character's own paranoia since all events and personas are channelled through one character. In the Galway production, oppressive attitudes towards Francie no longer echoed within the character's mind but were brought to life by a range of performers. While the character Frank remained as narrative framing device, the actual stage presence of so many actors within an intimate space served to implicate the community in Francie's downfall, and to make palpable our shared responsibility for protecting vulnerable members of society. The Galway production, with its large cast, extended the way in which transitioning from page to stage creates action from narration. This resulted in a multiplicity less mediated by the singular, authorial voice of both the novel and the original play. Immediacy was added to Flynn's production by pushing the narrative mode of 'there and then,' further towards the dramatic mode of 'here and now' (Elam 110-111). The revised *Frank Pig* did not suggest alternative ways of living like Fregoli's *Home*, but left its audience only with the starkness of Francie's tragedy as a resonant reminder of wrongs in Irish society. Despite its conclusive starkness, however, this production still offered possibilities to promote utopian performatives which, according to Dolan, 'exceed the content of a play or performance; spectators might draw a utopian performative from even the most dystopian theatrical universe' (8). The spontaneous standing ovation that took place on the night I attended indicated this production's power, through 'a complex alchemy of form and content, context and location' (*ibid*), to produce a communal, affective moment in which to imagine an improved future.

Conclusion

The 2012 productions of *Home*, *King Alfred* and *Frank Pig* showcase a range of ways in which devising is practiced in contemporary Irish theatre, be it in repeating and revising historical material, collectively creating original work, or adapting fiction to expand existing scripts. Looking at these case studies together suggests that devised performance within regional urban centres such as Galway is characterized by negotiating marketability, practicality and conceptions of artistic integrity. The production of *Frank Pig* was successful in utilizing devised performance to include a large ensemble, accommodate a range of varying expertise and achieve a well-attended production of a professional standard. Although *Frank Pig* and Side-Show's *King Alfred* continued to foreground singular authors and directors, each also made a significant effort to acknowledge the collaboration involved in their productions. GAF TV, a selection of promotional videos on Galway Arts Festival's website, is littered with material that highlights the intergenerational, amateur and professional teamwork underlying the 2012 production of *Frank Pig*. Side-Show exhibited the community input in the making of *King Alfred* by staging the play in conjunction with a documentary film including interviews with locals. With *King Alfred*, Side-Show fulfilled its artistic goals but could learn from Flynn and Fregoli who attracted much wider audiences by embracing the potential publicity of working with local communities and by using events such as Galway Arts Festival and Galway Theatre Festival respectively as platforms for staging their work. Fregoli, on the other hand, could channel some of the attention it has given to promotional strategies and practicality into offering a more rigorous engagement with contemporary Irish culture particularly in terms of a deeper engagement with increased racial and ethnic diversity. Yet each of these works shows the potential of devised performance, through its processes and outcomes, to challenge broader cultural stratifications and promote a revisionist questioning of deep-seated national values.

When performance practices known as devising proliferated internationally in the 1960s and 1970s, these were associated with a counter-cultural fringe that reacted against oppressive hierarchies. However – in the UK in particular – these modes of work seem to have become institutionalized. Even in a monograph on devising that is now over two decades old, Oddey's 1994 volume, the author acknowledges that by the early 1990s the radical associations of such practices were already beginning to wane (9). Goven, Nicholson and Normington also argue that, due to the mainstream adoption of devised practices, these can be scarcely still viewed as counter-cultural. However, the recentness of this current surge of devised practices in Ireland might reveal a present need for more inclusive communities, for bringing people together, and for sharing resources and recognition in a climate of diminished arts funding post-2008. In this context, and considering Dolan's theorizing of utopian performatives as effectively and affectively pointing towards a better future, devising might offer rehearsals for more socially democratic ways of living. Each of the works I have discussed interrogates the workings of privilege and exclusion; each can be aligned with challenging dominant historical constructions. Together, these productions showcase a move towards reconceiving ownership of theatre work in a country where an obsession with owning property has recently had devastating consequences, and where – in the theatre specifically – the prominence of authors and their plays has led to lack of recognition for diverse creative contributions. Overall, the 2012 productions of *King Alfred*, *Home* and *Frank Pig* reveal the ways in which sharing different stories and perspectives through devising 'can help to construct communities' *and* 'to question the nature of what constitutes community' (Govan et. al. 89).

Works Cited

'About Fregoli.' *Fregoli Theatre Company.* Rob McFeely, 2007. Web. 26 May 2014.

Central Statistics Office. *Census 2011 – Results for County Galway.* Galway: Galway County Council Social Inclusion Unit, 2011. Web. 21 November 2013.

Crosbie, Judith. 'Irish Anti-immigrant Attitudes Growing, Report Shows.' *The Irish Times* 26 June 2013. Web. 2 October 2013.

Dolan, Jill. *Utopia in Performance: Finding Hope at the Theater.* Ann Arbor:University of Michigan, 2005. Print.

Elam, Keir. *The Semiotics of Theatre and Drama.* London: Methuen, 1980. Print.

Etchells, Tim. *Certain Fragments: Contemporary Performance and Forced Entertainment.* London: Routledge, 1999. Print.

Flynn, Andrew. 'On *Frank Pig.*' Telephone interview. 9 Oct. 2013.

Govan, Emma, Katie Normington, and Helen Nicholson. *Making a Performance: Devising Histories and Contemporary Practices*. London: Routledge, 2007. Print.

Grehan, Ida. 'Alfred the Great at Kilchreest.' *The Irish Times* 26 Oct 1968: 10. *ProQuest Historical Newspapers*. Web. 25 Sept 2013.

Heddon, Deirdre, and Jane Milling. *Devising Performance: A Critical History*. Basingstoke: Palgrave Macmillan, 2006. Print.

Jacobus, Lee A. *The Bedford Introduction to Drama*. Boston: Bedford, 1997. Print.

Jürs-Munby, Karen. 'Introduction.' *Postdramatic Theatre*. Hans-Thies Lehmann. Trans. Karen Jürs-Munby. London: Routledge, 2006. 1-15. Print.

Oddey, Alison. *Devising Theatre: A Practical and Theoretical Handbook*. London: Routledge, 1994. Print.

O'Gorman, Siobhan. 'King Alfred: A Mystery Play.' Rev. of *King Alfred: A Mystery Play*. *Irish Theatre Magazine* 15 Mar. 2012. Web. 12 Oct. 2013.

Parks, Suzan-Lori. 'From Elements of Style' 1994. *The America Play and Other Works*. New York: Theatre Communications Group, 1995. 6-22. Print.

---. 'Possession' 1994. *The America Play and Other Works*. New York: Theatre Communications Group, 1995. 3-5. Print.

Sharry, Martin. 'Side-Show.' Personal interview. 19 June 2013.

Tivnan, Maria. 'Re: *Home*.' E-mail interview. 16 July 2013.

Walsh, Dick. 'Richard Walsh.' Telephone interview. 30 Sept. 2013.

12 | An Interview with Máiréad Ní Chróinín, Moonfish Theatre

Charlotte McIvor

Founded in 2006, Moonfish Theatre is a Galway-based company that creates work in English and Irish and is led by co-directors Máiréad and Ionia Ní Chróinín. They describe their work as 'creating work in English and Irish that is rooted in the limitless possibilities of the imagination' (Moonfish Theatre, 'About'). They work in a variety of genres and their body of work includes the restaging of classics, new writing, adaptations and devised work. Their approach to theatre-making is characterized by a blending of artistic mediums including shadow work, live music, dance, and puppetry. Their strong collaborative ethos means that the materials such as puppets (as well as the content) of their performances is created in-house, often in the rehearsal rooom, by a rotating and continually expanding team of collaborators called the 'Moonfish Gang' which includes Grace Kiely, Kate Costello, Matt Burke, Simon Boyle, Joanne Cummins and Zita Monahan. The company noted in a recent programme note for their 2014 adaptation of Joseph O'Connor's *Star of the Sea* that 'The ensemble directs each other. This gives every member of the company faith in and ownership of the production' (Ionia Ní Chróinín). They have also worked with collaborators from Scotland including Joanne Cummins, and their work has been seen throughout Ireland and in the UK.

They are strongly based in the West of Ireland and in the Galway community, making work that continually tests the limits of how Irish and English can be joined in performance for Irish and non-Irish speaking audiences alike as they make work adjacent to the Gaeltacht. Their own genesis is attributed by Máiréad Ní Chróinín to a 2006 Galway-based festival 'Project '06' and in addition to making their own work, they contribute significantly to the performance ecology of Galway at large. They do so through an ongoing association with the Galway Early Music Festival (a frequent commissioner of their work), collaborating with Taibhdhearc na Gaillimhe (the national Irish-language theatre), as well as participating actively in the steering of the Galway Theatre Festival, with Máiréad Ní Chróinín serving on the board.

Whether reimagining classic texts in local circumstances (and in Irish) such as their 2009 *Namhaid don Phobal,* a version of Henrik Ibsen's *Enemy of the People,* or bringing the legend of Mad Sweeney to Galway Early Music Festival audiences, Moonfish Theatre consistently revisit the stories and legends that audiences think they know, expanding their possibilities through their multidisciplinary and collaborative approach to making theatre. Another strong hallmark of their work is the creation of material for both adult and youth audiences, again challenging perceived binaries between theatre for adults and theatre for youth in works including *Noah's Ark* (2008), *The Secret Garden* (2009), and *Tromluí Phinocchio* (2010), which won the Stewart Parker Trust/BBC Northern Ireland Irish Language Theatre Award.

A contestation of history has remained at the centre of their work since their inaugural 2006 production of *Bonny & Read,* the tale of two eighteenth-century female pirates, Anne Bonny and Mary Read which retrieved these 'minor' figures from the footnotes of history. Their largest scale project to date, a 2014 adaptation of Joseph O'Connor's epic novel, *Star of the Sea*, engaged with the Famine, emigration and the erosion of the Irish language through a multi-media theatrical spectacle. The production however also remained stripped back (as is Moonfish's signature style) through their masterful use of a poor theatre aesthetic drawing on Brechtian theatre mechanics and the company's own recurring aesthetic tropes including the use of live music and onstage operation of technical elements. Moonfish Theatre's adaptation of *Star of the Sea* distilled the novel expertly to its thematic core, decisively revealing the skills of a company that is both epic and local in its scope. Currently, the company is preparing for a national and international tour of *Star of the Sea* as they continue to push the boundaries of their own practice and their audiences' imaginations in the West of Ireland and beyond.

Charlotte McIvor: Máiréad, you are the co-director of Moonfish Theatre. Can you talk about your company's mission?

Máiréad Ní Chróinín: Our mission is to create theatre that's rooted in the imagination, and that taps into understanding on a lot of different levels for different ages. Our mission has become more defined and more realized over the past few years, though. We've always aspired to create the kind of theatre that inspired us when we were growing up in Galway. We saw a lot of international theatre, particularly from Europe, as part of the Galway Arts Festival, and of course we also had the Macnas shows and parades. That theatre was often non-verbal, dynamic and magical, and it created really strong moments of immersion and wonder that stayed with us. So part of our mission is to capture that magic of theatre in our own shows. We also wanted to explore the fact that we have Irish and English and the access that gives us to questioning language in performance. But I would say that it took us a while to figure out how we were going to make theatre that would realize those aspirations. We did it instinctively with our first production, but then after that we did some productions of previously scripted work including British playwright Dennis Kelly's *After the End*, which took us in a different direction for a while.

C: So you would make a distinction in your work between script work and the devised performances in terms of your working process?

M: Yes, definitely. With a script, particularly a script by a living author, you're often not half as free to chop and change. Also, most scripts focus on dialogue, so it is harder to get away from language. You can definitely do it, but you have to make a very conscious decision to do that, and to have an approach that will allow you to do that, which we didn't have at the time. I think if we went back to scripts now we might have a different approach, but when we first started working with them we were quite reverential – you are taught to be, and once you have a script in front of you you start thinking about the whole process of creating theatre in a much more 'traditional' way. For example, with our first all-Irish production, *Namhaid don Phobal*, a version of Ibsen's *Enemy of the People*, we followed the model that was (and still is) common in Irish theatre – have a casting process for the roles; have a four week rehearsal period; do the show. We only realized in the middle of that production that that model didn't feel comfortable for us at all, and things that we were trying to do, like have an unrealistic set and bring movement elements into the production, were very difficult to achieve within that model. But that was a very valuable experience because we became conscious of how we like to work, whereas before we had only done it instinctively.

We do like working with scripts, but I think the kind of script that attracts us is quite rare, which is why we often chose to devise instead. The first script we did was *After the End* by Dennis Kelly, in 2008, which is a very dark story, but appealed to us because its premise – two people trapped together in a bunker after a nuclear disaster – was so unusual and gripping. We did *Namhaid don Phobal* in 2009 for a number of reasons – Irish had just been declared an official European language and we wanted to revive a script that showed the potential of Irish to bring European theatre to Ireland (*An Enemy of the People* had never been done in Ireland in English – the only time it was ever performed in Ireland was in Irish). Then, as well, Galway had just gone through the cryptosporidium crisis and we felt the script perfectly captured the conflict between self-interest and the common good that that health scare showed up. And, in general, it is just a masterful example of how to write a really absorbing political play, which is something we felt wasn't being seen onstage in Ireland much at the time. I suppose the thing that attracts us to scripts, when we do decide to do them, is a strong and unusual story, and the scope to create a show that has real integrity and theatricality. That's really exactly the same as what we always try to do – we always try to make the kind of theatre that we would like to see.

C: The first show that you did as a company was *Bonny & Read*. How then did Moonfish come together? Did you come together to produce that show or intending to start a company, and that just happened to be the first show?

M: We came together to do the show. I had just come back from working in Brussels and had worked with Róise Goan and Wayne Jordan's company Randalph SD, up in Dublin. I was stage manager on their show *The Public*, by Lorca, and one of the lines from that play is 'I wish you were a moonfish.' I just loved that image. In the way of a lot of young theatre companies, I think, we wanted to do a show and needed a company name, and that came to mind. *Bonny & Read* basically came about because of Project '06 in Galway. Project '06 was a one-off festival that was organized in 2006 as a kind of fringe (although they didn't want to call it that) while the Galway Arts Festival was on. Ionia and I arrived back in Galway in 2006 and there was just an incredible energy coming from Project '06. I think a lot of Galway companies started then, on the back of it. We just decided to produce *Bonny & Read* on the spur of the moment, to be a part of it all although we were too late to be included in the official programme. We ended up the fringe of the Fringe!

We produced it at the time and then waited a whole year before we did it again. Jo Cummins, who was in it with us, is Ionia's friend from Royal Scottish Academy of Music and Drama [now] in Glasgow, and she encouraged us to take it over to the Edinburgh Fringe in 2007. So there was a year-long gap between coming together to do that one show and then revising it completely and taking it over to the Fringe.

C: What was the process of making that work like?

M: It was great, actually – we loved it. We wanted to do a show for two women and we originally had the concept of the Gráinne Mhaol and Queen Elizabeth meeting. But I read up on that and it turned out that they were both quite old at the time, so we thought that wouldn't really suit Ionia and Jo. In the course of reading about Gráinne Mhaol, though, I came across two other female pirates in the 1700s called Anne Bonny and Mary Read. There was actually a lot of documentation about them because they were so unusual – there was the transcript of their trial, there were a lot of contemporary histories, and some eyewitness accounts, so there was a lot of really chunky stuff from the period. The other factor was that *Pirates of the Caribbean* had just come out, with its central character of Jack Sparrow (played by Johnny Depp), and that intrigued us because in the story of Anne Bonny and Mary Read they both end up on a pirate ship led by a captain called Calico Jack. There were a lot of parallels between the real-life character Calico Jack and Jack Sparrow, and it kind of annoyed us that the makers of *Pirates of the Caribbean* had seemingly taken the character of Calico Jack and put him in this really cool film, and had completely ignored the equally interesting characters of Anne Bonny and Mary Read.

So one of the things that drew us to the piece was that these two great characters were just sitting there ready to be embodied as interesting women with incredible, true stories. Mary Read went off to find her love who was fighting on the battlefields, and, as in a lot of folk songs, she dressed up as a man to go find him. She did find him, and they married, but he died and she decided that she would have a lot more freedom if she dressed as a man. So she did, and finally took to the seas as a pirate. Anne Bonny had a different, but similarly incredible trajectory, so there was so much there to be mined.

Because we had a background in song, one of the ways that we wanted to tell the story was to investigate all the kind of folk songs that could tell parts of the women's stories. So we took folk-songs like 'Will You Go to Flanders,' and songs about sailing the high seas, and things like that, and used them as a key way of telling the stories. It wasn't a musical, but there were a lot of songs taking the audience through the story.

C: This has continued to be a hallmark of your work through the years. It seems like most productions employ music in some way, so was that an intention to continue that as a thread through the work of the company from the beginning?

M: I think it happened organically. A lot of what we now recognize as our hallmarks were just elements we liked employing, we didn't necessarily sit down and think, how will we use music in this show? I suppose the idea of live music stems again from shows that we've seen and enjoyed. Having live music on stage was an aspect of theatre that wasn't very common when we started, although it seems like everyone is doing it now. It was a bit ignored, the fact that you can use live music and live song in performance, as opposed to just taping everything and pushing the button. For us, pre-recorded sound and music lacked that kind of sensual texture you get on stage. Also, it's just interesting to watch musicians and how they interact – think of a jazz band, and how they're all constantly talking to each other with their eyes or their gestures. It's just so interesting to watch. We've been lucky so far to work with musicians who are also really good performers, because it seems like a lot of musicians just want to hide when they're in a theatre piece – they're behind the scrim, or in the pit, or something like that. But for us, we didn't just want the music live, we wanted the performer – we wanted the audience to see the musicians and to see that they were a part of it. So in *Bonny & Read* we had three musicians live onstage when we went to Edinburgh, and they were a part of the action as well – they would sometimes take on the role of other pirates and things. More and more, we work with people who can sing and play.

C: So there's the Moonfish gang, who started out as you and Ionia and Jo. How do you determine who is in the collective and how are decisions made amongst the group of you?

M: Well, through *Bonny & Read* we met Grace, who has been in most of our shows since, and who's really another Moonfish founder member (the other founder member is Úna, who hasn't been in many shows recently but is always there supporting us). A lot of the time we've met people through other productions: I directed Zita in a Mephisto production, and Ionia worked with Morgan on a few shows with Branar. We tend to meet people that way and then often we've invited them to do one of our 'mini-shows,' which are shows that we've made for the 'family event' in the Galway Early Music Festival. *Bonny & Read* (the revived version) was one, and the others were *Noah's Ark*,

Aucassin & Nicolette and *Buile Shuibhne*. Our mom, who runs the festival, usually wants shows with a medieval theme, and often she'd just give us a medieval text and say, riff on that. These are our 'mini-shows.' They're usually about half an hour long, and developed over a week or two weeks, but I think actually they've really contributed to building up our aesthetic and our methodology, because we're devising from texts that aren't necessarily intelligible for our audiences. So we have to try to keep the old-style language but then we also have to think, how are we going to interpret this to an audience of kids and adults? And we're also trying to make theatre that will appeal to different generations, so we're also asking, what's going to get the adults laughing, what's going to get the kids into it?

They're always a lot of fun to make. We all get together for a week or two, everybody makes all the set and props, everybody composes the songs, everybody just figures out how things are going to work. So it's a great introduction to the Moonfish way of working, which is very collaborative, and depends a lot on working with like-minded people. Looking back now, those projects were just fantastic for getting people inspired, and for figuring out who we could work with and how we could work together. It let us establish a good short-hand with people – for example, for *Star of the Sea* we used a lot of the overhead projector stuff we experimented with on *Buile Shuibhne*. And the fact that Grace, Ionia and I had all worked on *Buile Shuibhne* meant it was easier to jump in and figure out quickly what would work and what wouldn't for *Star of the Sea*. The 'mini-shows' are also good in the sense that we all like to work on every aspect of the show, so the performers rarely just perform, they've also had a role in the writing, or the composing, or the sewing of props, or the gathering of costumes. Everyone just kind of chips in and does what needs to be done. We'd say, we need really big puppet feet for the Dad (in *Aucassin & Nicolette*) because all you're ever going to see are his feet, kind of like in a *Tom & Jerry* cartoon. And Orlagh [de Bhaldraithe], who has worked with us on a few shows, would say, 'I'll make them this evening', and she'd come in the next day with huge puppet legs on sticks. Or we'd decide that we needed some shadow puppets [for *Buile Shuibhne*, for example] so we'd put aside a day for making-and-doing and all sit down and mess with feathers and gels and things like that on an overhead projector to see what worked.

Because everyone has a say in every aspect of the production our process is intensely collaborative and consensual, and so working with people on a 'mini-show' is a good way for them and us to figure out if they suit that style of working, and if they enjoy it.

It's hard to pick apart the process of decision-making because it's so collaborative. In terms of the shows we've done so far, usually myself or Ionia suggest an idea for a show and we see what people think. So far, everyone has liked the suggestions, and I suppose that has a lot to do with the fact that we work with people who have a similar approach to theatre. Then, a lot of the process has to do with questions, usually posed by Ionia or me, like: What is the best thing to focus on today? What do we want to show about this character? How do we convey this particular type of atmosphere? ... And all of us giving suggestions. Even the order of the day is up for discussion. Often someone will give a suggestion and then someone else will tweak it a bit, and it'll go on like that, so at the end it's very hard to point to anything onstage and say – that was so-and-so's idea. Usually it's an amalgamation of a few ideas. I always use a soap-bubble analogy – watching the ideas come together in the room is like watching small soap bubbles slowly start to combine and become one big bubble.

When there's a lot of voices in the room and we need to make a decision, usually Ionia or I have the role of making a call and deciding what idea we're going to focus on. But often we'll try one idea and then if that doesn't work we'll try another idea – usually it's fairly obvious to everyone what works and what doesn't. It takes more time but it's definitely worth it. One of the things we've discovered is that when people are very involved in the creation of the show they make decisions based on the good of the show as a whole, rather than just defending their own character or role, so a lot of decisions that you would think would be very difficult, like cutting a whole scene, are actually not, because the people who are in that scene recognize that the show works better without it. In our process you have to be up for trying as many ideas as possible, but you also have to be able to let ideas go, and not to take it personally if one of your ideas doesn't work. It's impossible to say which ideas will work and which won't – you don't know until you try, so you have to be ready to throw them in but then throw them out again.

C: What kind of research or table work would the company do before coming into the room? Would everyone come in with resources and ideas or would you present people with ideas to work with at the beginning of a process and then go on from there?

M: Prior to *Star of the Sea* we didn't do a lot of research beforehand, apart from reading the book we were going to work from (in the case of *The Secret Garden*, and *Tromluí Phinocchio*). One of the first things we did for *The Secret Garden*, because we wanted to get away from the text, was to ask the gang – if this was a Macnas parade, what would the floats be? And then we took a day and drew our parade ideas on huge bits of paper. For *Tromluí* we made a map with pictures to show all the different episodes in the book. For the first stage of *Star of the Sea* we didn't do any research either, we just asked people to read the book and then on the first day we created a huge mind map of images and quotes from the book. But for the second and third stages of *Star of the Sea* we did do a good bit of research – more on the aesthetic side than the historical side of things. We kept having to pull ourselves away from the idea that we were making a show directly about the Famine, and come back to the fact that we were making a show based on *Star of the Sea* (the novel). We didn't really try to bring in much more history than was already in the novel. But we did do a lot of research to try to find inspirations for how we were going to tell the story; Ionia and I gathered YouTube clips and images and audio files and showed them to the gang, and then everyone went away and sent in their own images and clips. We ended up putting together a huge Prezi file, with loads of inspirations from puppetry, music, dance, sculpture, painting ... and a lot of them ended up in one way or another influencing the show. For example, we had a video of a puppet show about the concentration camps, called *Kamp*, and their approach to representing the people in the concentration camps ended up influencing our stick-figure representations of the Famine victims that we put up on the overhead projector and used in the 'Steerage' passages in the show.

C: You've had such a huge range of work as we've discussed, everything from stories that are devised out of fairy-tales to folktales to translated work. Given the work you produce is diverse in terms of genre, how do you approach positioning your company for funding?

M: We usually focus on what we've done post-*Namhaid don Phobal* because that's when we started to consciously think about the type of theatre we wanted to make and our methodology, particularly the longer time-frame we take to develop projects. So we usually say that we are a company that focuses on devising from texts, that we create work for all ages, and that we enjoy working bilingually. We do try to emphasize that we don't always work bilingually – it's very much dependent on the text. Not every text that we might want to do would work bilingually – there mightn't be a reason for it, or it just mightn't work theatrically to have two languages going on at the same time. And then, on the other hand, we might one day decide to devise a show completely through Irish. That's definitely one of our goals, to see what happens when you devise completely through Irish, through a language that isn't English.

C: What has the reaction been to having that flexibility or espousing that flexibility as the core of what you do?

M: Well, it is difficult to get people to get their heads around that flexibility and we have to be very careful with our publicity that we make it clear who our audience is. For example, a lot of people would have known us from *The Secret Garden* and *Tromluí Phinocchio*, both of which were for younger audiences, which *Star of the Sea* is not, so for *Star of the Sea* we had to make sure we emphasized that it was for over sixteen-year-olds. But it wasn't a huge problem, I think because *Star of the Sea* was so well known as a novel, and also because we didn't approach schools, which we would when we're publicizing the shows for younger audiences. People do tend to want to see you in one bracket or the other, though, and it doesn't help that a lot of the time people don't think of theatre for young audiences as being of the same quality as theatre for adult audiences. Whereas for us, it all has the potential to be high quality theatre. One of the companies we would be inspired by are Kneehigh, a company based in Cornwall in the UK, and they started out doing pantomimes and then moved into doing shows for adults (although they still do shows for young audiences too, I think). But they brought their pantomime aesthetic into their adult shows and because of that they created shows that were unusual and exciting for adults. I think we're the same in that we've brought the aesthetic that we've had for the shows like *The Secret Garden* and *Tromluí Phinocchio* into *Star of the Sea*, and that's meant that the show is a very different experience for our adult audiences than they would usually get at the theatre.

In terms of the bilingual theatre, once you start bringing Irish into shows people like to place you into that bracket: 'Oh you make theatre in Irish.' A lot of people don't really understand the concept of bilingual; they think, oh it's through Irish but there's English subtitles, or something like that, and you have to try to explain that there's actually equal amounts of each language in the show. But when you talk to people about it, and particularly when they experience it themselves, they get very excited by the idea that Irish and English are both there as languages on stage. When they see the potential there is to use language, even if it's not directly intelligible, as a way of telling you something about a character, or about a situation, people get very excited about that. For example, in *Tromluí Phinocchio* we decided we wanted Pinocchio to be a rebellious teenager, and the way we communicated that to the audience was that, while his father spoke

Irish to him, he refused to speak Irish back and only ever spoke English until the end. That was a short-hand the audience immediately understood – even if they didn't understand what Geppetto was saying they understood the rebellion in Pinocchio not speaking Irish back to him. With *Star of the Sea* people reacted really strongly to the way the difference between the statuses and fortunes of the characters was emphasized by whether they were English speakers or native Irish speakers. And, again, at the end, Mary Duane chooses to give her name in English instead of Irish, which for many audience members was a reminder of everything Irish emigrants chose to reject and leave behind them when they left Ireland. You don't need to speak Irish to understand those moments, but you can only create those moments if you work with both languages. I think there's a real openness to that potential.

C: Your work sometimes uses cross-gender casting. What makes you decide to work this way in the context of an individual production? Is this something that characterizes Moonfish's approach to thinking about the role of the actor in storytelling?

M: For us, the priority really is the ensemble – our process only works if we're working with people who have the right kind of energy and approach and skills, so getting that is a priority for us over any kind of gender consideration. Then, our approach in terms of an individual production is to look at how the energy of a particular performer works with a particular character. Sometimes that has to do with age and gender, but sometimes it has to do with the performer's presence, their voice ... lots of things. Again, it's something we've done organically and we're only now starting to think about it and its ramifications because it was questioned a lot by ourselves and others during the development of *Star of the Sea*.

I suppose it comes back to the fact that we feel that the audience can handle having dual experience of the theatre piece, where they see it from the outside and from the inside. So they see the world being made at the same time as they are allowing themselves to be immersed in the world. Creating that kind of dual perspective is part of the reason we like having the foley live on stage, and with the cross-gender casting it's the same: we feel that the audience can make a distinction between the character they're identifying with and the actor who is bringing that character to life. It's actually part of what the audience enjoy, and when we asked audiences at our works-in-progress for *Star of the Sea* about the cross-gender casting they told us it didn't bother them at all – most of them forgot that Zita and Grace were women in male roles. And the feedback we've had since from a lot of audience members who saw the show in the Galway International Arts Festival was that they found it very exciting. We've had a few people spontaneously come up to us and say things like, 'you see a lot of men playing women, but you never see women playing men. But it really works; people should do it more often.' Something *Star of the Sea* taught us is that audiences can cope with a lot more than you think.

C: In terms of your experience with Arts Council and other funding, what are the consequences of defining yourself as working through devised performance when you apply for funding?

M: Well, I think the Arts Council are open to devised performance. In fact, I think they're more open to that than if you went to them and said you wanted to do another production of a Martin McDonagh play – because they emphasize the creation of new work, particularly by young companies I think, and new ways of working. The way the funding is structured now, it also helps, because if you're like us and you devise over a long period of time, you can apply for the development strand first, and then apply for the production strand to create the actual production. I think, though, that you do have to prove yourself and find funding elsewhere for the first few years. We just got our first Arts Council grant so previously we've had to find other sources of funding. But that seems to be par for the course – you apply three or four times and then, if they can see that you are committed and developing your practice, they'll try to support you. Of course, it's never guaranteed, but I wouldn't say that defining yourself as working through devised performance is a disadvantage.

The flexibility we spoke about is probably more of an issue for us, because there are often separate funding sources for 'children's theatre' and 'adult theatre.' Because of the work we do we tend to move between both and that can be difficult, because if you're not making theatre for young audiences all the time you don't build up the same relationship with those funding sources as other companies that make that their sole focus.

C: There is often a binary made between devised performance and then the writer's theatre, or a writerly theatre. Breaking this binary down seems to increasingly be a priority of Moonfish's work, so how would you respond to this perceived binary in the field?

M: Well I'd love if there wasn't, because I think that it'd be great to have a writer in the room. I would see people like Shaun Dunne traversing that barrier, definitely. When I see a Shaun Dunne performance it's very hard to figure out if someone wrote it from scratch or if it was workshopped ... it has the aesthetics of a devised piece but the kind of language he uses is like the language of 'writerly' theatre: he uses language very beautifully and I think that it would be great to have more writers who work that way. I suppose there's two ways to look at writing for theatre: you can see it as a process of creating the entire piece – the plot, the characters, and the words the performers speak; or you can see it as just writing the actual words spoken by the performers. I think maybe there is definitely a way to bring writers into devising if we look at writing for theatre from the second perspective. So the writer as an ensemble member is a co-creator of the overarching piece, but as the writer, she or he is responsible for what is spoken. For me, speech and words are another theatrical element, and I think with *Star of the Sea* we found that, as we create bigger productions, it's great to work with people who have an area of specific expertise. We all feed into the ideas about the set and the costumes, but at the end of the day there's one person whose responsibility is to go and spend time coming up with a design and making that design happen. It's just a question of time and focus – it's good to have people who can focus on each area of the work. But, having said that, they have to be able to come back and take suggestions, changes, and all that, and they have to be able to work alongside the development of the show; they can't just come along beforehand and give us something finished. Everything has to grow together, and that often means that a change in how we decide to tell the story will mean a change in the costumes or in the sound ... and similarly in the script, if we had a writer working with us. We might decide we need a whole new dialogue, or we might decide to cut a dialogue out. Obviously, of course, the performers then have to be able to adapt to that as well and learn new lines all the time, or unlearn lines sometimes.

C: How do you handle documentation of your work if it isn't entirely based on a textual score?

M: We do a lot of video recording – that would be how we document a lot of stuff. Unfortunately not usually the final performances because at that point we lack the resources and money – all our energy is focused on making the show happen. But the rehearsal process is documented on film, for ourselves mostly so that we can go back and figure out what we thought worked and what didn't. I suppose if it came down to publication, it would just be a matter of going back over those revisions and rewriting them and figuring out which one we're kind of happy with. But one of the interesting things about the process is that, because everything is intertwined, the script for a Moonfish show is often two lines of dialogue and then the rest of the page is all stage directions – so and so walks here, so and so picks this up, so and so pushes this button, so and so says this line while so and so is putting on this hat ... So it's actually really hard to write it in the traditional form in a way that someone could possibly re-stage it. You really probably would need a video of *Tromluí Phinocchio* to understand how the script worked.

It's very hard to get down every single beat of everybody's performance because it's grown organically, so each performer has a kind of bodily memory – this is how I move here, this is how I'm going here – and nobody else has that particular experience. We've tried to improve with *Star of the Sea* and keep detailed records, and work with a stage manager, but things always keep changing, so keeping the script up to date is very difficult. But again, it's something we've become more aware of as a recurring trait of our process so we've started to think about how we can address that. I've been wondering if something like dance notation might work, but I haven't had the chance to look into that in any detail yet.

C: How would you yourself ultimately define devising as a practice?

M: For us anyway, devising is a way of creating a story or experience that grows out of the combination of lots of different imaginations and intelligences in the room. So that it's never just the product of one consciousness or one individual intent, and what you end up with then is something that is more than the sum of its parts. Obviously, that also happens when a director takes a script and actors take characters, and stuff like that, but I suppose with devised performance it's different because everything is equal in the room at the beginning. Nothing has priority – script, character, set, movement, they're all there but there's no pre-defined idea about how they are going to come together, and what priority they're going to be given at any particular moment in the show.

C: What are the potential benefits and drawbacks of the devised approach in terms of driving your own theatre practice forward?

M: I suppose the drawbacks of working with a piece that is in a constant state of evolution is that you do have to find a way to make space for the performers to learn lines and get to grips with character – if that is something that's important to the show. It is important in *Star of the Sea* so at a certain point we had to draw a line under the script and decide that was that – for this iteration of the production anyhow. The other drawback is that the work is very ephemeral. It's the creation of a certain group of people at a certain moment of time – I'm not sure how easy it would be to bring a show like *Tromluí Phinocchio* back now that we've put it to bed, for example. We did do *The Secret Garden* with a different cast, but we still had it on the road at that point. If we were to bring either of those shows back with a different cast I think we'd have to find some way of allowing the new performers to own the show – maybe to do some workshopping first and even change the script a bit. Because of that the number of shows we can have in production is limited by our own and the gang's availability.

The benefits of working this way are, I suppose, that we are completely involved in the whole life of the production, and that is how we like to work, so there's great job satisfaction involved. We also get to create the kind of theatre we find exciting and invigorating, and I suppose because our process is quite unique, the outcome is quite unique too.

Works Cited

'About.' Moonfish Theatre. Moonfish Theatre, n.d. Web. 17 Dec. 2014

Section Four: Northern Approaches

13 | Reawakening Belfast's Streets: Tourism and Education in Site-Specific Northern Irish Theatre

Eleanor Owicki

In the wake of 'the Troubles,' the thirty-year period of sectarian violence that shook Northern Ireland, the city of Belfast has struggled to find a new identity in the face of competing needs and goals. Many living in the area want Belfast (and indeed all of Northern Ireland) to imagine itself as undivided. These people speak of the importance of creating a 'shared future' or a 'shared society' in which Catholics and Protestants will not only refrain from conflict, but actually will consider themselves one community. In contrast, some emphasize the different values and histories of the two traditional communities, worrying that the effort to create a shared society will require them to sacrifice their understanding of their distinct, cultural identities. While these concerns primarily relate to the ways Belfast sees itself, there are also worries about the image Belfast projects to outsiders. Those who would like to see Belfast become a popular tourist destination struggle with how to address the city's divided past (and, indeed, present). While so-called 'Troubles tourism' is popular, there are also people working to create more optimistic visions of Belfast for public consumption.

This chapter explores two 2010 plays staged on the streets of Belfast that embrace these tensions. *The West Awakes* and *Belfast Bred* take the form of highly theatrical walking tours. *The West Awakes* focuses on the history of the Falls Road, a Catholic neighbourhood in West Belfast; *Belfast Bred* focuses on the city's culinary history and contemporary 'foodie scene.' The plays were devised by the site-specific theatre company Kabosh under the direction of Paula McFetridge, also the company's Artistic Director. The processes of creating the two plays were highly collaborative. For each, Kabosh partnered with a preexisting organization to craft a piece that would be theatrically innovative while also supporting the organization's specific goals. To create *The West Awakes,* Kabosh partnered with Coiste, an organization of former republican prisoners and a team of writers including Jimmy McAleavey, Laurence McKeown, Kieron Magee and Roseleen Walsh while *Belfast Bred* was developed in collaboration with the owners of several Belfast restaurants and playwright Seth Linder. The two plays speak directly to the moments and spaces for which they were devised. As a result, the finished products represent a negotiation between Kabosh's artistic goals, the organizations' missions, and the larger concerns of the tourism industry.

The goals of both plays may be broken into three major categories: creating compelling theatrical events, educating audiences, and fostering a positive image of the parts of the city in which the performances are staged. To fulfill the first goal, the creators drew on their experience with more traditional theatre; while both plays maintain the structure of a tour, the authors introduce tension through conflicts between characters (in the case of *Two Roads West*) and a race against the clock (in the case of *Belfast Bred*). These stories are then put in the service of the second goal, educating the audiences. In particular, both plays focus on the history of Belfast before the troubles. They draw attention to aspects of the city's history that are overlooked when citizens and visitors focus only on the bloody conflict of the late twentieth century. These histories are in part shaped by the final goal of 'selling' Belfast. While acknowledging the less savoury parts of the city's history, both plays present the areas in which they are staged as vibrant and attractive sites, open to locals and visitors alike.[1]

Kabosh is intimately and inextricably tied to its performance locations. The company has devised plays for a number of non-traditional venues, including Gavin Kostick's *This is What We Sang* (2009) in the Belfast Synagogue and Jimmy McAleavey's *Titans* (2012) in the new Belfast Titanic centre. Before *The West Awake* and *Belfast Bred* the company had already structured a play around the idea of tourism. In 2008, they staged Laurence McKeown's *Two Roads West*, which took place in a taxi during a political tour of the sectarian neighbourhoods of the Falls and the Shankill roads. By staging theatre

---

[1] Anthony Jackson and Jenny Kidd's *Performing Heritage* offers significant insight and explanations on the ways audiences may respond to the different goals of theatre in museum contexts.

in and explicitly about iconic locations, Kabosh hopes to enact a two-way transfer of meaning: audiences' understandings of the play will be informed by their knowledge of the space, and their understanding of the space will be changed by the performance. Joanne Tompkins notes that, in site-specific theatre, 'space, place, site, landscape and location are regularly characterized by ambiguity, contingency, and unsettlement' (1). The inevitability of shifting meanings is particularly important in Belfast, a city where space is frequently segregated and imbued with deep political symbolism. Projects like Kabosh's site specific plays challenge the audience's assumptions about the spaces and those who inhabit them, and in doing so have the potential to transform relationships between the people of Belfast as well as the city's tourist image.

Finally, while both plays largely depict the past, they are also invested in showcasing Belfast's current modern status. In her book *Destination Culture,* Barbara Kirshenblatt-Gimblett argues that this is common to performances of heritage in developing nations. Although Northern Ireland does not precisely fit into this category, the legacy of conflict means that it has frequently been viewed as 'savage' and 'uncivilized' by many outsiders. According to Kirshenblatt-Gimblett, technologies allow tourist performances to emphasize the state's movement into modernity even as the content creates the appearance of viewing the past (8). Although neither *The West Awakes* nor *Belfast Bred* uses modern technology to achieve their effects, they do draw attention to the ways in which the city has moved beyond its past. *The West Awakes* reassures audiences that the Falls road is now a safe place for tourists to wander and investigate. *Belfast Bred*, for example, promises that gourmet food is readily available in Belfast for visitors who want a more 'high end' experience. In this way, the plays point to the better, brighter present and future envisioned by much of Belfast's tourism industry.

The West Awakes

The West Awakes showcases the tension between tourism narratives designed to unify Belfast and the more divisive narratives associated with the two traditional communities (in this case, Catholic nationalists). In devising the performance, the creators navigated this tension, attempting to create a piece that looks optimistically towards the future without airbrushing the past. *The West Awakes* is staged in one of the most iconic neighbourhoods of the Troubles; the Falls is a working-class, Catholic district in West Belfast which was both the site and origin of much of the violence during the conflict. In August 1969 a Loyalist mob attacked the nearby Bombay Street, driving Catholic residents from their homes, many of which were entirely destroyed. Similarly, during the Troubles, the British Army maintained a base on the top floor of the Divis Flats, which housed more than 2,400 residents. This allowed the Army to closely monitor activity along the Falls Road and increased the nationalists' feeling that their community was singled out for special scrutiny. In addition to their suffering, many residents of the Falls were members or supporters of the IRA and thus contributed to the organization's attacks on state forces, loyalist paramilitary groups, and civilians from both communities. The street therefore provided rich history and symbolism for *The West Awakes*. The changes it has undergone since the Good Friday Agreement also shaped the performance.

Since the end of the Troubles, the Falls has become an important destination for visitors to Belfast. Its complicated history and the many murals created during and after the violence draw tourists hoping to understand the conflict. While some visitors simply pass through the Falls on bus tours, others stop on the street; the money this latter group spends has noticeably improved the economic conditions of the area. The Coiste tours have been one effort to both court these visitors and share the republican narrative of the Troubles. The organization is composed of former republican prisoners – Coiste translates to 'committee' in Gaelic – who lead tours of the Falls with particular attention to the area's political history. These tours begin at the one remaining tower of the Divis Flats and then travel west, ending at the Milltown Cemetery where hunger-striker Bobby Sands and many other prominent republicans are buried. The guides describe the history of the area, emphasizing the ways Protestant control of the state brought suffering to Catholics before and during the Troubles.

In addition to its explicit political stance, Coiste is also a part of the city's commercial tourism industry. Indeed, its website (www.coiste.ie) presents the tours as sightseeing and educational opportunities rather than foregrounding their political message. Tickets for the tour can be purchased from the Belfast Welcome Centre; this cooperation between a government agency and a group of people who had long refused to acknowledge that government's legitimacy would have been unthinkable in previous decades. Guides generally present an optimistic take on the current status of both Belfast and the Falls, depicting them as vibrant and welcoming locations. During the tours they greet people on the street warmly and by name; they frequently recommend pubs, cafes, and shops and encourage visitors to spend more money in the area. Thus, the tours fill both commercial and political roles.

In devising *The West Awakes*, Kabosh needed to create a piece that would work within this complex framework but also introduce a new element into the pre-existing Coiste tour. *The West Awakes* uses the structure of the tours, but inserts five short plays at iconic locations along its route: St Comgalls School, the Conway Mill, An Cultúrlann McAdam Ó Fiaich (a centre for Irish culture and language), the City Cemetery, and the Milltown Cemetery. Each play consists of a male and female character, played by the same two actors. In between the Kabosh short plays, the tours continue as normal; the guides are not asked to alter their presentations to fit the performances.

The short plays bring dramatic tension that is not otherwise present in the tour. The guides are typically compelling storytellers, but they relate past events rather than allowing spectators to see the stories unfold. In contrast, the plays allow audiences to 'step back in time' and get a glimpse at the ways people (apparently) lived in the past. The stories are simple: each play centres around one specific conflict between the two characters. This conflict is generally personal, although it also has political overtones. For example, in the scene at the Conway Mill, a woman begs a foreman who had raped her to bend the rules and allow her eight-year-old daughter (a product of that rape) to work in the mill. The audience sees the woman standing in front of them, and the powerlessness caused by her gender and poverty becomes 'real' in a way that would have been unlikely if the guide had merely told the story of such a woman. Freddie Rokem argues that performances of history can uniquely eliminate (or at least diminish) the sense of distance that exists between past and present. 'The theatre "performing history" seeks to overcome both the separation and exclusion from the past, striving to create a community where the events from the past will matter again' (xii). This is certainly the case with the plays in *The West Awakes*, which allow audiences to see and feel the effects of the poverty and oppression described by the guides.

As part of its educational goal, *The West Awakes* works to unsettle preconceptions about the area. The Coiste tours arguably conform to most tourists' expectations about the Falls by focusing on republican politics through iconic images such as murals. In contrast, the dramatic structure of the plays in *The West Awakes* allows a wider array of opinions to be voiced. In particular, the first play works to put the audience in a mindset where they will be open to having their preconceptions about the area challenged. This is staged in front of St

Comgalls School and is the only play to be set during the Troubles. Set in 1969, it features a news reporter and her cameraman arguing over the best way to present a shooting from the night before. The play begins with the reporter speaking to camera; in a formal and crisp English accent, she describes the tense situation on the Falls and claims that their camera was stolen and held for ransom. The cameraman stops recording to scoff at this assertion. Switching to her natural Belfast accent now that she is no longer being recorded, the reporter replies: 'Well we can't just say we're on the Falls Road and the area is very quiet. Mothers are doing their shopping, kids are playing in the streets and the people are very warm and hospitable.' Thus, the performance argues that the images of the Falls Road broadcast internationally during the Troubles did not necessarily represent the lived experience of its residents. The play tells audiences to forget the things they think they know, and open themselves up to being surprised.

In many ways this sentiment echoes the 'tourism' goal of both *The West Awakes* and the Coiste tours. This first play suggests that the Falls was never as hostile to outsiders as its reputation suggested, and that it has only become more welcoming. Even the performance's title highlights this goal; the idea of 'awakening' mirrors much of the rhetoric of the post-Troubles tourist industry. The site-specific nature of the play becomes particularly important here – the 'rethinking' encouraged by the play is supported by walking along the Falls and seeing that it is, indeed, safe. The scenes of residents going about their business echo the reporter's claim that daily life continues as normal.

The West Awakes also works to counter some of the tour's actual or perceived sectarian biases. In their regular tours, the Coiste guides explicitly acknowledge that their position – as both republicans and ex-prisoners – shapes their understandings of the conflict. These understandings emphasize the wrong that was done to Catholics during the state's history and minimize the violence done by republicans (the guides acknowledge this, but generally in drier, more matter-of-fact language). They generally do not comment on the events that led to their own imprisonment, further distancing spectators from the specific violent actions of the IRA (or, of course, the miscarriages of the justice system that imprisoned many without a fair trial). The strongest message of the Coiste tour is that the people of the Falls (and, indeed, all nationalists in Northern Ireland), have been oppressed by state forces and the Protestant hegemony that controlled the state since its creation. When I have taken the tour, the guides have been clear that they support the peace process and believe that Northern Ireland is much more just than it was before and during the Troubles. At the same time, the guides have routinely articulated that they do not believe that full equity has been achieved; they see the Good Friday Agreement as a transition in the tactics of achieving a united Ireland rather than an abandonment of that goal.

While the tours do not present all Protestants as oppressive or immoral, they make little effort to directly convey the experiences or opinions of the 'other' community. The structure of *The West Awakes* allows Kabosh to create space for a wider variety of viewpoints. For example, several plays reference James Connolly, who lived for a time on the street and was executed for his part in the Easter Rising of 1916. The play at the City Cemetery is set at the time that the news of his death reached Belfast; it depicts an argument about Connolly's legacy. A nationalist woman and a unionist soldier discuss the merits of independence and the role the British Empire has played in the world. They passionately disagree, but treat each other with a respect grounded in their shared concern for the working class and future generations. The play certainly favours the woman's pro-Connolly point of view, but it also makes space for those who disagree to do so with respect and dignity.

The desire to introduce voices from outside the tour's republican viewpoint is particularly evident in the performance at An Cultúrlann. The building is a cultural centre for Irish identity, and in particular for the Irish language, but the play focuses on its more distant history as a Presbyterian church. It depicts the ghosts of a fictional young man and woman who met and fell in love through their attendance at the church but were eventually separated. This love story runs counter to the common narratives of segregation around Belfast – it reminds audiences that the Falls had not always been a 'no-go' area for Protestants. It also imagines a blending between identities of Irish and British lineage (as well as the building's past and present) when the characters' spirits began to slip into the Irish language. In this way, the play embodies the idea of a 'shared society' and explicitly presents sympathetic, non-sectarian Protestant voices in ways that the tours generally do not.

It is also important to note, however, that this goal of 'selling' both Belfast and the Falls means that the plays do not address some of the most traumatic moments in the street's history. Indeed, the only piece set during the Troubles – the play outside St Comgall's school – is the story of a non-event overblown by the press. Had those who devised

The West Awakes taken a different approach to balancing the three imperatives of dramatic tension, education, and tourism, the play might have looked very different. The plays could have drawn attention to the specific injustices suffered by those on the Falls during the Troubles; plays around the burning of Bombay Street or the oppressive surveillance of the army could have been both educational and dramatically compelling. For the play in the Milltown Cemetery, Kabosh made the decision not to focus on the graves of the hunger strikers. Instead, they depicted a conversation between two lesser-known residents who had played important roles in earlier Belfast history. This decision was made primarily because the hunger strikers were already prominent in both the tour and the public imagination, but it also seems likely that focusing on them could have embroiled the performance in sectarian politics in a way it sought to avoid. The overall effects of these choices were that *The West Awakes* was gentler than it might have been, but remained far from apolitical.

Belfast Bred

While *The West Awake*'s tone is ultimately hopeful, offering visions of a revitalized neighbourhood and connections across political divides, it focuses on the serious social issues of poverty and labour rights. Seth Linder's *Belfast Bred*, in contrast, takes a far more lighthearted, celebratory tone. It also more explicitly foregrounds its commercial and tourist connections. The performance has been immensely popular in Belfast, being remounted a number of times since its 2010 premiere. It offers a tour of Belfast's culinary history led by a most unlikely guide – Barney (played by Fra Gunn in the performance's initial iterations), who had served as a chef on the Titanic, and been frozen in the infamous iceberg on the fatal night in April 1912. Global warming released him from this frozen captivity, and Barney has only just returned to his native city where he has been challenged to recreate the banquet from the launch of the Titanic. To do so, he needs the audience to help him collect the right ingredients from shops and restaurants around the Belfast City Centre. His costume reflects the whimsical, out of place nature of his character – he is dressed in spotless chef whites (apparently undamaged by the crash or their time in the iceberg), but draped with seaweed, fishing nets, and even a crab. His appearance immediately sets the tone of the piece – light hearted, but with a very specific mission and story.

During the performance, Barney ushers the audience from one shop or restaurant to another, giving them insight into Belfast's culinary history. At each destination, Barney turns the group over to a representative from the business, who gives an overview of the institution's history as well as the history of particular foods in Northern Ireland. The stops have varied slightly in different iterations of the tour, but the first is generally Sawer's Deli, which opened in 1897. Here, owner Kieran Sloan draws the audience's attention to the broad range of local produce present, emphasizing its quality and abundance. Other stops on the tour have included the John Hewitt Bar (for a discussion of Northern Irish microbreweries) and Nick's Warehouse (where founder and food personality Nick Price discusses local cheeses). The tour ends at St George's Market, where producers from throughout the state gather to sell their wares.

Belfast Bred is structurally an inversion of *The West Awakes*. In the latter play, a member of the sponsoring organization leads the tour, while the drama is contained in a small number of stops. In *Belfast Bred*, however, an actor leads the tour while non-actors speak at the stops. In many ways, the tour portions of the two plays are similar – in each, one man walks audiences through 'living' neighbourhoods, drawing their attention to locations of important events and filling in general history. However, Barney's quest adds an extra dimension of urgency to *Belfast Bred*. McFetridge and Linder deliberately incorporated this element of dramatic tension in order to make the play truly 'theatrical.' Barney is not simply a costumed tour guide, he is a character with a specific history and motivation (even if neither is explored in great detail).

Belfast Bred is more explicitly tied to commercialism and the tourism industry than *The West Awakes*. Its primary goal is to create an image in which Belfast (and particularly its City Centre) is sophisticated, welcoming, and full of pleasant non-political history. Much of the play's education mission focuses on selling local food. For example, both Barney and the chef at the Mourne's Seafood Bar stop emphasize the connection between oysters and 'the common man.' While oysters are now associated with the elite, earlier in Irish history they were considered 'peasant food.' This will be a moment of education – and likely a surprise – for most audience members, but more importantly it works to encourage audiences to view the shellfish as something that they can (and should) purchase. It depicts the oysters as sophisticated but unpretentious and turns obtaining them into a foray into local culture.

The tourist narrative of *Belfast Bred* ties directly into larger Belfast tourist initiatives; the connection lacks the ambivalence of *The West*

Awakes. Unlike the Falls Road, the space of the City Centre was never explicitly sectarian, but it too has been overwhelmingly shaped by Belfast's tumultuous history. It particularly suffered during the Troubles. Shops were open during the day, but gates around the area kept it empty during the night. Shoppers would generally be searched for weapons once when passing through the gates into the centre and again as they entered each shop. In addition, for reasons of both safety and comfort, Belfast's residents were hesitant to socialize outside of their immediate neighbourhoods. As a result, at the end of the Troubles the City Centre was a far from appealing area. There was no infrastructure for any kind of nightlife, and Belfast's residents felt little ownership of the area or desire to spend time there.

Combatting this history and turning the city centre into a vibrant destination for locals and tourists alike has been one of the major efforts of the post-Troubles transformation projects. One of the earliest examples was the revitalization of the Cathedral Quarter (where Nick's Warehouse is located), which turned the area into a cultural and culinary hot spot. This has been followed by transformations in other parts of the City Centre, and the area now boasts a wide array of restaurants and leisure activities. Stuart Emmrich reflects on this transformation in a 2005 *New York Times* article. Comparing contemporary Belfast to his one earlier experience of the city in 1989, he enthused:

> Belfast is almost unrecognizable. The city centre is now a thriving social hub – with young, well-dressed couples whiling away their weekend afternoons at a series of fashionable cafes. A clutch of boutique hotels and first-class restaurants has opened up in recent years, and there have been sightings of visiting celebrities like Bono, Colin Farrell and Brad Pitt regularly reported by *The Belfast Telegraph*.

Although the city has worked to maintain this new metropolitan allure, it has struggled against the decrease in tourism caused by the global economic downturn. It is thus understandable that business owners in the City Centre are eager to support initiatives like *Belfast Bred* which promise to increase the area's tourist profile. It is also understandable that they would prefer these events to offer a less ambivalent view of the city's history than was present in *The West Awakes*.

Belfast Bred bridges the city's pre- and post-Troubles history even more explicitly than *The West Awakes*. Barney represents a link between two highly successful times in Belfast – the booming industrial age that created the Titanic and the (still developing) tourism and service oriented economy of the 'new' Northern Ireland. Barney's time in the iceberg has coincided with both the Troubles and the city's post-industrial stagnation – for him, these periods never happened. The play thus avoids many of the worst years of Belfast's sectarianism. In addition, however, Barney glosses over the sectarianism present in Belfast in the late-nineteenth and early-twentieth centuries. Although discrimination in Barney's Belfast was in many ways less blatant than it would have been in the lead up to and during the Troubles, it was certainly still a problem. By keeping Barney distanced from these tensions, the performance was able to maintain a more cheerful feeling and could avoid embroiling its audience members in politics that remain divisive. In doing so, however, it sacrifices the opportunity to show audiences the effects of the sectarianism and poverty that have long been part of the city.

This is not to say that the play entirely avoids political issues, however. While *The West Awakes* looks back to Connolly, *Belfast Bred* looks further into history. Barney frequently discusses the United Irishmen, who fought for Irish independence at the end of the eighteenth century. While passing by Kelly's Cellars, for example, Barney tells a story about Henry Joy McCracken hiding from British soldiers behind the bar. The United Irishmen offer a less divisive version of nationalism than many later movements. Since many of the organization's most prominent members were Protestant, it lacks the sectarian connotations normally associated with Irish nationalism. Similarly, its logic was primarily drawn from the Enlightenment values that had led to the revolutions in France and America. The cultural Irish nationalism of later independence movements – which would alienate many who consider themselves British – was absent.

While *Belfast Bred's* primary goal is rooted in tourism and commercialism, it also arguably expresses a subtle Irish nationalism. Barney never explicitly expresses a political opinion about the Belfast of his day or of the present, but much of his language seems to treat the island of Ireland as one unit. Since the Titanic sailed and sank before the partition of the island, this is perhaps not surprising. Further, while he never addresses either partition or Northern Ireland's constitutional status, Barney seemed to feel more connection to the places that are now in the Republic of Ireland than with those in Britain. Along with his several references to the United Irishmen, this suggests a certain sympathy towards the goal of reuniting the island. This sympathy remains subtle, however. Barney's primary focus on Northern Ireland tempers the political implications of these moments. While he seems to feel more Irish than British, he most explicitly projects the 'Northern Irish' identity that many in the peace process have worked to establish as both a compromise and a point of unity for the divided community.

Belfast Bred has proved immensely popular – it has been remounted many times, and has even been transformed into an iPhone app. Here users can view video recordings of the stops on the tour, including commentary by Barney and the presentations of the shop owners (naturally, this version of the tour lacks the taste-testing element). The performance has also increased the business to the shops on the tour – many report seeing noticeable rises in profits on tour days. The proprietors play an important role in the performance; they are in many ways its body, providing a majority of the specific information as well as the food itself. As with *The West Awakes*, this collaboration between theatre makers and local organizations grounds *Belfast Bred* in its location. When the tour is not operating, former audience members can relive it simply by returning to the shops, armed with a newfound culinary confidence. In that way, the performance truly serves its primary function of both increasing pride in the City Centre and directly contributing to the area's economic success. Its ability to do so, however, is bolstered by Kabosh's attention to creating a dramatic narrative and an enjoyable educational experience.

Conclusion

In devising *The West Awakes* and *Belfast Bred*, Kabosh needed to balance many different goals. The plays reflect these negotiations in both content and form; they steer away from the more divisive or controversial events that affected the areas depicted. The violence of the Troubles is only tangentially present in one play of *The West Awakes*, although the Coiste tour ensures that audiences will hear (although not see) these stories. Similarly, *Belfast Bred* avoids almost all discussion of sectarianism and only hints at the economic inequality that undergirded Belfast's industrial prowess. This does not mean, however, that the stories told in the plays are necessarily less true than the grittier stories more often told about the city. Both plays acknowledge the more unsavoury elements of Belfast's history, even if they (and particularly *Belfast Bred*) do not dwell on them. In a city where much of the tourism focuses on repeating stories of trauma and death, an attempt to find other narratives can be beneficial and healing.

Further, by pairing with local organizations – Coiste and the culinary proprietors – Kabosh ensured that the plays are rooted in the needs and goals of the areas depicted. McFetridge believes this is an important part of the projects' successes. Rather than 'parachuting' artists in and having them leave after the performance without offering anything of significance to the community, the plays provide true partnerships. The company is also working to make the tours more widely available to potential tourists to Belfast. In addition to the *Belfast Bred* iPhone application, a similar but even more ambitious project is underway for *The West Awakes*. The goal is to create an app that will be able to host video tours of many areas of the city. At the time of writing, Kabosh is partnering with community organizations on the traditionally-Protestant Shankill Road to create a similar performance detailing the working-class Protestant experience in that area. Since there is no well-established equivalent of Coiste there, the project includes helping residents of the Shankill develop the tour itself – one that will hopefully be available whether or not the Kabosh plays are taking place.

Works Cited

Belfast Bred. Computer software. *Apple App Store*. Vers. 1.0.2. Kabosh Theatre Company, 5 Sept. 2012. Web. 10 Apr. 2013.

Birch, Anna, and Joanne Tompkins. *Performing Site-Specific Theatre: Politics, Place, Practice*. Performance Interventions. New York: Palgrave Macmillan, 2012. Print.

Emmrich, Stuart. 'Belfast Is Ready for the Party to Begin.' *New York Times* 21 August 2005, sec. Travel: 1. Print.

Jackson, Anthony, and Jenny Kidd. *Performing Heritage: Research, Practice and Innovation in Museum Theatre and Live Interpretation*. Manchester: Manchester UP, 2011. Print.

Kirshenblatt-Gimblett, Barbara. *Destination Culture: Tourism, Museums, and Heritage*. Berkeley: U of California P, 1998. Print.

Magee, Kieron, Jimmy McAleavey, Laurence McKeown, and Rosemary Walsh. *The West Awakes*. Unpublished Playscript. Belfast: Kabosh Theatre Company, 2010.

Rokem, Freddie. *Performing History: Theatrical Representations of the Past in Contemporary Theatre*. Iowa City: U of Iowa P, 2000. Print.

McFetridge, Paula. Personal Interview. 7 Feb. 2011.

---. Personal Interview. 6 June 2013.

Shirlow, Peter. 'Belfast: A Segregated City.' *Northern Ireland after the Troubles: A Society in Transition*. Eds. Coulter, Colin and Michael Murray. Manchester: Manchester UP, 2008.73-87. Print.

'*West Awakes, The.*' Belfast: Northern Visions, 2010. Web. 27 July 2013.

14 | Politics, Pride and Performance: TheatreofplucK's Devised Queer Dramaturgies in Northern Ireland

Caitriona Mary Reilly

Patriarchal society and hegemonic identities are sites of critique in numerous theatrical productions and live performances. The evocation of a particular political agenda in live performance is common practice, serving to raise consciousness of important social issues such as those relating to gender, sexuality, and class. Specifically, feminist theorists challenge 'patriarchal discourse' (Greer 8) whilst queer discourses eschew 'fixed categories for identity in recognition of openness, fluidity and flux' (Greer 6). Within feminist performance, practitioners and performers have used the female body to politicize and critique hegemonic notions of womanhood, femininity and motherhood. Gender and sexuality remain contested issues for feminist and queer theorists alike.[1]

Stephen Greer argues that queer theory has sought to 'understand identity and sexuality as a regime of knowledge and power rather than as pre-given facts' (7). Greer argues that queer performance 'might work to disrupt or otherwise intervene in the processes of cultural production' (11). Greer also calls into question 'conventional understandings of sexual identity by deconstructing the categories, oppositions and equations that sustain them' (Jagose 97). Greer

---

[1] Consider the feminist performance work of Carolee Schneemann as well as the lesbian and feminist practice of Split Britches. In a contemporary Irish context, Amanda Coogan and Áine Phillips are two noteworthy feminist practitioners who utilise the female body in performance.

deconstructs normative notions of gender, sexuality and hegemony. This essay will discuss the different queer strategies and queer thinking utilized in devised performance practices and productions by the Northern Irish theatre company, TheatreofplucK. The essay will examine how the company uses queer practice and performance to disrupt and deconstruct hegemonic Northern Irish identities in the context of the Troubles.[2]

TheatreofplucK is Northern Ireland's first publicly funded gay theatre company that aims to 'produce quality theatre for everyone but with a queer slant.' Considering Northern Ireland's particular notoriety for trouble, TheatreofplucK creates a different kind of theatrical trouble, disturbing and inverting Northern Irish identities. Ruth Goldman describes queer theory as one which 'intends to problematize identity and challenge the normative' (173). Through the realization of queer identities and dramaturgies, TheatreofplucK seeks to interrogate the complex weaving of masculinities, femininities and transgender identities in 'post-conflict'[3] Northern Ireland. Performances such as *Bison, Divided, Radical and Gorgeous* (2011) and *Lesbyterian MissConceptions* (2013) confront the paradoxes of Northern Irish identities which are trapped in the queer limbo of nationalist/unionist

---

[2] 'The Troubles' lasted from the late 1960s and continued until the late 1990s. More than 3,700 people were killed in the violence, an 'average of just over 2 a week for the thirty years that the conflict lasted' (Moloney xiii). Ed Moloney describes how by the summer of 1969 Northern Ireland 'had been simmering for months as Protestant resentment at a hugely successful civil rights campaign by Catholics, fuelled by years of political and economic discrimination, threatened to spill onto the streets in violence' (7). By August the Troubles had officially begun. Tensions between the Catholic and Protestant communities in Northern Ireland heightened and 'soon led to armed conflict, forcing the British government to intervene for the first time since the 1920s, by sending the British army to support NI's police force in containing the conflict' (McMahon 15).

[3] The perception that Northern Ireland is a post-conflict society is treated with cynicism in this essay. Given the discord in the Northern Ireland Assembly between rivalling parties such as the Democratic Unionist Party (DUP) and Sinn Féin, one cannot assume that the Troubles of Northern Ireland have been resolved and are in the past. Dawson uses 'post-conflict' to signify 'a society and culture emerging from a period of intense political violence, engaged in efforts towards conflict transformation but overshadowed by a still unresolved past and subject to ongoing conflict which might include – as in Northern Ireland – further resort to political violence' (286).

allegiances and hegemonies. From this perspective, the following essay will examine the conception, devising and production of the performances *Automatic Bastard* (2006) and *Divided, Radical and Gorgeous (D.R.A.G.)*.

Automatic Bastard is a part dance, stand-up comedy which uses autobiographical material inspired by the lives of Niall Rea and Karl Schappell whilst *D.R.A.G* is a 'one man/woman' cabaret act exploring one person's own experience of growing up and 'coming out' during the Troubles. The Northern Irish Troubles were a conflict spanning thirty years, ostensibly coming to an end in 1998 with the signing of the Good Friday Agreement. Whilst *Automatic Bastard* premiered in Belfast and is written from an American perspective, *D.R.A.G.* is contextualized within the premise of a current peaceful Northern Irish society. The two performances demonstrate how one's identity is shaped and moulded by society's prejudices and conflicting politics, whilst also revealing how a queer identity can still emerge despite exposure to intense, bigoted prejudices and homophobia.

In Northern Ireland, religious and cultural segregation has been apparent in the division between Catholic and Protestant communities. The tense relations between these communities have overshadowed the experiences of other marginalized groups. As political tensions continue to simmer, the experiences of these diverse social groups have been coming to the fore. The gay community is one group which has been experiencing discrimination and social segregation. Gay men seeking to donate blood have been discriminated against, for example, and there are still issues concerning the equality of civil partnerships to heterosexual marriages. However, despite such enduring prejudices, Northern Ireland is slowly adapting to diversity. In December 2013, a ban was lifted on gay and unmarried couples applying to adopt children in Northern Ireland (BBC News).[4] Most recently, a study found a growing 'tolerance of same-sex relationships' (Communications and External Affairs Office).[5] The study compared the percentage of survey

---

[4] The Northern Ireland Health Minister Edwin Poots unsuccessfully tried to 'challenge an appeal court decision to extend adoption rights to gay couples' (BBC News).

[5] The article quotes Dr Nicola Carr: 'Over half of the survey's respondents expressed support for same-sex marriage, however, over one third disapproved of gay adoption and also to lesbians having access to fertility treatment on the same basis as heterosexual women. At least one in four people did not believe that a lesbian or gay parent or parents with a child constituted a "family."' The survey

participants who believed that same sex relations are 'always wrong.' The percentage of those who thought same sex relations were always wrong dropped from '76 percent in 1989 to 28 percent in 2012' (Communications and External Affairs Office).

Northern Ireland's queer arts scene is thriving with the OUTburst Queer Arts Festival growing year on year since it was established in 2007. OUTburst has provided TheatreofplucK with an audience who are actively seeking queer performances. The festival is described as a registered charity and not-for-profit initiative, 'dedicated to exploring and celebrating lesbian, gay, bisexual and transgender stories and experiences through the Arts in Northern Ireland' ('OUTBURST'). OUTburst 'aims to support, encourage and inspire local LGBT creativity, in addition to bringing the best in international queer Arts to the city of Belfast' ('OUTBURST'). Together TheatreofplucK and OUTburst provide a unifying space for members of the LGBTQ community in Northern Ireland, where queer identities can be critiqued, interrogated but also unified. The continuation and growth of the festival highlights the visibility of the gay community in Northern Ireland and suggests that the festival is offering events which cater to a wide range of people beyond the LGBTQ community.

TheatreofplucK was originally known as 'PLUCK' and was created in 1995 by Karl Schappell, an American choreographer; Niall Rea, an Irish director/designer; Robin Patchefsky, an American performer; and Jon Stark, a Scottish photographer. PLUCK derived its name from a phrase used by Schappell and Rea's friend, Christopher Hawks, a dancer who passed away in 1994. Rea describes 'Pluck!' having been used by Hawks in good humour as an exclamation referring to someone who seemed a little queer: a little out of the ordinary. In 2007, the company changed its name to TheatreofplucK after unfortunately discovering that there was a string trio already touring under the name 'Pluck.' Having spent a number of years living in London, Schappell and Rea moved to Amsterdam in the 1990s where Rea worked with a number of practitioners such as Marina Abramović and Michael Laub. It was during this time that Rea and Schappell developed a dramaturgy which would be the basis for TheatreofplucK. Laub's work as a director-choreographer would prove particularly of influence to PLUCK in the

---

was carried out by ARK, a joint resources between Queen's University Belfast and the University of Ulster, and interpreted data from the 2012 NI LIFE and Times Survey (NILT), which 'use a random sample of 1,200 people living across Northern Ireland' (Communications and External Affairs Office).

construction of *Automatic Bastard* given the performance's dance theatre characteristics.

Performed by Karl Schappell, *Automatic Bastard* was designed and directed by Rea. It toured internationally, with performances taking place in Philadelphia, Dublin, and Belfast. The performance mixed 'elements of European avant-garde, theater and dance,' and took the audience 'on a journey into the depths of a lunatic's mind' (Cooper Robb 28). The performance encapsulated contemporary dance theatre incorporating Schappell's skills as a choreographer, as well as drawing on Rea's theatrical experience. *Automatic Bastard* was developed and scripted through a series of workshops held at The Lyric Theatre in Belfast, facilitated by a grant of rehearsal space through the 'Space Access Programme' in 2005. Richard Conway quotes Rea when he describes the performance as 'looking at fame' and the 'whole obsession with celebrity' (26). Conway's review focuses on the Dublin performance of *Automatic Bastard* and therefore the political resonances of the performance in relation to Northern Ireland may not have been as evident as when it was performed in Belfast. It is possible also that Rea downplayed these aspects of the performance for Dublin audiences, suspecting that they might be weary or tired of their Northern Irish neighbours' conflict. Tom Maguire argues:

> In the service of its own internal cohesion which has been threatened by the Troubles 'up North' and in its most recent processes of modernization, the Republic of Ireland has sought to redefine itself in ways to which militant republicanism and northern nationalism have been, at the very least, an embarrassment. (11)

The audiences in the Republic were assumed to be alienated and disassociated from the Troubles in Northern Ireland. Their embarrassment of the conflict perhaps led to a disinterest into the politics of the Troubles as well as theatre which depicted such conflict.

Immersive research comprised the preliminary work for the creation of *Automatic Bastard*. Before Rea explored queer theory academically, he began by looking at issues of identity and violence in Northern Ireland. Given that Schappell is North American, he and Rea began to tackle issues of 'identity and violence in terms of racism and homophobia' drawing on their different cultural perspectives (Rea). They sought to create a multi-biographical format where the 'identifying pronoun was always changing' (Rea). Rea describes this use and queering of pronouns: '[It changed] [f]rom He to Her to I to Us to You almost haphazardly – we wanted a jarring affect [sic] of one minute identifying and the next minute disidentifying [sic] with the protagonist of whatever story we were recounting/playing with.' Rea and Schappell purposely queered pronouns so as to play with shifting identities, realizing the fluidity of identity in their performance. The audience members may have been able to recognize the autobiographical quality of the performance, but they were then alienated given the changing pronoun.

During the devising process for *Automatic Bastard*, Rea and Schappell came up with a list of eight 'Text' ideas and four 'Dance' ideas. They organized the text ideas under such labels as: drunk in paper with microphone; set in silence & I discovered modern dance; religious fundamentalism and honour killings; dwarf porn & she was an average woman; call her name into telephone conversation; afraid of other people; ear wig; and funeral. The dance descriptions included: Eric Satie – body image; Violent – Reservoir Dogs; Replacing paper; and intimate in a corner [dropping paper]. By using queer pronouns from the beginning of their devising process, the collaborators were able to elaborate their text and movement based on their initial list of text and dance ideas. Improvisation was important to developing these ideas. By playing with the pronouns, the collaborators were able to mould queer identities for the performance.

Rea states that he prefers a 'hands-off' approach to directing wishing instead to develop his work through improvisation. The scripting of a performance is only ever finalized towards the end of the rehearsal process. This allows TheatreofplucK's performers to develop their characters organically and encourages them gradually to add their queer autobiographies and ideas to the performance. In turn, because of the ongoing input of performers and other collaborators during the devising process, the resulting production was marked by each contributor's personal experiences or prejudices. The narrative of the performance distanced itself from objectivity and became more subjective. The combination of theatre and dance, therefore, foregrounded a sharing of the collaborators' past experiences and personal behaviours.

Automatic Bastard was a personal performance which incorporated autobiographical situations. It critiqued the use of violence in families and relationships whilst contrasting this domestic violence to violence in society. In a review of *Automatic Bastard*, David Warner argued that PLUCK's international perspective 'ought to place a fresh spin on the subject of violence in America.' Warner quotes Rea who states he is more 'frightened' in the USA than in Belfast: 'In Ireland people are killed because of a religious war, but they're not killed for any other reason. Here [in the USA] you see women pulling knives, men with baseball bats — in Belfast you'd just see a kind of a bomb in the distance.' Rea's statement suggests that he is somewhat desensitized to the violence in Northern Ireland. For Rea, the violence in the USA is queer (strange). In America people commit violent acts based on distinct motivations compared to the sectarian, political violence associated with Northern Ireland. There appears to be no single, overarching conflict underpinning violence in America like the overarching sectarian conflict Rea can identify in Northern Ireland. *Automatic Bastard* challenges Rea's assumptions through the juxtaposition of the violent imagery and language of Schappell (the American performer) within the context of a Northern Irish theatre space and audience.

Automatic Bastard began with the stage lit in a soft red glow. The only other light source was a single light bulb hanging mysteriously in the darkness. A cube frame marked the parameters of the performance space, and was completed with a single wooden chair and mass of crumpled paper. The paper mass shifted into life and recoiled in agony. The layers of paper started to shift and fall off the moving mound. Schappell emerged slowly out of the crumpled heap gagging and clearly distressed. His first words were abrupt and spoken into a microphone: 'It's yellow – the vomit.'[6] Wearing only a white vest, Schappell proceeded to stand and put on his white briefs. He moved to the microphone stand and stated, '[i]t's not a biography' before swiftly moving to the centre of the stage, stretching himself into a series of rhythmic gestures. Schappell's assertion that the performance was 'not' a biography promoted disorientation in the audience, considering the queer autobiographical strategies the company is known for using.

The performance drew on a wide range of public paranoia surrounding violence, interweaving anecdotes relating to the sectarian violence of Northern Ireland with the racism specifically in Allentown, Pennsylvania (Schappell's hometown). One of the most troubling scenes of *Automatic Bastard* involves Schappell telling the audience, 'There's a serial killer loose in our town.' It is revealed that the serial killer watched his mother being 'raped in a closet' and now he is 'raping and killing women.' Schappell slowly relayed a list of stereotyped characters targeted by the serial killer including fat blonde women,

---

[6] This essay refers to a recording of *Automatic Bastard* staged at the Lyric Theatre Studio in September 2005.

Latino men, people who put their jeans inside their boots, gay men who lie about their age on Gaydar, and lesbians with bad asymmetrical haircuts. The serial killer's victims are referred to by their queer identities and characteristics. They are marginalized in society, marked by their physical, sexual, and ethnic differences.

When the slow atonal music which has been accompanying Schappell cut out, the audience was once again disorientated by the sudden shift in tone. Schappell clutched the microphone stand once again, and strutted to the front of the stage. Within the next performance sequence there was an increased pace and tension in his voice. He alerted the audience now to the 'terrorist loose in our town.' The audience were told of the young men wearing long dark trench coats; people who poop into paper bags, light them on fire and leave them at your front door; girls who wear veils on their heads; and dark-skinned men who are driving taxi cabs. Schappell's performed self was disturbed when a phone rang from beneath the paper pile. Answering the phone he started yelling, 'Who the fuck are you talking to?' Music faded in and Schappell proceeded to perform an extended movement piece. During the dance, the audience saw the performer at his most vulnerable. The contrast between Schappel's yelling to a slow moving dance evoked a newfound sensitivity. He gracefully moved his arms outwards towards the audience and raised them invoking the image of Christ on the cross. His fragile, sick persona from the opening moments of the play was again inferred in his solitude and unkemptness. As he sat down, he became aware of his isolation, gazing into the dark, claustrophobic performance space. He no longer engaged with the audience, instead he was distracted by his own loneliness. His elegant gestures created a beautiful, emotive tableau as the cathartic movement released Schappell's dance character from the multiple personae which have been tormenting him throughout the performance.

Within the final moments of the performance, Schappell regained his composure and reasserted his normative masculinity by dressing in a suit and partaking in violence. He became angrier and aggressive as he paced the stage and told the audience about his relationship with his 'sister' Sheryl. He talked about their specific childhood moments together before she got 'knocked up' by a Puerto Rican guy called Jesus. Schappell told the audience how he and two friends went to confront Jesus with baseball bats. The audience learned that during the confrontation, Sheryl was injured. Schappell appeared panicked, saying, 'I don't know. She gets hit a couple times, and I guess Stevie, I don't know, I guess he cuts her. She gets cut bad.' Schappell screams,

'It's not my fault. It's not my fucking fault.' Rea draws attention to the roles of sisters in both *Automatic Bastard* and *D.R.A.G.* explaining that they had an influential role in both his and Schappell's everyday lives as children. The reason for the inclusion of Sheryl's story was to highlight how racist tensions have had disastrous consequences. As such, the production subverted notions of violence as a characteristic of hegemonic masculinities by making it an alienating and a destructive force.

Divided, Radical and Gorgeous (D.R.A.G.) was devised in part for Niall Rea's doctoral research in 2011. *D.R.A.G.* critiques the post-conflict optimism within Northern Ireland, instead drawing attention to issues such as homophobia, transphobia, sectarianism and racism. The audience bears witness to one queer character, 'P,' questioning others' closeted and fluid queer identities. There have been two incarnations of *D.R.A.G.* to date. Gordon Crawford, otherwise known as Trudy Scrumptious, a Belfast drag performance artist, first performed *D.R.A.G.* as part of the OUTburst Queer Arts Festival in 2011. Paul C. Boyd took over the role in the second production of *D.R.A.G.* in 2012.[7] Boyd's succession of performances lasted several dates throughout August 2012 with performances in Belfast and Newtownabbey, as part of the Belfast Pride festivities. *D.R.A.G.* focuses completely on the experience of one individual coming out in Northern Ireland during the time of the Troubles. Whilst *Automatic Bastard* was influenced more by the autobiographical stories of North American company member Schappell, *D.R.A.G.* specifically offers up a Northern Irish perspective provided by Niall Rea and his collaborators, Crawford and Boyd.

Here, as with *Automatic Bastard*, Rea chose a hands-off directing approach preferring the actors gradually to play with the development of characters. To encourage improvisation during the rehearsal process, Rea would write notes on pieces of paper which would then be chosen at random. Each actor then had to perform a spontaneous short dialogue based on each note. Notes from the *D.R.A.G.* rehearsal process include, 'Tell us the first time you tried on women's clothing,' 'Make a love scene with the balaclava,' and 'Do a terrorist dance.' With each rehearsal, Rea was able to collaborate with the performers to devise new segments for *D.R.A.G.*. Rea, Crawford and Boyd used improvisation, drawing on their personal stories. Referring to the queer

---

[7] This essay refers to a recording of Divided, Radical and Gorgeous (DRAG), as performed by Paul C. Boyd at The Belfast Barge, Lanyon Quay, Belfast, July/August 2012.

strategies and queer thinking that were brought to the devising process, Rea explains that he followed the 'strategy' of using a 'real cross-dressed queer person' (i.e. Crawford) for 'the first two periods of development.' This allowed for a 'queer validity' in the developing script (Rea). Crawford's experiences as a working-class Protestant and Rea's experiences as a working-class Catholic, offered two narratives from both sides of the 'sectarian binary' in Northern Ireland (Rea). Rea argues that the queer community in Northern Ireland was and still is a non-sectarian community and that this cross-community collaboration was perhaps 'doubly queer' because of this.

Rea describes the devising process of *D.R.A.G.* as being part of a 'queer memory,' a 'kind of queer historiography in performance.' Using his memories of Belfast in the Troubles, Rea was able to reflect back on the conflict through a queer lens. Drawing on his personal experiences and those of Crawford and Boyd, Rea utilized the concept of 'Queer autobiography' which allowed all the collaborators to describe 'hidden queer stories' (Rea). These hidden stories described the experiences of what Alyson Campbell calls 'marginalized subjectivities' (196). With reference to the plays of Frank McGuinness, David Cregan argues that 'notions of queer identity' can be seen to 'intersect with ideas of national identity and fragment essentialist concepts of who or what constitutes both contemporary and historical Irish national identities' (60). Cregan's statement is also applicable to TheatreofplucK's productions. In *D.R.A.G.*, TheatreofplucK specifically deals with notions of queer Northern Irish identities intersecting with essentialist national identities. The essentialist identity presented in *D.R.A.G.* is a combination of a hegemonic Republican and Loyalist masculinity (the result of Rea and Crawford's original collaboration and experience from different cultural backgrounds). By using the characterization of a drag queen, Rea creates a queer identity which, through the parody of other queer identities, intersects and conflicts with the essentialist Northern Irish hegemonic hybrid.

Drag has long been a political tool, used to critique gender stereotypes. Roger Baker, et al. discuss how drag was 'embraced back to the bosom of the gay activism in the 1990s' with queer politics celebrating 'difference and the breaking of gender rules' (255). Judith Butler argues:

> In imitating gender, drag implicitly reveals the imitative structure of gender itself – as well as its contingency. Indeed, part of the pleasure, the giddiness of the performance is in the recognition of a radical contingency in the relation between sex and gender in the face of cultural configurations of casual unities that are regularly

assumed to be natural and necessary. (*Gender Trouble* 187).

The humour and subversive intervention in *D.R.A.G.* comes from the absurdity of the feminized Boyd partaking in paramilitary activities and the positioning of drag within the context of a warzone. Drag already disturbs hegemonic identities but the drag performance becomes more alienated and complexly disruptive in Northern Ireland, where the sectarian binary negates the existence of a single, hegemonic masculine identity.

In his analysis of Frank McGuinness's work, Cregan argues for the application of queer theory as an attempt to interpret McGuinness's dramaturgy as a 'cultural discourse' (3). For Cregan queer theory demands 'historical contextualization in order to illuminate how normativity has impacted and, in fact, restricted the development of identity' (3). This raises questions in relation to the conflict in Northern Ireland where the dominant hegemony has consisted of Catholic and Protestant communities. As such, cultural background has served as the dominant identity marker in Northern Ireland whilst 'marginalized subjectivities' are lost amongst these heteronormative political discourses. As Campbell argues, Northern Ireland is an extremely conservative society where politics is 'overwhelmingly' driven by religious affiliation (204).

Comparisons can be made between Boyd's character P in *D.R.A.G.* and the character of Dido in Frank McGuinness's *Carthaginians*. In Scene Four of *Carthaginians*, Dido enters in 'drag' wearing 'a black miniskirt, black tights, high-heels and beret' (301). By performing in drag, Dido queers what Nikki Sullivan describes as 'the essentialized or naturalized notions of gender, sexuality, and the subject that are integral to hegemonic discourses and institutions' (86). In Scene One, Dido enters wheeling a 'pram' (McGuinness 301). The pram is a signifier of motherhood and femininity. Through drag and his feminine props, Dido reveals his queer identity. Kenneth Clatterbaugh argues that queer or 'gay masculinities' present perhaps the greatest single challenge to dominant forms of masculinity in that this challenge in part stems from the widely held belief that '"gay masculinity" is an oxymoron, because to be gay is to fail to be masculine' (138). Fintan Walsh argues that 'homosexuality and queerness typically function to destabilize history, widely accepted truths and grand narratives' (7). He continues: 'This is especially true of McGuinness's oeuvre, which has consistently explored the relationship between homosexuality and the production of knowledge in an Irish context' (7). Like Dido, P in *D.R.A.G.* uses drag and femininity to undermine hegemonic notions of

Northern Irish masculinity. In his performance of *D.R.A.G.*, Boyd slowly began his transformation into his drag persona P, but paused this transformation by pulling a gun from his dressing table and threateningly pointing it at the audience. The use of the gun situated the transvestite persona within the politics and violence of Northern Ireland. The interruption of the gun created alienation between the performer and the spectator. Spectators witnessed a queer character in flux with P in gender purgatory. The use of the gun evoked typical images of the hyper-masculine paramilitary, but was queered by Boyd being part dressed in female clothing. Both Dido and P threaten the hyper masculinity of the invisible paramilitaries who mark their masculinity using violence. Dido's queerness threatens the 'hyper-masculine republican identity' (Curtin 34) of Hark, whilst in *D.R.A.G.*, P's queerness undoes the hyper-masculinity of his beloved freedom fighter with whom he forges a secret relationship. The flamboyancy and campness of both characters serve to challenge hegemonic masculinities at times of political and civil unrest in Northern Ireland.

D.R.A.G. opens in a very similar way to *Automatic Bastard*. P is hidden under a mass of black cards. Naked, he emerges from the black heap stating, 'It's all my fucking fault.' The stage has a cubic frame with a single white chair and dressing table complete with a vanity mirror. P approaches the table applying some makeup, before returning to the pre-set microphone to make a statement. The pace is slow, punctuated by the act of applying the makeup. He seductively stated, 'I don't want to take you on some angst-ridden journey through my troubles … Your troubles … Our troubles …' Then, he looked at the audience, lingering before proceeding to the table for one final time to apply another item of makeup. He drew the microphone down to his genitals before getting onto his knees. He suddenly put on a balaclava threatening to tell the audience some of the 'dirty sins that might make your pants that little bit tighter.' The balaclava again evoked a reference to the hyper-masculinity of the Republican paramilitaries. P moved to the dressing table, removed the balaclava and put on a dress. P flicked on the lights of the vanity mirror and the audience saw his face projected onto a screen at the back of the stage. He carefully applied his makeup, punctuating each application with a humorous quip: 'Maybe we're all procrastinating bitches. We should have solved all these things ages ago but it *dragged* on and on … Dragged – on and on. L.O.L.' He flirted with the camera, eyeing the audience from the projection screen, applying bronzer whilst pouting in the mirror.

D.R.A.G. is broken into a series of chapters with one entitled 'Mummy's boy: Bullying and Guilty Bombs.' P tells the story of his optimistic, pre-conflict, youth: 'He discovered drag when he was eighteen years old at a time of raves and new-wave music. Now imagine a much younger Paul in a tight little skirt: full of hope; idealistic; young; pure; untainted by life. Happy ...' The reference to 'raves' is an ode to Rea's punk youth and his queer autobiography. In this section of the production, P discussed his relationship with his mother juxtaposing his reapplication of make-up with a tale of his mother's beauty. He romanticized her referring to her beautiful 'porcelain skin.' The audience became a younger P, watching him in the same way he watched his mother apply makeup. He talked about his mother's shifting attitude to him, from being called 'dear' and 'special' to 'queer' and 'homo.'

In the script, Rea highlights the use of the word queer as a derogatory term. Butler argues that 'the term "queer" has operated as one linguistic practice whose purpose has been the shaming of the subject it names or, rather, the producing of a subject *through* that shaming interpellation' ('Critically Queer' 12). Queer, Butler continues, 'derives its force precisely through the repeated invocation by which it has become linked to accusation, pathologization, and insult' ('Critically Queer' 12). As P continues to rhyme off a list of derogatory names, he starts to include references to physical violence. In the production, he became more hysterical, as the list went on, culminating in the shout: 'And then there were fists. And then there were kicks. And then there were bombs. And then there was destruction. And then there was annihilation.' The noise of gunshots and bomb blasts followed his rant. The diva persona, clearly distressed by the prior sequence and noise, whimpered into a corner of the stage. The anger and violence demonstrated by P is a reminder of his masculinity. However, his cowardice and whimpering are signifiers of his queerness in that he appears more vulnerable and archetypally feminine.

P describes how two of his 'friends' went on to join paramilitary organizations in Northern Ireland. The script queers the paramilitaries, provocatively poking fun at their acronyms, for example, referring to the LVF as the 'Loyalist Volunteer Faggots.' Boyd's alter ego attempts to make light of the paramilitary organizations and violence in Northern Ireland. During the performance, he picked a member of the audience to act as his paramilitary friend, forcing her/him to wear a balaclava. The balaclava is an intimidating item of clothing associated with paramilitaries. P's balaclava was queered with the addition of glitter and bling. The chosen audience participant at one of the Barge performances laughed during her participation in the scene. Though embarrassed, she also seemed at ease in taking part. P is not threatening. He's endearing. The performative campness and glittered balaclava subverted the hyper-masculine and violent associations of the balaclava wearing paramilitaries.

In the staging of the section entitled 'An Ode to Our Silence,' P proceeded once again to his vanity mirror. Parallels with *Automatic Bastard* again appear in the script with a reference to a 'serial killer loose in this town.' P completed his drag transformation by putting on his blonde wig, glittered red lipstick and a pair of patent red shoes. Suddenly the audience were engaged in another performance segment, 'The Queer Club and the Tranny Gaze.' This act begins with Boyd's imaginary journey into Belfast city in a black taxi where the taxi swerved to avoid another vehicle in flames. Undeterred P states, 'Nothing was going to stop us from our wee night out together.' This line reveals how the club scene provided a unifying space where 'faggots' and punks from both sides were able to enjoy the company of each other in a neutral space. During the Troubles, Rea was a punk who like others distanced himself from the political and paramilitary influences. United in their indignation at the daily violence on the streets of Belfast, Rea explains nothing would stop them from going out. *D.R.A.G.* depicts a frustration with the normalization of violence during the Troubles. Going out was an attempt to reinstate some sense of ordinariness into people's lives. People had to abide by daily evening curfews, thus sacrificing social interactions because Belfast city was deemed too dangerous. Going out as such became a subversive attempt to reclaim the conflicted streets of Belfast from the police, the British army and paramilitaries. Raves offered a queer social space wherein members of all communities and cultures (Queer, Catholic, Protestant etc.) could enjoy a level of freedom from the enduring conflict.

In the staging of the 'Ballad of the Closeted Freedom Fighter' P sung of his past lover who 'killed a cop.' He played a concertina singing of the woes of being in a relationship with someone who was more concerned about fighting for the greater political good. It is revealed that the Closeted Freedom Fighter is put in prison for having shot a police officer in the head, diminishing all hope for an apolitical future. In the final moments, P read a letter from the Closeted Freedom Fighter:

> Dear P, I've been doing a lot of reading in here. I wanted to sort out in my head what happened and where we fitted. I mean, after we had been through all that, was there anyone really to blame? I

think you are brave in your skirt looking for something different, some other way of being. We shouldn't be normalized. Or bloody globalized!

Following this, P became upset, crumpling the letter and throwing it away. Choosing to ignore the romantic illusion of a united relationship with his Freedom Fighter, P tore off his wig. He communicated his wish for '[a] queer future, in a new place, in a new time' but acknowledged that we have to somehow rewrite history and tell stories from everyone involved and affected by the political conflict and Troubles. He proclaimed: 'Show what happened behind those doors with the wee windows. Yes – show our pride but talk about it all! All the false turns, all the dead ends. All the abuse.' Boyd's character ended the performance by indignantly shouting, 'I will not be some tranny in a wig.' Instead he put on his glamorous balaclava and proceeded to sing 'Belfast Punk Torch Song' (by Robert Brown) ending the show with a uniting crescendo of 'I am Divided, Radical and Gorgeous!'

TheatreofplucK is a theatre company concerned with critiquing the everyday social and political situation in Northern Ireland within a queer framework. *Automatic Bastard* may have theatricalized Schappell's experiences of racism and violence in North America, but its Belfast production reminded the audience of the violence of the Troubles. It positioned Northern Ireland within a globalized society, marked by terrorism ever more intensely since 9/11. Through the performance of drag, *Divided, Radical and Gorgeous* critiqued the politics of Northern Ireland and masculinized cultural identities. Within the two productions, the characters were presented as flawed individuals with personal, psychological traumas. However, this was a trauma shared with the audience. The shared theatrical experience was potentially cathartic as it happened within a queer, neutral, non-sectarian space. TheatreofplucK is committed to creating political, queer productions which bring visibility to the queer community in Northern Ireland as well as to issues relating to HIV and AIDS.[8] The company offers an alternative to the typical theatrical Troubles narrative, which has predominantly focused on the violence of the conflict and the associated hegemonic masculinities. TheatreofplucK continues to diversify with its most recent production, *Lesbyterian MissConceptions* (2012), offering the drag king, lesbian alternative to D.R.A.G. By using a collaborative, devising process, TheatreofplucK

---

[8] See: TheatreofplucK's production of Lachlan Philpott's *Bison* (2009-10), directed by Alyson Campbell.

brings together a range of queer autobiographies and experiences. Staging diverse queer experiences in this way places centre stage queer politics and typically marginalized identities in contemporary, post-conflict Northern Ireland, serving productively to 'trouble' simplistic constructions of Northern Irish identity.

Works Cited

Baker, Roger, et al. *Drag: A History of Female Impersonation in the Performing Arts*. New York: New York University Press, 1994. Print.

BBC News. 'Gay adoption: Northern Ireland ban lifted.' *BBC*. 11 Dec. 2013. Web. 15 Feb. 2014. <http://www.bbc.co.uk/news/uk-northern-ireland-25332917>.

Butler, Judith. 'Critically Queer.' *Playing With Fire: Queer Politics, Queer Theories*. Ed. Shane Phelan. New York and London: Routledge, 1997. 11-29. Print.

---. *Gender Trouble: Feminism and the Subversion of Identity*. New York and London:Routledge, 2006. Print.

Campbell, Alyson. 'From *Bogeyman* to *Bison*: A Herd-Like Amnesia of HIV/AIDS in Theatre?' *Theatre Research International* 36.3 (2011): 196-212. Print.

Clatterbaugh, Kenneth. 'Gay Men: The Challenge of Homophobia.' *Contemporary Perspectives on Masculinity: Men, Women, and Politics in Modern Society*. 2nd ed. Boulder, Colo. and Oxford: Westview Press, 1997. 117-156. Print.

Communications and External Affairs Office. 'Attitudes towards same-sex relationships changing according to new survey.' *Queen's University Belfast*. Web. 24 Feb. 2014. <http://www.qub.ac.uk/home/ceao/News/Title,437092,en.html>

Conway, Richard. 'Fringe Fancies.' *GCN*. September 2006: 26. Print.

Cooper Robb, J.. 'Tania Isaac: Disposable and In the Name Of / Puck: Automatic Bastard.' *Philadelphia Weekly* 24-30 January 2007. Print.

Cregan, David. *Frank McGuinness's Dramaturgy of Difference and the Irish Theatre*. New York: Peter Lang, 2011. Print.

Curtin, Nancy J. '"A Nation of Abortive Men": Gendered Citizenship and Early Irish Republicanism.' *Reclaiming Gender: Transgressive Identities in Modern Ireland*. Eds. Marilyn Cohen and Nancy J. Curtin. Basingstoke: Macmillan, 1999. 33-52. Print.

Dawson, Graham. 'The desire for justice, psychic reparation and the politics of memory in 'post-conflict' Northern Ireland.' *Rethinking History: The Journal of Theory and Practice* 18.2 (2014): 265-288. Print.

Goldman, Ruth. 'Who is That *Queer* Queer?: Exploring Norms around Sexuality, Race, and Class in Queer Theory.' *Queer Studies: A*

Lesbian, Gay, Bisexual & Transgender Anthology. Ed. Brett Beemyn and Mickey Eliason. New York and London: New York University Press, 1996. 167-182. Print.

Greer, Stephen. *Contemporary British Queer Performance*. Hampshire and New York: Palgrave Macmillan, 2012. Print.

Jagose, Annamarie. *Queer Theory: An Introduction*. New York: New York University Press, 1996. Print.

Maguire, Tom. *Making Theatre in Northern Ireland: Through and Beyond the Troubles*. Exeter: University of Exeter Press, 2006. Print.

McGuinness, Frank. *Carthaginians. Plays One*. London: Faber, 1996. 291-379. Print.

McMahon, Margery. *Government and Politics of Northern Ireland*. 3rd ed. Newtownards: Colourpoint Books, 2011. Print.

Moloney, Ed. *A Secret History of the IRA*. London: Penguin Books, 2003. Print.

'OUTBURST Queer Arts Festival.' *Cathedral Quarter*. Web. 24 Feb 2013. <http://www.thecathedralquarter.com/about.aspx?title=Festivals&id=3045&dataid=895638>

Rea, Niall. 'Re: Fw: Thanks and Help.' Message to Caitriona Reilly. 20 Feb. 2014. E-mail.

Sullivan, Nikki. *A Critical Introduction to Queer Theory*. Edinburgh: Edinburgh University Press, 2003. Print.

Walsh, Fintan. 'Introduction: The Flaming Archive.' *Queer Notions: New Plays and Performances from Ireland*. Ed. Fintan Walsh. Cork: Cork University Press, 2010. 1-16. Print.

Warner, David. 'Ya Gotta Have Pluck: A fearsome foursome is about to debut at the Arts Bank.' *Philadelphia Citypaper*. Web. 15 July 2013. <http://archives.citypaper.net/articles/101295/article028.shtml>.

15 | Interview with Will Chamberlain, Director of Belfast Community Circus

Siobhán O'Gorman

Will Chamberlain moved from Switzerland to Ireland in the late 1990s, when he took up his current role as director of Belfast Community Circus School. Prior to this, he was a professional clown and community circus teacher for twelve years. He also worked as a more general arts practitioner and advocate for community arts, serving for three years as chair of the Community Arts Forum (CAF). CAF had been founded at a meeting of community arts activists in Belfast in 1993. The forum has since ceased operation due to cuts in Arts Council funding. The conversation below took place across from CAF's former headquarters, in the middle of Writer's Square, in July 2013.

For three decades, Belfast Community Circus has operated as a forum for fostering the personal development of young people from some of the most disadvantaged communities in Northern Ireland. In the early 1980s, Donal McKendry and Mike Moloney had responded to diverse Northern Irish young people's pressing needs for positive shared experiences by introducing community circus in Northern Ireland. With the help of McKendry and Moloney, Belfast Community Circus was established in 1985. Since then, the initiative has become 'one of the most prolific arts organizations in Northern Ireland and a leading light in the international world of social circus' ('History'), winning such honours as the final Guardian Jerwood Award for Excellence in The Community (1999).

The school itself is located on Gordon Street and offers a range of youth circus programmes for children and young people from different communities, training for professional performers and circus arts teachers, and a venue for hosting local, national and international circus productions. In 2012, for example, Belfast Community Circus School provided training for Karen Anderson, Emily Aoibheann and Elaine McCague, the trio who had formed in 2011 PaperDolls, a Dublin-based performance group specializing in contemporary circus in addition to multidisciplinary, live, immersive and experimental art. In addition, the activities of the school featured prominently in the 2013 RTÉ four-part documentary series, *John Lonergan's Circus*, offering – with the facilitation of Lonergan, former governor of Mountjoy Prison – circus training for young people from disadvantaged regions of Dublin city as a way of boosting creativity, self-esteem, teamwork and discipline. In 2004, Belfast Community Circus launched its annual international street arts festival, the Festival of Fools. The festival has been growing from strength to strength, receiving in 2006 an Arts and Business award for work in the community undertaken with the Laganside Corporation.

The ultimate mission of Belfast Community Circus is to: 'Transform lives and communities through the power of circus arts and street theatre' ('Ethos and Mission'). In Chamberlain's view, the democratic leanings of genres such as community arts and street theatre can bridge social and cultural divides by fostering a sense of togetherness in the moment for performers and audiences alike, as well as helping to overcome perceptions of the arts as the special provenance of cultural elites. He sees the potential of the arts to have an important impact on everyday lives and lived experiences, on people's relationships with space and place, and even on commerce – although he remains steadfast in promoting the ideal of arts as an experience rather than just a commodity. In his 2004 essay, 'Access, Authorship, Participation and Ownership,' Chamberlain writes in detail about misconceptions concerning, and insufficient funding for, community arts. Based on this interview conducted more than a decade later, it appears that the ways in which community arts are funded and valued still need to improve. Yet, Chamberlain remains determined to fulfill a range of goals in the arts that he believes can foster positive social change.

Siobhán O'Gorman: Can you tell me firstly about the kinds of devising work that you do?

Will Chamberlain: Okay … most of the devising work we do would be working with children and young people who are part of our youth circus. There are different levels of that depending on the resources that we have available for the show. Normally one of the biggest problems for us is that accessing money for creating performances is really difficult. The participatory bit is what funders seem to be interested in *funding*, but they don't seem to get the idea that, actually, without an end product then the process *is* slightly diminished. So there is a range of devising processes that we do but nearly all involve engagement with the artists, whether they be young people or professionals – for them to be part of a devising process. The reasons for that, with the young people, would be that it is about trying to empower and trying to harness their creativity, and trying to encourage them to think for themselves and to take ownership of the show. Circus children, by and large, are not the most gregarious and outgoing. There are a lot of introverts who come into circus. They can hide behind props, you know, particularly jugglers. They've got their clubs or their balls in front of them and they're focused in on that and that's what they imagine the audience is seeing. They don't really think the audience is seeing *them* – to begin with anyway. So obviously one of the things we have to work on is getting them to understand that, actually, it helps if they smile, it helps if they're enjoying themselves. And as they progress in terms of proficiency and confidence, we start to bring in elements of clown, elements of movement and dance (although we never call it dance). To begin with, though, these young people are often not the most expressive.

S: How do young people get involved with the school?

W: They come to us, mainly. We have outreach programmes, although the more complex shows that we do are nearly all to do with the young people that come to us. Seventy-five young people come to us every Saturday, another twenty-five on a Sunday, fifty on Thursdays, and we've a waiting list of about a thousand. Just through word of mouth, children want to be involved with us. The pinnacle is our third group on a Saturday. Everybody is on the waiting list to get onto the Saturday programme and then go from beginners to intermediate to advanced. But the shows that we do, by and large, with the young people are with the whole of the Saturday group – so up to seventy-five children and young people between the ages of eight and eighteen. We have a policy of making it an inclusive process so we're not auditioning; everybody who wants to be in the show from those seventy-five kids can be in the show. Even if they join us a few weeks before the rehearsals start, they'll still be in the show if they want to be. We'll find a way to build them in. We try to tap into *their* creativity and get them to take ownership so that they're then less inhibited about performing. If you're a bit shy, performing somebody else's work is a bit harder because you're pretending a bit more, you're less comfortable about it; whereas if you've been able to get excited about the *idea*, then you're more likely to buy into the actual process of delivering the creativity and the performance. So that's one of the reasons why we would look to the young people to engage.

S: Would that work be staged publicly then?

W: Yes ... at the moment we have a cycle where we'd have a big show every Christmas. That will sometimes be a themed show, sometimes it'll be a cabaret – maybe with a theme running between different acts. If we have the resources it will then become a more elaborate show and will be a bit more, sort of, scripted. The last themed show we did was *The Grinch who Stole Christmas*, with a circus theme and it was lovely.

S: Where did that take place?

W: That was in the Circus School. So we had a cast of about fifty – which is a tight squeeze when your backstage area isn't really big enough to accommodate fifty people – and we performed for six nights to about 120 people a night. There was character work involved, and there was of course the age-old problem that we have of trying to make, say – I use this as the most graphic example – juggling look like it's not just juggling; so trying to get some sort of engagement in. We often look to see if we can explore how juggling can become more that just three balls, three clubs, four, five, whatever, so that it's actually about juxtaposition of objects and it's about movement. I've seen wonderful dance pieces that are, effectively, juggling pieces as well. It doesn't need to always have the same props. It *is* about movement, and that movement can be people movement or it can be object movement, it can be suitcases passed from one person to another, rather than, necessarily, a placid pattern of juggling.

S: So how about telling the story of *The Grinch who Stole Christmas*? How did you go about that?

W: We slightly cheated and had a bit of narrative going on there, a bit of a voice-over, yea. I don't know if it's my indulgence or punishment but I'm allowed to write scripts for the Christmas shows. And in the spirit of Christmas pantos, it's a lot of rhyming couplets; it's very basic, getting a story from A to B. I put a little bit of humour into it, and arrange it so that the young people can say something – often in chorus. Again, they're a bit shy about taking centre stage. If they're together it's a lot less scary. Of course there are some exhibitionists and natural performers in there, and we find the channels for them to perform; although *The Grinch who Stole Christmas* was interesting because the young person who played the Grinch, who sort of volunteered himself for it, was *very much* the opposite of an exhibitionist. I mean he was a great juggler. Maybe that was something to do with the fact that there was going to be a costume and, say, he was less recognizable or I don't know. He was sixteen at the time so he would have been with us for seven or eight years and always kind of hiding behind the juggling.

S: So, if you have someone with you for seven or eight years, can you see evidence of this particular kind of work helping with their personal development?

W: I think absolutely, and not only can we see it but the parents can see it and we get a lot – *a lot* – of stories from parents. Now we can actually start our young performers at the age of two. Six years ago we started our Itty-Bitty Circus programme, which is two to three year-olds and is more about physical literacy and play in a group context; it's about taking instruction and communication. It's also about parental and grandparental interaction with the children. Then with four and five year-olds, parents are out the door, and we start to work on a few more skills. Six and seven: much more skill. Then they go into Youth Circus. So we have somebody who started at the age of two and he's now eight. He rides a giraffe unicycle. But for us it's not about 'how can we get them to be incredibly skilled?' It is all about giving them an environment where they feel safe, where they feel valued, and where they feel that they have a contribution. It's born out of the specifics of Belfast and Northern Ireland in terms of safe, neutral space, shared space, cross-community interaction. Even since the Good Friday Agreement, the level of interaction between Catholic and Protestant young people is less than it was before. So there are still things to overcome. The medium of circus has an advantage in that there has never, in the history of circus, to my knowledge, been a Catholic circus or a Protestant circus. In the Soviet era, the circus was used in part as a political tool, but there was still subversion going on the whole time. So it's never really been something that is seen as being *owned*. Even if you look at Fossett's, if you look at Duffy's – the two biggest Irish circuses – they're still full of artists from other countries, other continents. So it's always been this kind of inclusive form. It's an embracing and welcoming form.

S: Do you think that one reason for this might be its physicality, the fact that it's less rooted in language perhaps?

W: I think that's one reason. But I think it's also the very nature of circus. Interdependence is really important. By very definition it's a collaborative form. This is a hackneyed example, but I use it still because it does work. When you have a human pyramid, and the kid at the top of the human pyramid, say, is from a Loyalist background and the kids at the bottom of the pyramid are from a Republican background. You can ask [from the top] 'where are you from?' But it would be insane to say to the Republican kids 'right, bugger off,' 'cause you're the one that suffers. There's a very real interdependence and connection between everybody involved in circus. It's hard to dissociate this from the form. In traditional circus, that runs through from the Big Top up through to eating together, through to forming that circle of caravans. There are lots of ways in which circus is demonstrably about a togetherness.

S: Do you think that those involved in Belfast Community Circus apply those practices beyond the circus? How does it inform their behaviour elsewhere?

W: You know, those involved form friendships that they wouldn't have formed anywhere else. I mean my daughter is a case in point. She would have been going, 'Can I go to the park, there's a group of us going to the park to do a unicycle' and those are kids that wouldn't otherwise mix. They're from different parts of the town, one's from another town altogether. They're coming together – Protestants, Catholics, non-believers. It is definitely a reality that people involved connect outside of circus. I think they're more open-minded; they see that you don't judge people by where they're from. Here, in Belfast, in Northern Ireland, there's a massive tendency to do that. So a lot of what we do is about creating environments where that doesn't matter. And going back to the Festival of Fools, you know, we started that in 2004. By 2004, theoretically, peace was embedded, and we were in a post-conflict situation. But post-conflict doesn't necessarily mean 'normal' –

S: And 'post' doesn't always mean over; 'post' is always processual ...

W: It *is* a process. So, the city centre, for example was somewhere that, during the Troubles, was a ring of steel. It was a hostile place; it was a place where people were going in to shop, and out. There was risk involved. Post the ceasefire it was a much more functioning place as a place of commerce, but not what I would describe as a living city. Yes, more people now were going in to do their shopping, but that was all the city centre was about. Okay, there were some people working in offices, some people working in the shops, but basically people are coming in to shop. And what that experience meant was that you're either dragging your kids around kicking and screaming or you're bribing them to get from A to B. The streets and the public spaces were just what you had to get across to get from one shop to another. There was no sense that this is a city of leisure, that this can be a place where you can dwell, where you can enjoy the architecture, where you can actually can sit down and take it in. You'll see that the street furniture is still oriented around older people with bags who might *need* to sit down. The thinking has still to catch up.

S: So, do you think that people still just want to get in and get out?

W: They used to. What we brought with the street festival was a totally different relationship with the city. With the first edition, we had no idea if anyone was going to come down because there'd not been any street theatre for thirty years.

S: So, is moving Belfast more towards the 'city of leisure' model one of the goals of the Festival of Fools?

W: Well, to a mixed city, to a contemporary European city really. It's always been an international festival so our opening show was a Sardinian company, Theatre En Vol, who started off with vertical dance coming down from Castle Court which is our modern – I would say quite hideous – shopping centre. But the idea of their work is to get the audience, to get the public, to be looking beyond shops at street level because that's the bit that's been sterilized. That's the bit that's uniform. In towns and cities across Europe, often the ground level is where they rip out the actual essence of the building and they replace it with frontage and goods in the window. When your eye line rises above that, then you'll see that, wow, there are some really glorious buildings here. And that's what they were about as a company, and it's something that they have given to us as an extra mission, to just connect people with the city. So I think that was *more* what it was about. It was connecting people with the reality and the possibility of the city of Belfast. So, from the very opening show, people were being encouraged to look above. If you go to any shopping town, people are often focused downwards. They're on a mission. So, getting them just to lift their eyes up changes their mentality as well as their understanding of the environment. But also just to get people in a space together, to relax and to enjoy laughter. The theme of our festival is laughter: the Festival of Fools. And, again this is an example I've used ever since we started the festival, but it's no less true: if you're standing side-by-side with a complete stranger and you're looking at somebody over there who's acting the fool, and you're enjoying the fact that there's somebody doing something stupid there – obviously you've got some superiority because you're laughing at somebody … But then you exchange a glance with your neighbour and you've both been laughing at the same thing: you've shared a moment. I have nothing scientific to back this up but I'm pretty sure that if you did a test, there's less aggression between two people who've shared a moment of laughter than two people who haven't. So you're connecting people through the medium of humour, which transcends cultural backgrounds. The festival is about extending our idea of what circus does, in terms of bringing different people together and making the boundaries and barriers irrelevant, but doing that on a much more public platform. At the same time, we're saying to people, 'Look, this is a city. You don't have to just shop.' We've forged links with hospitality businesses so I think the last festival had nineteen restaurants and cafés as sponsors and you'll see in the brochure that there are vouchers for everyone, kids eat free, etc. The businesses understand that we want people to come in and enjoy themselves in the city. The transformation that has taken place – and I'm not, obviously, taking credit for that – over the last ten years is phenomenal. We don't claim credit but we have been part of that story of moving things forward. We played St. Anne's Square when it was a car-park. Then the property developers sponsored the festival when they'd finished building the square but they hadn't any occupants in yet, and we had this beautiful Russian company, Mr Pejo's Wandering Dolls, who did a processional piece. They were all in white with large masks and very precise movement at dusk coming into that white square. Aw, it was phenomenal ... So we were the first to play there, and we were the first to play in Custom House Square too.

S: That piece by Mr Pejo's Wandering Dolls sounds like a more sombre piece?

W: Well, the final part was joyous; the rest of it was intriguing. I wouldn't say sombre because it was fascinating in a true sense of the word. And people were drawn in and intrigued and almost hypnotized by the piece. So, not every piece that we do has to be comedic. But if you look at any of the programmes, it'll be the thing that defines ninety per cent of it. This year we had a production bringing hip-hop and circus together, a European production called HipCirq, with some partners that we're involved with. And ironically, we took it indoors. We took the hip-hop dance inside.

S: Who were the partners?

W: There were two young, emerging artists from France, others from Finland, Holland, Belgium, and Guadeloupe. Then there was a French choreographer and a French circus director. The third outing of the show was here. It was devised in two parts in France and Brussels, with the whole group. Then it played in each of those countries, then here. And it sold out on two nights, even though it was an unconventional location – a bit far out of town. It took place on a massive hanger by the docks which lay empty for years and is now occupied by skaters and BMXers. That was very gratifying to see that the festival can have that potential. Another thing that we *do* want to do, which has not been possible so far due to resources, is to try and create those pathways from people watching street theatre to people going into theatres, to try to break down some of those inhibitors.

S: What do you see as the inhibitors to getting bums on seats in theatres?

W: Well, I think theatres themselves can be seen as elitist ... I used to be a member of the Arts Council and so I would get invited to things and all the rest of it. And obviously I'm a relatively confident individual but I hated going to some of those things. I'd go to an opening night at the Lyric, and I absolutely detested everything about it. I detested the fact that all the people who were there for free could easily afford to pay. I detested the fact that they were all just so up-market and up themselves; same with opening nights at the orchestra. So, that was my experience as a confident person working in the Arts. I think that it's a massive problem, trying to get people in. And also there's that investment that you have to make, without knowing what it is you're going to see. It's alright for those in the know, those who are experts ...

S: Some 'experts' take issue with what they perceive as the 'quality' of devised and/or community theatre. But it can be just as much of a risk to attend a production by a long-established or national theatre company. Not everything they are producing is enjoyable or 'worth the money,' and it's often a lot more expensive.

W: Yea, and I think as well if it gets to the point where theatres only produce something that's a banker then where's the art and the creativity? So, for me, street theatre is the ultimate democracy in audience and performance because it takes place in *your* space. And, some people will walk straight through that space like they have done every other Saturday, and that's kind of a great thing and a good street artist will make something of that moment. So people aren't intimidated. They stay for as long as they want to ...

S: They're not trapped ...?

W: Nooo. And the thing is, in the theatre, you're only trapped by convention.

S: You can go ...

W: You *can*, but ... I think that the biggest preventer of people leaving is 'what will other people think?' I've done it, I'm afraid, at the last couple of plays I've been to I only lasted till the interval. Even then, it's a bit radical to leave at the interval. Whereas with street theatre, not only can you leave any time you like, you can also arrive late *and*, if you don't like it, not only can you walk away but you can bloody-well tell them that you don't like it. You can shout, 'You're shit, mate!' or whatever. So I think it's a really democratic form. Then of course at the end, if you have liked it and you have stayed, then you give what you feel it is worth to you – rather than somebody telling you beforehand it's twenty-five pounds, and then you come out going, 'But that was shit.' And of course they have to do it because of the economics of maintaining the building and all the rest of it. I think, you know, there needs to be some kind of a mass breakthrough to make a difference to whether people feel comfortable going to something or not, which probably isn't going to happen with the Festival of Fools leading people to a new 'promised land.' But when we did the HipCirq programme, we took it into T13, that venue I mentioned for urban extreme sports, or street-sports – you know skateboarding, BMXing – in the massive industrial hanger. They created a black box in the midst of this vast hanger. So, you had the kind of convention of theatre, but a completely unconventional venue for it. And somehow it worked beautifully as a location, and I think it introduced some of the skaters to this more structured form, and also some theatre-goers went down going 'oh, what's this place?,' you know? So it was an interesting thing. There is an ambition to do that, to try to detoxify clown because in the UK and Ireland, if you say 'I'm a clown,' then it's a no-no. The image people have is associated with children. It's the same with circus. You say circus, most people go, 'oh, that's children's stuff.' I've had this conversation with a number of people. Even if you say 'it's suitable for families,' then automatically everyone thinks it's for children when in fact it's suitable for everyone *in* a family. This means that everyone in a family might get something out of it, but we filter it all out. Clown is particularly vulnerable to this kind of thinking. I lived in Switzerland for a while and I used to be a professional clown. When I moved to Switzerland and people would say 'What do you do?' and I'd say 'I'm a clown.' The different reaction I got when I would say this when I was in England – they were worlds apart. In England people would scoff, but in Switzerland, anybody I ever said that to, said 'Oh, have you seen Dimitri' or 'You must see Gary Heuter!' These are two iconic clowns who do wear red nose. Well, one wears red nose; one's more of a mime, white-faced character. But they pack out theatres. Proper, tuxedo-wearing, theatre-goers will flood to see them. So, their artistry is accepted. The closest we've got to it is Slava and his *Snowshow*, where I think it's seen as glamorous because it's from somewhere else. So we're allowed to like it.

S: Do you think we have to 'other' it in order to accept it?

W: Yea, we do, absolutely. For a while I toyed with the idea of creating a Czech persona for myself. I mean, I'd have to act as my agent on the phone, and I'd say 'Well, he doesn't speak any English.' Then just hope that they don't get a Czech translator! Anyway, it didn't transpire. So, where were we? In terms of creating a different dynamic in the city, it's about playing with public space. I mean, look at this space where we are now and it's deserted, of course. We've done a great job of spending a lot of money on public space, with all of the emphasis going on 'space,' and none of the thought going on 'public.' So, during this year's festival, we had a trapeze rig there [pointing to the centre of Writer's Square], we had visual artists around the outside. We invited them and it was the first time that visual artists had displayed their work in that setting in Belfast. We had some tables and chairs in here, so it was like a café-style ambiance. Later on in the weekend, there was a mobile cinema down the end. And the space was a lovely place to come and hang out.

S: Did you get a good crowd for the very first Festival of Fools? And has it been growing?

W: Yes we did.... And this year – without a doubt – was the best year. Overall there were about 40,000 people, of whom there would be repeat viewers. We usually have six pitches simultaneously around the city centre. Although, I say around the city centre when this year we had one here, one in St Anne's Square, and one in Cotton Court, which is the other side of the Circus School, so three of them in this area. So three of them in Cathedral Quarter, which is the sort of arts and cultural hub, and it's till neutral which is an important thing. The fact that we provide this free stuff is really important. I'm part of a trust for this area so for me it's vital that we retain the mix – that this will always be a place where families can come, where you can see something for nothing. In St Anne's Square, we've got stuff every Sunday. And people come down and they don't have to spend anything to be in the Cathedral Quarter. Families come down *with* whatever they need so they won't necessarily have to go and buy anything.

S: So that's every Sunday you do this?

W: Well, every Sunday in July and August, yea. So we've been doing that for eight years now.

S: And what work is presented on these Sundays?

W: It's like the Festival of Fools only that it's just two shows every Sunday. So, we'll bring some people back from the festival. It's also quite a good place for me to see some of the new shows. If I'm not convinced about bringing them for the next festival, I can get a look at them. Again, it's a bit of pioneering because we're the only people who have been presenting work on Sundays for years. Well, there's now starting to be a little bit, but for years everyone was going 'there's nothing to do on the Sundays' and 'there's no arts on Sundays' and we were going 'Um, we're here ...' We weren't getting funded for it but we were still doing it. It needs a critical mass for it to really take off, and slowly, slowly, we're getting there.

S: Where do you get your budget from?

W: For the festival itself, about fifty-per-cent comes from the Arts Council Lottery. We also get funding from the Department of Social Development, which has a remit for events in this area. The City Council gives us some money. Then there's sponsorship, and then donations from the audience. Again, from the beginning, we've always asked audiences to contribute to the festival because one of the things I wanted to do was to try and create the environment where this was worth people coming to perform in the streets. So we always say to people, 'look, if you've enjoyed this, donate,' and it went towards the next year's festival or, more often than not, it went towards the shortfall that we had in any one festival. Immensely complex financial situations arise from the fact that our funders will only fund on a zero-sum basis. And then, you know, because it's an international festival, the exchange rate fluctuates by seven per cent from when you submit your application to when you stage the festival and you're going, 'where am I gonna get *that* from?' So there are all sorts of complications that donations generally tend to make up for. *And* funding often comes in late. This year, the City Council reduced their funding to us, so we would have been totally screwed without donations. Luckily donations were at record levels so it worked out okay.

S: How do you integrate the work of Belfast Community Circus School with the Festival of Fools?

W: We create a show from our performance troupe of young people every year for the festival. So that, again, would be a devised piece and the young people in that performance troupe will have been with us for five or six years anyway by the time they get into the performance troupe. So they're encouraged to do a lot of shaping of their own routines. The whole troupe sits down at the start of the devising process and they look at different themes, they look at how they want to costume themselves, they just toss ideas about between themselves, and there are normally three trainers that work with them on that process.

Out of that evolves the idea for the show, and the separate pieces. Then the trainers and circus director will shape those and give them enough coherence and cohesion.

S: What about the work Belfast Community Circus does with adults and professional performers?

W: So, with the adults, there are a few different things. At the moment, there's an adult cabaret going on in the school, just from adult circus, which is full of enthusiasts and hobbyists – which is very interesting because they're actually starting to create work that is, to my mind in the cabaret setting, more fun than I've seen for years. They're quite camp, the cabarets, in an absolutely delightful way. There's such a pleasure taken by the people staging the performances, and at the same time there's an incredible atmosphere within the audience. The audience is all friends, family or people who've heard about these adult circus cabarets. So, that sense of mutual support is *raging* throughout the building. There are 120 people there to enjoy the cabaret. And, you know, they're having a few beers, and then you've got, probably, twenty-five people from the adult circus who are working together. Some of them are only backstage doing make-up, but then there are also performance pieces that they're doing that may involve five or six of them. And they're putting stories in their own pieces and they're getting very playful with it. They're using films to inspire their works. They're inspired by popular culture, by what they like, and they've got a real unfettered sense of fun. And it's lovely to see. They don't give a shit about whether anyone's gonna like it in the *profession*, 'lovie,' or whatever. It doesn't matter to them whether they get booked for doing it. They don't do it to get booked. They do it for the love of it. And for fun!

S: When did fun become so trivial?

W: I know, I know! And the last show I saw them do, it was so uplifting. You know, I was beaming for the whole show! As was the whole audience and, yea, it was just lovely. So *they* do some stuff, and they get input from professionals, and they get some direction from professionals, but they also very much support each other. They brought in a big dance number to finish the whole piece as well, choreographed to the James Bond theme. And it was marvellous.

S: What other involvement does the school have with professional practitioners?

W: In terms of the work that the Circus School itself has overseen, and produced, that would be more ensemble stuff. But it's not frequent. I think my favourite piece was back in 2005. It was kind of at this time of change – so it was a year after the Festival had started. And it was this thing where the face of Belfast was definitely changing. We called the show *Hardhats and Lattes*. It was kind of a history of Belfast, with the dockyards, the shipyards, you know … the hardhats in terms of those going to work there. But *now*, the changing face of Belfast – it's a bit like Dublin has been for a long time. You know, this perpetual building site, with cranes everywhere, and the hardhats for a *different* reason. Building had been sort of put on hold for thirty years here. Then there's this emergence of a café culture. So, it kind of told the story of an old bar being ripped out and a new, trendy coffee shop. The theme gave rise to a lot of slapstick – with the building scenes, and the use of planks. But with a through-line as well.

S: Who was involved?

W: We had a director in from Australia that we'd worked with before, who is a fantastic circus guy himself. All of the performers in it were professional performers in their own right, so they all would have had their own acts, but they came together for this production. I gave the director a brief, in terms of 'this is the story that we want to try and tell, but then it's up to you and the guys to *devise* it.' So then there was a lot of play and devising in rehearsal, and everybody was able to create their own characters and scenarios, as long as it fitted within the whole.

S: Was this a non-verbal show?

W: Well, there were a few words, but mainly it was non-verbal. There was a live band there as well, with original music. So it had a nicely rounded feel as a production. In 2012, we had *Land of Giants*. *Land of Giants* was a massive production of which we were a part. It was Northern Ireland's biggest, ever, outdoor arts production. In the end, I think it involved about 300 performers. It took place on the slipway of the Titanic – where the Titanic was actually built. And it involved PaperDolls. The reason they were here was because I was running this ten month course and the graduate show was *Land of Giants*. Some of the PaperDolls and others were up thirty metres on cranes doing some aerial harness work. There were over a hundred drummers involved. There was a lot of physical theatre. It was storytelling on a massive scale. It was my idea originally; we gave the director/writer the brief and it was incredible the way he was able to make that into something that could bring in all these people; there were about 18,000 people watching the show. Everybody had to have something that was close to them. It was no good having everything down at the end with people, sort of, squinting. So, there was a 150 metre stage, effectively, made up of shipping containers and people on top. The scenes were being reproduced right down the spine of the stage. It was a phenomenal performance.

S: So, that was a collaboration between you guys and various different groups?

W: Yeah, there was The Beat Carnival; we got about 120 drummers involved, and the Belfast Children's Festival as well. Through our community engagement work, we got some choirs involved. So, it was very much a multi-art-form production, involving a diverse range of people including amateurs and professionals.

But mainly, in relation to professional companies, what we are is really a platform and a facilitator. We provide them with the space; we bring in a lot of master class work. We have a strong thread of clown in that master class. We'll often bring somebody in and we'll say, 'Well, can you work with the group?' and then also 'Can you do, like, clown surgery?' So we look at their work with the group and then they might spend half a day or a day trying to work up a piece. So we kind of provide that support and development for them. In this year's festival, we had Barren Carrousel with their show, *Squash*. The company has existed for a while but only one of the original founder members is still there. So there were two new people coming in and we provided the space for them to train and rehearse, and our Youth Circus director gave them some direction on their work. They also had some workshops with Mooky Cornish, who was involved in this year's festival as well. So, it's not so much a sort of concerted, coherent investment there. We put the resources out there and then it's up to people to put the pieces together. And that way it allows for and encourages more artistic freedom from the individuals. If it was always down to *my* artistic vision, or something, there would be too much sameness about it.

What circus artists and street theatre artists really value is their freedom. That comes over time and time again, that they want to be doing what *they* want to be doing, and that they don't like being *told* what to do – which is also great and it's part of the street festival. It's part of where the name 'Festival of Fools' comes from. It comes from the '70s in Amsterdam where there was a very anarchic festival, and we want that kind of anarchy going on; we want artists to be doing what they want to do, not to be doing what they're told. So, it kind of works, yeah.

S: What about actors who are usually more involved in institutional or mainstream theatre? Have many trained with you, and how might they benefit from this?

W: Definitely they have. And there have been instances where circus people have been fitted into more, sort of, straight theatre. So, I mean, Kabosh Theatre, for the past ten to twelve years, would have, from time to time, used circus people in their productions. Cahoots, which is a children's theatre company, are always using our folk.

S: That kind of training for actors could also, I think, really revitalize some conventional theatre.

W: Yea, but I think what's missing are the resources to be able to explore it. I mean, we would work with Stephen Beggs from Bruiser Theatre Company. He's done some directing for us. And he gets quite inspired by working with the circus. About ten years ago, I think, we created kind of a lab – a share lab – for circus and actors. I think what we found was that the circus people had a lot more stuff that people were interested in learning than the actors did. You know, so it didn't quite work. But I'd like to do something where it's a bit more facilitated, and structured, so that there could still be the 'share' ethos, but also we would be bringing people in for master classes. What would be really good would be if, say, once a month, we could have an experimental production, and it could be cabaret, it could be ensemble – it doesn't matter – but there'd be this pool of people one week, come who may. You know, whoever comes, that informs what happens. And whatever show happens – it might be ten minutes, it might be an hour and ten minutes – it doesn't matter. And we wouldn't, obviously, charge people in. But just have a, sort of, experimental crossover; maybe bring some dance in as well. I mean, actually, there has been a little bit more happening with dance and circus.

S: Have you worked with any dance companies?

W: Yeah, Ponydance, who are doing quite well as a contemporary dance company. And they're quite humorous as well. They've done quite a few workshops with us. They've even done some training in acrobatics, and then we have the same clown teacher that comes and works with both of us. So I think undoubtedly there's loads of scope there for cross-pollination. But, you know, we get so poorly-resourced. We're open, pretty much, seven days a week for fifty-one weeks of the year. And the numbers of performances that we facilitate – and the number of participants that we work with – are vast. But we get a fraction of, what, say a theatre company that does one production a year – and is very, very, very stale – might get. And that's just the reality that we face. And, I think, if we could get resourced to the point – or *valued*, even – to the point that theatre, and dance, is valued – or even better, opera and orchestra – that would be fabulous. Then I think we could do absolutely amazing things. Only there just isn't the willingness to break free from certain mindsets, and actually say, 'this might be the direction that we need to invest in.' I think they're making a huge mistake; I think the arts council, and various others, are trying to prop up dying forms by putting more and more money into them. And they're not realizing that those forms need to move forward and innovate. In everything, just from audience development for example, they could do so much. But I think they're stagnant.

I was just thinking, in relation to the orchestra, for example, its forums can be very elitist, whereas they need to be coming out and engaging properly. They'll argue 'Oh we do have community engagement; we have musicians going to schools.' I know the musicians who go into schools because my daughters were at one of the schools where they went. There was no engagement whatsoever. They ended up being on the same stage in some sort of performance but my kids didn't even know who they were. And it's like, they've ticked that box: 'oh, we do outreach. We've engaged with 70,000 children in schools.' No, you haven't.

S: You haven't engaged with them. You appeared with them!

W: Yea, you were in the same, sort of, physical reality as them. So, I think there's a real reluctance to address that here. I think it happens to a certain extent in England but maybe not nearly as much as it should. But here, you know, there are still some very unpleasant statistics as to where the money goes. And when they've said, in the past, that a figure of fifty-seven per cent, or something, goes to areas of social need, and I'm going, 'No, it doesn't.' That's just because you classify this area – I mean this area here – is actually classified as 'disadvantaged.' Or it's in one of the wards of the highest levels of disadvantage just because right across the road there *is* massively disadvantaged. So, for every Arts organization that's based here, the funding is going into an area of disadvantage. That's a bit of a statistical massage, really, when you actually look at what the impact of that money is. And by the way, this building here used to be the Community Arts Forum.

S: What is it now?

W: It's empty. The Community Arts Forum closed down. It was throttled by Arts Council cuts. It was the umbrella body for community arts and I'm still quite angry that it was allowed to go. That was a hotbed of activism and passion at one stage. Yea ... very sad. Listen, I'm gonna have to go.

S: Yea, I'm gonna have to go too. Thank you so much for your time Will!

Works Cited

Chamberlain, Will. 'Access, Authorship, Participation and Ownership.' *An Outburst of Frankness: Community Arts in Ireland: A Reader.* Ed. Sandy Fitzgerald. Dublin: Tasc at New Island, 2004. 195-212. Print.

'Ethos and Mission.' *Belfast Community Circus School.* Belfast Community Circus School, n.d. Web. 09 Dec. 2014.

'History.' *Belfast Community Circus School.* Belfast Community Circus School, n.d. Web. 09 Dec. 2014.

Contributors

Laura Farrell-Wortman is a PhD candidate in Theatre and Drama at the University of Wisconsin, Madison. Her dissertation, 'Theatre After Anglo: Irish Drama Responds to the Great Recession,' examines post-2008 Irish theatre in the context of the global financial crisis and considers the role of theatre in creating an alternative documentation of the Irish debt crisis. Her research is focused on the intersection between theatre and political economics in the contemporary Republic of Ireland. Previous work has appeared in *Studies in Musical Theatre*, *The New York Irish History Roundtable Journal* and *Irish America Magazine*. She holds degrees from New York University and the University of Arizona, and has previously worked with the Abbey Theatre, Arizona Theatre Company and the Atlantic Theater Company.

Miriam Haughton is Lecturer in Drama, Theatre and Performance at NUI Galway. Her research field encompasses contemporary theatre, feminisms, trauma and memory studies, and cultural politics. Her monograph *Staging Trauma* is forthcoming with Palgrave MacMillan. Miriam co-edited the third volume of *Irish Theatre International* (2014), and the forthcoming collection *Radical Contemporary Theatre Practices by Women in Ireland* (Carysfort). Miriam's research is included in multiple international journals, and she is an Executive Member of the Irish Society for Theatre Research.

Michael Jaros is Associate Professor of English at Salem State University in Salem, Massachusetts, where he teaches graduate and undergraduate courses in dramatic literature, Irish literature and culture, as well as working with the Honors Program and as a dramaturg to the theatre program. His research and publications focus primarily on Irish culture and performance in the 20th and 21st centuries. He holds a PhD from The University of California, San Diego and an MPhil from Trinity College Dublin.

Charlotte McIvor is Lecturer in Drama, Theatre and Performance at NUI Galway and Director of Postgraduate Studies in Drama, Theatre and Performance. She is currently at work on her Irish Research Council funded project, 'Interculturalism, Migration and Performance in Contemporary Ireland' and completing a monograph, *Towards A New Interculturalism: Migration and Performance in Contemporary Ireland* (forthcoming from Palgrave Macmillan). Her publications include *Staging Intercultural Ireland: Plays and Practitioner Perspectives*, co-edited with Matthew Spangler (Cork University Press). Her work has appeared or is forthcoming in *Modern Drama, Irish Studies Review* and *Irish University Review* among others and multiple edited collections including *'That Was Us' Essays on Contemporary Irish Theatre and Performance*.

Siobhán O'Gorman is a Government of Ireland Postdoctoral Fellow (2013-2015) at the School of Drama, Film and Music, Trinity College Dublin. There, she is working on her monograph project entitled 'A Stage of Re-Vision: Scenography in Irish Theatre 1950-1990.' She is one of three co-convenors for the Theatre and Performance Research Association's scenography working group. Her work has appeared in such international publications as *Scene, Irish Studies Review, Irish Theatre International, Verbal* and *Precarious Parenthood: Doing Family in Literature and Film*. From 2008 to 2013, she was a critic for *Irish Theatre Magazine*, in addition to lecturing in drama and literature at NUI Galway. Her current research interests include theatre historiography, gender and performance, twentieth-century and contemporary theatre, collaborative performance practices and scenography.

Eleanor Owicki is a Visiting Assistant Professor in Indiana University's Department of Theatre and Drama and previously worked as lecturer in the Department of Performance Studies at Texas A&M University, where she taught courses on theatre history. Her research focuses on theatre in Northern Ireland, and particularly the relationship between performance and the ongoing peace process. She has published articles and reviews in *Theatre Symposium, Theatre Journal*, and *Eccumenica*, and is a past Assistant Editor of *Theatre Research International*. She received her PhD from the University of

Texas in 2013. She is also the resident dramaturg at This is Water Theatre in Bryan, TX.

Caitriona Mary Reilly is a PhD candidate in Drama Studies, School of Creative Arts at Queen's University Belfast. Caitriona was formerly a recipient of the Michael Barnes MA Scholarship (2011). She was awarded a Department for Employment and Learning (DEL) Research Studentship to continue her PhD study at Queen's. The working title of her doctoral thesis is 'Postfeminist Irish Performance, Theatre and Culture.' The thesis draws on the historiography and dramaturgical analysis of performances and productions by Irish practitioners such as Áine Phillips, ANU, and Marina Carr. It examines the impact of postfeminist culture within contemporary Irish society and discusses representations of girlhood, motherhood, and prostitution. Through an interrogation of contemporary gender issues, the thesis aims to understand what is still at stake for Irish women in the increasingly globalized twenty-first century.

Noelia Ruiz lectures in the School of English, Drama and Film, University College Dublin. Her doctoral research specialized in contemporary theatre-making processes and aesthetics, using as case studies Pan Pan Theatre and The Performance Corporation. She worked with both companies as a participant observer using ethnographic methodologies. She recently co-organized with Siobhan O'Gorman the Dublin Theatre Festival/ Trinity Long Room Hub 2014 symposium on scenography, 'Performing Space.' Publications include 'Positive Acts: The Evolution of Pan Pan Theatre Company,' in *No More Drama* edited by Peter Crawley and Willie White (2011) and 'A Estética da Pan Pan Theatre' in *Revista Brasileira de Estudos da Presença* (2013).

Rhona Trench is Programme Chair and Lecturer in Performing Arts at IT Sligo, where she teaches Drama Studies and Directing for Theatre. She is Treasurer of the Irish Society for Theatre Research. She is author of *Blue Raincoat Theatre Company* published by Carysfort Press (2015) and editor of *Staging Thought: Essays on Irish Theatre, Scholarship and Practice* (Oxford: Peter Lang, 2012). In 2010, she published the only monograph to date on the work of Marina Carr entitled *Bloody Living: The Loss of Selfhood in the Plays of Marina Carr* (Peter Lang). She has contributed peer reviewed essays to *Dublin City Comedy: Doing Things with Laughter in Irish Society* (Carysfort 2014) edited by Eric Weitz, *The Theatre of Conor McPherson: Right Beside the Beyond*

(Carysfort 2012) edited by Lilian Chambers and Eamonn Jordan, *Irish Drama: Local and Global Perspectives* edited by Patrick Lonergan and Nicholas Grene (Carysfort 2012), and *The Binding Strength of Irish Studies* edited by Marianna Gula, Mária Kurdi, István D. Rácz (Debrecen, 2011). Currently, she is working on an essay on the theatre design of Sam Shepard's *A Particle of Dread* staged by Field Day Theatre Company and directed by Nancy Meckler in Derry in 2014, to be published in *Irish Drama and Theatre at Home and Abroad* (Debrecen 2017).

Jesse Weaver is an American writer and researcher based in Dublin. He received his doctorate from University College Cork, where his research focused on the changing role of the playwright in Irish theatre production. He was a reviewer for *Irish Theatre Magazine* from 2008 to 2013 and wrote several features for the magazine focusing on new writing for the Irish stage. A playwright himself, Jesse's work has been seen in Chicago, New York, Dublin and the U.K. Jesse is also a graduate of Boston University's actor training programme and has been seen on stage in Chicago with Next Theatre Company, Victory Gardens Theatre, and the Illinois Shakespeare Festival. His research interests include the work of Tom Murphy and Enda Walsh, as well as contemporary Irish theatre practice and the development of new writing for the stage.

Irene White is a lecturer and researcher in the School of Education Studies at Dublin City University. She is co-ordinator of the Professional Master of Education programme and lectures in Initial Teacher Education at undergraduate and postgraduate level. She also teaches on the Bachelor of Education and Training and Masters in Education and Training Management programmes. Her teaching is primarily in the areas of Drama in Education, English Pedagogy and Teaching and Learning Methodologies. Her current research interests include creativity in education; cross-curricular applications of arts-based pedagogies; transformative learning through the arts in formal and informal settings; community-engaged arts and human development; and the application of drama-based techniques in non-theatre contexts. She is currently on the Board of Directors for Upstate Theatre Project. She previously worked with the company as assistant director and stage manager for Upstate Live and as a facilitator and director with Upstate Local on a range of cross-border, cross-community projects. She has also worked with Smashing Times Theatre Company, a socially engaged theatre company based in Dublin, on their

'Acting for the Future' programme. This project, aimed at secondary schools, universities, and community-based youth and adult groups, uses the arts to engage with young people and adults to promote emotional wellbeing, positive mental health and suicide prevention. Irene is a member of the Association for Drama in Education in Ireland (ADEI) and a member of the Centre for Culturally Responsive Evaluation and Assessment (CREA) at Dublin City University.

Index

A

Abbey Theatre, 56, 132, 136, 279
Adigun, Bisi, 6
ANU Productions, 1, 5, 17, 21, 23, 34, 43, 47-51, 56, 60, 62, 65-69, 82, 85, 130-39, 142, 192, 281
Arden, John, 16, 21, 34-44

Arts Council (Republic of Ireland), 18, 48, 54, 58-63, 68, 75, 82, 133, 179, 222, 261, 269, 272, 277

B

Barabbas, 1, 4, 29, 61, 62
Beckett, Samuel, 17, 28, 156, 160, 165, 166
Bedrock Productions, 130
Belfast Community Circus, 12, 24, 56, 261, 262, 266, 272, 273, 278
Bernadette Players, 15
Blue Raincoat, 1, 4, 21, 23, 29, 61, 149, 162, 173-87, 281
Brecht, Bertolt 2, 33, 39-40, 44

Brokentalkers, 1, 5, 21, 27, 47-51, 62, 65-69, 75, 85, 87, 129, 131, 192
Brook, Peter, 148
Burke-Kennedy, Mary Elizabeth, 17, 56

C

Cannon, Feidlim, 48, 65, 68-69, 75, 82, 87-89, 93, 95
Carr, Marina, 20, 28, 245, 281
Chamberlain, Will, 12, 24, 261-62, 278
Charabanc Theatre, 20, 51, 64, 65
Chekhov, Anton, 17, 146, 153, 158, 160, 168
City Workshop, 21-22, 51, 56-57, 64
CoisCéim, 5, 130
Community Arts, 4, 26, 47, 50-53, 63-64, 95, 261, 277-78
Conroy, Amy, 6, 57, 129-32
Copeau, Jacques, 175, 184
Corcadorca, 1, 149, 162
Corn Exchange, 1-2, 61, 130
Cosgrove, Aedín, 149, 159

Craig, Edward Gordon, 154, 156, 175, 187-88
Crouch, Tim, 144, 151, 158, 160

D

Decroux, Etienne, 188
Devlin, Joe, 17, 26
Dowling, Gabby, 18
Druid Theatre, 26
Dublin Fringe Festival, 22, 34, 43, 80-81, 98-99, 102, 127-41, 159, 199-200, 214-15, 258
Dublin Theatre Festival, 5, 16, 19, 28, 47-49, 62, 97, 130, 132, 160, 198, 203, 208, 212, 281
Dublin Youth Theatre, 23, 48, 57, 190
Dunne, Shaun, 112, 117, 131, 222
Dyas, Grace, 6, 48, 129
Dyas, Veronica, 131

E

Edwards, Hilton, 13
ensemble, 8, 74, 98-99, 112, 145-48, 177-78, 181, 187, 190, 203-204, 208, 211, 221-23, 273, 276
Etchells, Tim, 190, 191, 209

F

Fabulous Beast, 5, 61
Flynn, Andrew, 190, 203
Focus Theatre, 16, 27
Forced Entertainment, 144, 153, 190, 197, 209
Frawley, Monica, 18
Fregoli Theatre, 23, 190, 198-201, 207-209

G

Galway Arts Centre Community Drama, 23, 62, 190, 203-204, 208, 213-14
Galway Youth Theatre, 23, 190
Glasshouse Productions, 20
Gorman, Declan, 6, 49, 53, 57, 60, 64, 68, 95
Gregory, Lady Augusta, 10, 12, 20, 28, 37
Grotowski, Jerzy, 147-48

H

Hickey, Tom, 17, 27, 57
Hot for Theatre, 132

I

Ibsen, Heinrich, 17, 38, 155, 165, 212, 213

J

junk ensemble, 48, 131

K

Kabosh Theatre, 12, 14, 24, 80, 229-36, 240-41, 276
Kavanagh, Patrick, 17, 57, 72, 149
Keegan, Gary, 65, 68, 75
Kinahan, Deirdre, 2
Kneehigh Theatre, 148

L

Lantern Theatre, 15, 28
Lecoq, Jacques, 9, 148
Littlewood, Joan, 9, 145, 147
Lowe, Louise, 17, 51, 65, 68, 82, 104, 129, 135

M

Mac Intyre, Tom, 17, 57
Mac Liammóir, Micheál, 13-14, 26
Macnas, 1, 4, 57, 61, 213, 219
Mallon, Declan, 6, 57-58, 64, 68, 95
Mason, Patrick, 17, 57
McFetridge, Paula, 229, 237, 241
McGuinness, Frank, 56, 252-53, 258-59
McKevitt, Una, 6, 22, 67, 97-98, 107
McPherson, Conor, 131, 281
Meade, Paul, 6
Meyerhold, Vsevolod, 8, 154
Mnouchkine, Ariane, 9, 145, 148
Moonfish Theatre, 24, 211-12, 225
Moving Theatre, 19, 21, 56, 57

N

Neighbourhood Open Workshop, 21, 56
Ní Chronin, Máiréad, 24

O

Oddey, Alison, 7, 28, 65, 178, 188, 190, 209-10
Operating Theatre, 18

P

Pan Pan, 1, 5, 11, 21, 23, 61, 98, 130, 143-44, 146, 149, 152-60, 281
Parks, Suzan-Lori, 189, 210
Peacock Theatre, 142
Pike Theatre, 15, 28

Project Arts Centre, 18-19, 40, 61

Q

Quinn, Gavin, 11, 23, 143, 159-60

R

Rea, Niall, 245-46, 251

S

Shakespeare, William, 72, 193, 282
Sheridan, Peter, 19, 22, 43, 50, 57, 59, 61, 64
Side-Show Productions, 189
Slot Players, 18, 28
Stanislavski, Konstantin, 16, 26-27, 146
Swift, Carolyn, 10, 28
Synge, John Millington, 12, 28

T

Talking Shop Ensemble, 22, 111, 125
TEAM Educational Theatre, 19, 56-57, 64
The Company, 1, 4, 29, 131
THEATREclub, 1, 5, 21, 47-50, 62, 131
TheatreofplucK, 24, 243-48, 252, 257
THISISPOPBABY, 1
Thompson, James, 9, 29, 138-39, 142
Troubles, The, 4, 24, 27, 41, 51, 65, 229-35, 238-41, 244-45, 247, 251-52, 256-59

U

Upstate Theatre Project, 6, 22, 29, 57, 64, 67-70, 89, 95, 282

W

Walsh, Enda, 2, 131, 149, 199, 282

Waterford Arts for All, 21, 56-57

West, Michael, 2

Y

Yeats, William Butler, 12, 23, 28, 37, 173-80, 186-88

Carysfort Press was formed in the summer of 1998. It receives annual funding from the Arts Council.

The directors believe that drama is playing an ever-increasing role in today's society and that enjoyment of the theatre, both professional and amateur, currently plays a central part in Irish culture.

The Press aims to produce high quality publications which, though written and/or edited by academics, will be made accessible to a general readership. The organisation would also like to provide a forum for critical thinking in the Arts in Ireland, again keeping the needs and interests of the general public in view.

The company publishes contemporary Irish writing for and about the theatre.

Editorial and publishing inquiries to:
Carysfort Press Ltd.,
58 Woodfield,
Scholarstown Road,
Rathfarnham,
Dublin 16,
Republic of Ireland.

T (353 1) 493 7383
E: info@carysfortpress.com
www.carysfortpress.com

HOW TO ORDER

TRADE ORDERS DIRECTLY TO:
Irish Book Distribution
Unit 12, North Park, North Road,
Finglas, Dublin 11.

T: (353 1) 8239580
E: mary@argosybooks.ie
www.argosybooks.ie

INDIVIDUAL ORDERS DIRECTLY TO:
eprint Ltd.
35 Coolmine Industrial Estate,
Blanchardstown, Dublin 15.
T: (353 1) 827 8860
E: books@eprint.ie
www.eprint.ie

FOR SALES IN NORTH AMERICA AND CANADA:
Dufour Editions Inc.,
124 Byers Road,
PO Box 7,
Chester Springs,
PA 19425,
USA

T: 1-610-458-5005
F: 1-610-458-7103

Sullied Magnificence: The Theatre of Mark O'Rowe

Edited by Sara Keating and Emma Creedon

"Mark O'Rowe is one of contemporary theatre's great extremists -- vivid, violent, beautiful, grotesque, each play a savage war between form and content. It takes some daring to explore the minefields he creates and in this very welcome volume, the authors do so with an intelligence that matches their intrepidity. Anyone with an interest in Irish theatre now will want to read it."
(Fintan O'Toole)

ISBN 978-1-909325-66-1   €20 (Paperback)

Radical Contemporary Theatre Practices by Women in Ireland

Edited by Miriam Haughton and Mária Kurdi

Radical Contemporary Theatre Practices by Women in Ireland is an important contribution to the fields of Irish theatre and performance studies, and gender and performance in Ireland. The essays and interviews explore the work of women directors, designers, and playwrights on both sides of the Irish Border, who are currently shaping theatre practice on the island. By gathering such an impressive range of material, Mária Kurdi and Miriam Haughton have produced a collection that offers a snapshot of radical practice on the Irish stage in the early 21st century.

ISBN 978-1-909325-75-3   €20 (Paperback)

The Theatre of Marie Jones: Telling Stories from the Ground up

Edited by Eugene McNulty and Tom Maguire

Marie Jones is one of the most prolific and popular writers working in Northern Irish theatre today. Her work has achieved local relevance and international recognition. From her earliest work with Charabanc in the early 1980s to the present day, Jones's work has engaged with Irish (and, more often than not, specifically Northern Irish) experience in ways that reveal the extent to which the personal is political in a distinctive form of popular theatre. This volume of essays engages critically with Jones's oeuvre, her reception in Ireland and beyond, and her position in the canon of contemporary drama.

ISBN 78-1-909325-65-4   €20 (Paperback)

Blue Raincoat Theatre Company

By Rhona Trench

Since its foundation in 1991, Blue Raincoat Theatre Company is Ireland's only full-time venue-based professional theatre ensemble and has become renowned for its movement, visual and aural proficiencies and precision. This book explores those signatures from a number of vantage points, conveying the complex challenges faced by Blue Raincoat as they respond to changing aesthetic and economic circumstances. Particular consideration is given to set, costume, sound and lighting design.

ISBN 78-1-909325-67-8   €20 (Paperback)

Across the Boundaries: Talking about Thomas Kilroy

Edited by: Guy Woodward

Thomas Kilroy's long and distinguished career is celebrated in this volume by new essays, panel discussions and an interview, reconsidering the work of one of Ireland's most intellectually ambitious and technically imaginative playwrights. Contributors are drawn from both the academic and theatrical spheres, and include Nicholas Grene, Wayne Jordan, Patrick Mason, Christopher Murray and Lynne Parker.

ISBN 78-1-909325-51-7   €15.00 (Paperback)

Tradition and Craft in Piano-Paying,
by Tilly Fleischmann

Edited by Ruth Fleischmann and John Buckley
DVD Musical examples: Gabriela Mayer

This is a document of considerable historical importance, offering an authoritative account of Liszt's teaching methods as imparted by two of his former students to whom he was particularly close. It contains much valuable information of a kind that is unavailable elsewhere. It records a direct and authentic oral tradition of continental European pianism going back to the nineteenth century.

ISBN 78-1-909325-524   €30 (Paperback)

Wexfour: John Banville, Eoin Colfer, Billy Roche, Colm Toibin

Edited by Ben Barnes
A dedication of four short plays by Wexford writers to celebrate the 40th Anniversary of Wexford Arts Centre.

ISBN 78-1-909325-548   €10

For the Sake of Sanity: Doing things with humour in Irish performance

Edited by Eric Weitz

Humour claims no ideological affiliation – its workings merit inspection in any and every individual case, in light of the who, what, where and when of a joke, including the manner of performance, the socio-cultural context, the dynamic amongst participants, and who knows how many other factors particular to the instance. There as many insights to be gained from the deployment of humour in performance as people to think about it – so herein lie a healthy handful of responses from a variety of perspectives.

For the Sake of Sanity: *Doing things with humour in Irish performance* assembles a range of essays from practitioners, academics, and journalists, all of whom address the attempt to make an audience laugh in various Irish contexts over the past century. With a general emphasis on theatre, the collection also includes essays on film, television and stand-up comedy for those insights into practice, society and culture revealed uniquely through instances of humour in performance.

ISBN 78-1-909-325-56-2   €20

Stanislavski in Ireland: Focus at Fifty

Edited by Brian McAvera and Steven Dedalus Burch

Stanislavski in Ireland: Focus at Fifty is an insight into Ireland's only arthouse theatre from the people who were there. Through interviews, articles, short memoirs and photographs, the book tracks the theatre from its inception, detailing the period under its founder Deirdre O'Connell and then the period following Joe Devlin's arrival as its new artistic director. Many of Ireland's leading theatre and film artists trained and worked at Focus, including Gabriel Byrne, Joan Bergin, Olwen Fouèrè, Brendan Coyle, Rebecca Schull, Johnny Murphy, Sean Campion, Tom Hickey and Mary Elizabeth and Declan Burke-Kennedy. The book comes complete with a chronological list of productions.

ISBN 78-1-909325-43-2 €20

Breaking Boundaries. An Anthology of Original Plays from the Focus Theatre

Edited by Steven Dedalus Burch

Almost from the beginning, since 1970, new plays became part of the Focus's repertory.
Of the seven plays in this anthology, all exhibit a range in styles from Lewis Carroll's fantastical world (*Alice in Wonderland* by Mary Elizabeth Burke-Kennedy), to a couple on the brink of a philandering weekend disaster (*The Day of the Mayfly* by Declan Burke-Kennedy), to a one-man show about Jonathan Swift (*Talking Through His Hat* by Michael Harding), an examination of two shoplifting thieves and the would-be writer who gets in their way (*Pinching For My Soul* by Elizabeth Moynihan), a battle royal between two sides of a world-famous painter (*Francis and Frances* by Brian McAvera), the reactions of multiple New Yorkers to that moment in September, 2011 (*New York Monologues* by Mike Poblete), to the final days of an iconic movie star (*Hollywood Valhalla* by Aidan Harney).

ISBN 78-1-909325-42-5 €20

The Art Of Billy Roche: Wexford As The World

Edited by Kevin Kerrane

Billy Roche – musician, actor, novelist, dramatist, screenwriter – is one of Ireland's most versatile talents. This anthology, the first comprehensive survey of Roche's work, focuses on his portrayal of one Irish town as a microcosm of human life itself, elemental and timeless. Among the contributors are fellow artists (Colm Tóibín, Conor McPherson, Belinda McKeon), theatre professionals (Benedict Nightingale, Dominic Dromgoole, Ingrid Craigie), and scholars on both sides of the Atlantic.

ISBN 78-1-904505-60-0 €20

The Theatre of Conor McPherson: 'Right beside the Beyond'

Edited by Lilian Chambers and Eamonn Jordan

Multiple productions and the international successes of plays like *The Weir* have led to Conor McPherson being regarded by many as one of the finest writers of his generation. McPherson has also been hugely prolific as a theatre director, as a screenwriter and film director, garnering many awards in these different roles. In this collection of essays, commentators from around the world address the substantial range of McPherson's output to date in theatre and film, a body of work written primarily during and in the aftermath of Ireland's Celtic Tiger period. These critics approach the work in challenging and dynamic ways, considering the crucial issues of morality, the rupturing of the real, storytelling, and the significance of space, violence and gender. Explicit considerations are given to comedy and humour, and to theatrical form, especially that of the monologue and to the ways that the otherworldly, the unconscious and supernatural are accommodated dramaturgically, with frequent emphasis placed on the specific aspects of performance in both theatre and film.

ISBN 78 1 904505 61 7 €20

The Story of Barabbas, The Company

Carmen Szabo

Acclaimed by audiences and critics alike for their highly innovative, adventurous and entertaining theatre, Barabbas The Company have created playful, intelligent and dynamic productions for over 17 years. Breaking the mould of Irish theatrical tradition and moving away from a text dominated theatre, Barabbas The Company's productions have established an instantly recognizable performance style influenced by the theatre of clown, circus, mime, puppetry, object manipulation and commedia dell'arte. This is the story of a unique company within the framework of Irish theatre, discussing the influences that shape their performances and establish their position within the history and development of contemporary Irish theatre. This book addresses the overwhelming necessity to reconsider Irish theatre history and to explore, in a language accessible to a wide range of readers, the issues of physicality and movement based theatre in Ireland.

ISBN 78-1-904505-59-4 €25

Irish Drama: Local and Global Perspectives

Edited by Nicholas Grene and Patrick Lonergan

Since the late 1970s there has been a marked internationalization of Irish drama, with individual plays, playwrights, and theatrical companies establishing newly global reputations. This book reflects upon these developments, drawing together leading scholars and playwrights to consider the consequences that arise when Irish theatre travels abroad.

Contributors: Chris Morash, Martine Pelletier, José Lanters, Richard Cave, James Moran, Werner Huber, Rhona Trench, Christopher Murray, Ursula Rani Sarma, Jesse Weaver, Enda Walsh, Elizabeth Kuti

ISBN 78-1-904505-63-1 €20

What Shakespeare Stole From Rome

Edited by Brian Arkins

What Shakespeare Stole From Rome analyses the multiple ways Shakespeare used material from Roman history and Latin poetry in his plays and poems. From the history of the Roman Republic to the tragedies of Seneca; from the Comedies of Platus to Ovid's poetry; this enlightening book examines the important influence of Rome and Greece on Shakespeare's work.

ISBN 78-1-904505-58-7 €20

Polite Forms

Harry White

Polite Forms is a sequence of poems that meditates on family life, remembering and reimagining scenes from childhood and adolescence through the formal composure of the sonnet, so that the uniformity of this framing device promotes a tension. Throughout the collection there is a constant preoccupation with the difference between actual remembrance and the illumination or meaning which poetry can afford. Some of the poems 'rewind the tapes of childhood' across two or three generations, and all of them are akin to pictures at an exhibition which survey individual impressions of childhood and parenthood in a thematically continuous series of portraits drawn from life. This is his first collection of poetry.

Harry White is Professor of Music at University College Dublin.

ISBN 78-1-904505-55-6 €10

Ibsen and Chekhov on the Irish Stage

Edited by Ros Dixon and Irina Ruppo Malone

Ibsen and Chekhov on the Irish Stage presents articles on the theories of translation and adaptation, new insights on the work of Brian Friel, Frank McGuinness, Thomas Kilroy, and Tom Murphy, historical analyses of theatrical productions during the Irish Revival, interviews with contemporary theatre directors, and a round-table discussion with the playwrights, Michael West and Thomas Kilroy.

Ibsen and Chekhov on the Irish Stage challenges the notion that a country's dramatic tradition develops in cultural isolation. It uncovers connections between past productions of plays by Ibsen and Chekhov and contemporary literary adaptations of their works by Irish playwrights, demonstrating the significance of international influence for the formation of national canon.

ISBN 78-1-904505-57-0 €20

Tom Swift Selected Plays

With an introduction by Peter Crawley.

The inaugural production of Performance Corporation in 2002 matched Voltaire's withering assault against the doctrine of optimism with a playful aesthetic and endlessly inventive stagecraft.

Each play in this collection was originally staged by the Performance Corporation and though Swift has explored different avenues ever since, such playfulness is a constant. The writing is precise, but leaves room for the discoveries of rehearsals, the flesh of the theatre. All plays are blueprints for performance, but several of these scripts – many of which are site-specific and all of them slyly topical – are documents for something unrepeatable.

ISBN 78-1-904505-56-3 €20

Synge and His Influences: Centenary Essays from the Synge Summer School

Edited by Patrick Lonergan

The year 2009 was the centenary of the death of John Millington Synge, one of the world's great dramatists. To mark the occasion, this book gathers essays by leading scholars of Irish drama, aiming to explore the writers and movements that shaped Synge, and to consider his enduring legacies. Essays discuss Synge's work in its Irish, European and world contexts – showing his engagement not just with the Irish literary revival but with European politics and culture too. The book also explores Synge's influence on later writers: Irish dramatists such as Brian Friel, Tom Murphy and Marina Carr, as well as international writers like Mustapha Matura and Erisa Kironde. It also considers Synge's place in Ireland today, revealing how *The Playboy of the Western World* has helped to shape Ireland's responses to globalisation and multiculturalism, in celebrated productions by the Abbey Theatre, Druid Theatre, and Pan Pan Theatre Company.

Contributors include Ann Saddlemyer, Ben Levitas, Mary Burke, Paige Reynolds, Eilís Ní Dhuibhne, Mark Phelan, Shaun Richards, Ondřej Pilný, Richard Pine, Alexandra Poulain, Emilie Pine, Melissa Sihra, Sara Keating, Bisi Adigun, Adrian Frazier and Anthony Roche.

ISBN 78-1-904505-50-1 €20.00

Constellations - The Life and Music of John Buckley

Benjamin Dwyer

Benjamin Dwyer provides a long overdue assessment of one of Ireland's most prolific composers of the last decades. He looks at John Buckley's music in the context of his biography and Irish cultural life. This is no hagiography but a critical assessment of Buckley's work, his roots and aesthetics. While looking closely at several of Buckley's compositions, the book is written in a comprehensible style that makes it easily accessible to anybody interested in Irish musical and cultural history.   *Wolfgang Marx*

As well as providing a very readable and comprehensive study of the life and music of John Buckley, Constellations also offers an up-to-date and informative catalogue of compositions, a complete discography, translations of set texts and the full libretto of his chamber opera, making this book an essential guide for both students and professional scholars alike.

ISBN 78-1-904505-52-5 €20.00

'Because We Are Poor': Irish Theatre in the 1990s

Victor Merriman

"Victor Merriman's work on Irish theatre is in the vanguard of a whole new paradigm in Irish theatre scholarship, one that is not content to contemplate monuments of past or present achievement, but for which the theatre is a lens that makes visible the hidden malaises in Irish society. That he has been able to do so by focusing on a period when so much else in Irish culture conspired to hide those problems is only testimony to the considerable power of his critical scrutiny." Chris Morash, NUI Maynooth.

ISBN 78-1-904505-51-8 €20.00

Buffoonery and Easy Sentiment':
Popular Irish Plays in the Decade Prior to the Opening of The Abbey Theatre

Christopher Fitz-Simon

In this fascinating reappraisal of the non-literary drama of the late 19th - early 20th century, Christopher Fitz-Simon discloses a unique world of plays, players and producers in metropolitan theatres in Ireland and other countries where Ireland was viewed as a source of extraordinary topics at once contemporary and comfortably remote: revolution, eviction, famine, agrarian agitation, political assassination.

The form was the fashionable one of melodrama, yet Irish melodrama was of a particular kind replete with hidden messages, and the language was far more allusive, colourful and entertaining than that of its English equivalent.

ISBN 78-1-9045505-49-5 €20.00

The Theatre of Tom Mac Intyre: 'Strays from the ether'

Eds. Bernadette Sweeney and Marie Kelly

This long overdue anthology captures the soul of Mac Intyre's dramatic canon – its ethereal qualities, its extraordinary diversity, its emphasis on the poetic and on performance – in an extensive range of visual, journalistic and scholarly contributions from writers, theatre practitioners.

ISBN 78-1-904505-46-4 €25

Irish Appropriation Of Greek Tragedy

Brian Arkins

This book presents an analysis of more than 30 plays written by Irish dramatists and poets that are based on the tragedies of Sophocles, Euripides and Aeschylus. These plays proceed from the time of Yeats and Synge through MacNeice and the Longfords on to many of today's leading writers.

ISBN 78-1-904505-47-1 €20

Alive in Time: The Enduring Drama of Tom Murphy

Ed. Christopher Murray

Almost 50 years after he first hit the headlines as Ireland's most challenging playwright, the 'angry young man' of those times Tom Murphy still commands his place at the pinnacle of Irish theatre. Here 17 new essays by prominent critics and academics, with an introduction by Christopher Murray, survey Murphy's dramatic oeuvre in a concerted attempt to define his greatness and enduring appeal, making this book a significant study of a unique genius.

ISBN 78-1-904505-45-7 €25

Performing Violence in Contemporary Ireland

Edited by Lisa Fitzpatrick

This interdisciplinary collection of fifteen new essays by scholars of theatre, Irish studies, music, design and politics explores aspects of the performance of violence in contemporary Ireland. With chapters on the work of playwrights Martin McDonagh, Martin Lynch, Conor McPherson and Gary Mitchell, on Republican commemorations and the 90th anniversary ceremonies for the Battle of the Somme and the Easter Rising, this book aims to contribute to the ongoing international debate on the performance of violence in contemporary societies.

ISBN 78-1-904505-44-0 €20

Deviant Acts: Essays on Queer Performance

Ed. David Cregan

This book contains an exciting collection of essays focusing on a variety of alternative performances happening in contemporary Ireland. While it highlights the particular representations of gay and lesbian identity it also brings to light how diversity has always been a part of Irish culture and is, in fact, shaping what it means to be Irish today.

ISBN 978-1-904505-42-6 €20

Plays and Controversies: Abbey Theatre Diaries 2000-2005

Ben Barnes

In diaries covering the period of his artistic directorship of the Abbey, Ben Barnes offers a frank, honest, and probing account of a much commented upon and controversial period in the history of the national theatre. These diaries also provide fascinating personal insights into the day-to-day pressures, joys, and frustrations of running one of Ireland's most iconic institutions.

ISBN 78-1-904505-38-9 €25

Interactions: Dublin Theatre Festival 1957-2007. Irish Theatrical Diaspora Series: 3

Eds. Nicholas Grene and Patrick Lonergan with Lilian Chambers

For over 50 years the Dublin Theatre Festival has been one of Ireland's most important cultural events, bringing countless new Irish plays to the world stage, while introducing Irish audiences to the most important international theatre companies and artists. Interactions explores and celebrates the achievements of the renowned Festival since 1957 and includes specially commissioned memoirs from past organizers, offering a unique perspective on the controversies and successes that have marked the event's history. An especially valuable feature of the volume, also, is a complete listing of the shows that have appeared at the Festival from 1957 to 2008.

ISBN 78-1-904505-36-5 €20

Synge: A Celebration

Edited by Colm Tóibín

A collection of essays by some of Ireland's most creative writers on the work of John Millington Synge, featuring Sebastian Barry, Marina Carr, Anthony Cronin, Roddy Doyle, Anne Enright, Hugo Hamilton, Joseph O'Connor, Mary O'Malley, Fintan O'Toole, Colm Toibin, Vincent Woods.

ISBN 978-1-904505-14-3 €15

www.ingramcontent.com/pod-product-compliance
Lightning Source LLC
Chambersburg PA
CBHW050334230426
43663CB00010B/1854